学术英语
论文写作与发表

ACADEMIC ENGLISH
PAPER WRITING & PUBLICATION

张英 田园 李秀立◎编著

清华大学出版社
北京

内 容 简 介

本教材共 12 个单元，系统涵盖了学术英语论文的主要组成部分，即学术英语论文各个部分的功能、基本逻辑发展、语言修辞特征和语言使用模板。此外，本教材还介绍了国际会议往来书信的写作与海报的制作以及论文发表的相关问题。同时，本教材还聚焦学生写作中常见的错误以及错误产生的原因。各单元的具体内容为：学术英语论文写作中的引言；文献综述；研究方法；研究结果；结果讨论；研究结论；摘要与标题；参考文献；学生写作常见错误分析；中式英语与标准英语对比；国际会议海报及数据展示；论文发表。教材配备 PPT 课件和练习答案，读者可登录 www.tsinghuaelt.com 下载使用。

本教材适用于非英语专业的硕士和博士研究生、本科高年级学生以及科技和人文学科的学者和教师。

版权所有，侵权必究。举报：010-62782989，beiqinquan@tup.tsinghua.edu.cn。

图书在版编目（CIP）数据

学术英语论文写作与发表 / 张英，田园，李秀立编著. —北京：清华大学出版社，2022.8（2024.9重印）
ISBN 978-7-302-61580-4

Ⅰ. ①学… Ⅱ. ①张… ②田… ③李… Ⅲ. ①英语—论文—写作—教材 Ⅳ. ①H315

中国版本图书馆 CIP 数据核字（2022）第 145565 号

责任编辑：刘　艳
封面设计：子　一
责任校对：王荣静
责任印制：宋　林

出版发行：清华大学出版社
　　　　网　　址：https://www.tup.com.cn, https://www.wqxuetang.com
　　　　地　　址：北京清华大学学研大厦 A 座　　邮　编：100084
　　　　社 总 机：010-83470000　　邮　购：010-62786544
　　　　投稿与读者服务：010-62776969, c-service@tup.tsinghua.edu.cn
　　　　质量反馈：010-62772015, zhiliang@tup.tsinghua.edu.cn
印 装 者：三河市铭诚印务有限公司
经　　销：全国新华书店
开　　本：185mm×260mm　　印　张：18.75　　字　数：398 千字
版　　次：2022 年 9 月第 1 版　　印　次：2024 年 9 月第 5 次印刷
定　　价：79.00 元

产品编号：098954-01

前言

近年来，国际化大背景对中国研究生的学术英语书面和口头交流能力提出了越来越高的要求。研究生在未来的学习、研究和工作生涯中，必须具备向世界讲好"中国故事"的学术交流能力。在此背景下，研究生学术英语教学已经成为研究生英语教学体系的主流。很多高校都设置了学术英语论文写作和学术英语交流等课程，并将其列为英语必修课程。目前，国外已经出版了一些学术英语论文写作和交流课程方面的教材，但是并不十分适合中国学生使用。我们应该汲取其精华内容，结合中国高校的实际情况，编写出更多适合中国学生学习的学术英语系列教材。这也是我们编写本教材的原因。

本教材是清华大学研究生学术英语系列教材中的一本。教材的编写基于语言"输入—输出"教学理论，并秉承"真实语料驱动""产出导向""任务驱动"和"体验式教学"等教学理念，力求引导学生将理论与实践并重，使学习与使用有机结合，从而达到有效学习的目的。

本教材在编写过程中力求从根本上实现两个转换：一是从通用英语教学向学术英语教学的转换；二是从语言知识点学习向学术英语交流能力和思维能力培养的转换。

从内容来看，本教材系统涵盖了学术英语论文的主要组成部分，即学术英语论文各个部分的功能、基本逻辑发展、语言修辞特征和语言使用模板。此外，教材还介绍了国际会议往来书信的写作与海报的制作以及论文发表的相关问题。同时，教材还聚焦学生写作中常见的错误以及错误产生的原因。全书共 12 个单元，具体内容为：学术英语论文写作中的引言；文献综述；研究方法；研究结果；结果讨论；研究结论；摘要与标题；参考文献；学生写作常见错误分析；中式英语与标准英语对比；国际会议海报及数据展示；论文发表。

本教材具有如下特色：

1. **选择新颖多样的文本，时效性强**。本教材的分析文本包括化学、生命科学、医学、环境科学、计算机科学、软件工程学、生物力学、统计学、管理学、传播学、哲学、法学、教育学、艺术学、社会学、语言教学等学科的新成果，使学生不仅能够习得语言，还能够了解各个学科的一些最新研究动向。

2. **融合一线教师的教学实践经验和理性认识。** 本教材以学生学习效果为中心，既包含学术英语论文写作的一般性内容，也包括教师在教学实践中所提炼出的适合中国学生的具体教学内容。

3. **结构编排科学合理，层次分明。** 在内容的编排方面，本教材循序渐进、条理清晰、层次分明、逻辑缜密、翔实周到。在词汇、句法、语篇三个层面上，教材展开并阐释了学术英语论文写作的步骤、方法和技巧。

4. **重视学术英语语言的表达规范。** 本教材前8个单元包含了对学术论文各个主要组成部分特有的语言特征的详细介绍和学术英语写作常用的表达方式；第9单元和第10单元聚焦学生写作中常见的错误以及错误产生的原因。

5. **注重学习与练习有机结合。** 本教材每个单元均提供大量练习题，题型新颖，采用任务驱动方式，针对论文的语篇结构、章节语步逻辑发展和语言特征等方面让学生充分练习。同时，注重鼓励学生积极发表自己的观点，并促使他们结合各自的专业领域强化论文各个章节的写作练习，在学习和操练论文写作的过程中，提升论文写作能力。

总体而言，本教材内容细致、重点突出、有的放矢、贴合实际、实用性强。

本教材适用于非英语专业的硕士和博士研究生、本科高年级学生及科技和人文学科的教师和学者。教材配备PPT课件和练习答案，方便教师备课和学生学习使用。

本教材由张英主笔编写第2单元、第6单元、第7单元和第10单元；田园主笔编写第3单元、第8单元、第9单元和第12单元；李秀立主笔编写第1单元、第4单元、第5单元和第11单元。全书的统稿工作由张英负责。

感谢清华大学研究生教育教学改革项目的支持；感谢清华大学语言教学中心的支持；感谢清华大学出版社的支持！

编者

2022年6月29日于清华园

Contents

Unit 1 Introduction 1

1.1 Overview 2
    1.1.1 Purpose of the Introduction Section 2
    1.1.2 Information Elements of the Introduction Section 2
    1.1.3 Main Focus of Writing the Introduction Section 2

1.2 Sample Analysis 4

1.3 Linguistic Features of the Introduction Section 8
    1.3.1 Lexical Features 8
    1.3.2 Syntactical Features 10

1.4 Useful Expressions for the Introduction Section 13

1.5 Reflections and Practice 15

Unit 2 Literature Review 27

2.1 Overview 28
    2.1.1 Purposes of the Literature Review Section 28
    2.1.2 Information Elements of the Literature Review Section 28
    2.1.3 Principles of Writing the Literature Review Section 30
    2.1.4 Citation Methods in the Literature Review 30
    2.1.5 Organizational Patterns of the Literature Review Section ...32
    2.1.6 Common Problems of Writing the Literature Review
          Section 34

2.2 Sample Analysis 34

2.3 Linguistic Features of the Literature Review Section 37
    2.3.1 Lexical Features 37
    2.3.2 Syntactical Features 39

  2.4 Plagiarism and Paraphrase 41
    2.4.1 Plagiarism 41
    2.4.2 Paraphrase 43
  2.5 Useful Expressions for the Literature Review Section 43
  2.6 Reflections and Practice 45

Unit 3   Methods 55

  3.1 Overview 56
    3.1.1 Purpose of the Methods Section 56
    3.1.2 Information Elements of the Methods Section 56
    3.1.3 Principles of Writing the Methods Section 58
  3.2 Sample Analysis 58
  3.3 Linguistic Features of the Methods Section 62
    3.3.1 Lexical Features 62
    3.3.2 Syntactical Features 63
  3.4 Useful Expressions for the Methods Section 68
  3.5 Reflections and Practice 70

Unit 4   Results 77

  4.1 Overview 78
    4.1.1 Purpose of the Results Section 78
    4.1.2 Information Elements of the Results Section 78
    4.1.3 Sequential Structure of the Results Section 79
    4.1.4 Principles of Results Presentation 80
    4.1.5 Common Mistakes in Writing a Results Section 81
    4.1.6 Criteria for Judging a Results Section 81
  4.2 Sample Analysis 82
  4.3 Linguistic Features of the Results Section 94
    4.3.1 Lexical Features 94

      4.3.2 Syntactical Features 95

  4.4 **Useful Expressions for the Results Section** 97

  4.5 **Reflections and Practice** 98

Unit 5   Discussion 107

  5.1 **Overview** 108

      5.1.1 Purpose of the Discussion Section 108

      5.1.2 Information Elements of the Discussion Section 108

      5.1.3 Principles of Writing the Discussion Section......................110

      5.1.4 Organizational Pattern of the Discussion Section 111

  5.2 **Sample Analysis**..111

  5.3 **Linguistic Features of the Discussion Section**............................118

      5.3.1 Lexical Features 118

      5.3.2 Syntactical Features 121

  5.4 **Useful Expressions for the Discussion Section**...........................122

  5.5 **Reflections and Practice** 124

Unit 6   Conclusion 133

  6.1 **Overview** 134

      6.1.1 Purpose of the Conclusion Section 134

      6.1.2 Information Elements of the Conclusion Section 134

      6.1.3 Principles of Writing the Conclusion Section......................136

      6.1.4 Common Problems of Writing a Conclusion Section 136

  6.2 **Sample Analysis**..137

  6.3 **Linguistic Features of the Conclusion Section**...........................141

      6.3.1 Lexical Features 141

      6.3.2 Syntactical Features 144

  6.4 **Useful Expressions for the Conclusion Section** 147

  6.5 **Reflections and Practice** 150

Unit 7 Title and Abstract 157

7.1 Overview 158
- 7.1.1 Purposes of the Title 158
- 7.1.2 Principles of Writing a Title 158
- 7.1.3 Types of Titles 159
- 7.1.4 Capitalization of the Title 160
- 7.1.5 Purposes of the Abstract 161
- 7.1.6 Information Elements of the Abstract 161
- 7.1.7 Types of Abstracts 162
- 7.1.8 Common Problems of Writing the Abstract 163

7.2 Sample Analysis 164
- 7.2.1 Title Analysis 164
- 7.2.2 Different Types of Abstracts 165
- 7.2.3 Textual Analysis of the Abstract 168

7.3 Linguistic Features of the Title and the Abstract 171
- 7.3.1 Lexical Features 171
- 7.3.2 Syntactical Features 174

7.4 Useful Expressions for the Abstract 177

7.5 Reflections and Practice 179

Unit 8 Referencing 187

8.1 Overview 188
- 8.1.1 Purpose of Referencing 188
- 8.1.2 Information Elements of Referencing 188
- 8.1.3 Referencing Styles 190

8.2 Sample Analysis 202

8.3 Reflections and Practice 205

Unit 9 Common Mistakes in Students' Writings 211

9.1 Common Mistakes 212

9.1.1 Lexical Level 212

9.1.2 Syntactical Level 214

9.1.3 Textual Level 217

9.1.4 Academic Conventions 224

9.2 Reflections and Practice 226

Unit 10 Chinglish vs. English 231

10.1 Overview 232

10.1.1 Interlingual Errors of Chinglish 232

10.1.2 Positive and Negative Transfer Between Two Languages 232

10.2 Sample Analysis of Representational Chinglish Structures 233

10.2.1 Interferences of Chinese Culture 233

10.2.2 Interferences of Chinese Thinking Pattern 234

10.2.3 Inappropriate Expressions 238

10.2.4 Confusion Between Coordination and Subordination 239

10.3 Some Salient Differences Between English and Chinese 240

10.3.1 Reversed Word Order 241

10.3.2 Postpositive Attributive in English 241

10.3.3 Static English and Dynamic Chinese 242

10.3.4 Multifunction of English Attributive Clauses 242

10.3.5 Compact English and Relatively Loose Chinese 243

10.3.6 Chinese Four-Character Sentences and English Words and Phrases 244

10.3.7 English Passive Sentences and Chinese Sentences with No Subjects 244

10.3.8 Inanimate Subjects in English and Chinese Sentences 245

10.4 Reflections and Practice 246

Unit 11 Posters for International Conferences and Data Presentation 251

11.1 Overview 252
11.2 Pre-Conference Correspondence 252
11.3 Making a Research Poster 255
    11.3.1 What Is a Research Poster? 255
    11.3.2 Instructions on Making a Poster for an International Conference 256
    11.3.3 Design Suggestions for Scientific Posters 258
11.4 Information Elements of Posters 259
11.5 Poster Samples 259
11.6 Linguistic Features of Posters 262
11.7 Data Presentation 265
11.8 Reflections and Practice 268

Unit 12 Manuscript Publication 271

12.1 Overview 272
    12.1.1 Aims and Scope of the Target Journal 272
    12.1.2 Guide for Authors 273
    12.1.3 Cover Letter 275
12.2 Response to Editors and Reviewers 276
    12.2.1 Peer-Review Process 276
    12.2.2 Three Golden Rules of Responding to Reviewers' Comments 277
12.3 Reflections and Practice 280

References 285

Unit 1
Introduction

Warm-up Questions

1. What is the purpose of the Introduction section?

2. What information elements are included in the Introduction section?

3. What are the salient linguistic features of the Introduction section?

1.1 Overview

1.1.1 Purpose of the Introduction Section

The main purpose of the Introduction section is to provide a reason for writing a particular paper, moving from a general discussion of the topic to the particular question of the hypothesis being investigated. It also aims to attract readers' interests in the topic. The reader will be more inclined to read a paper if the Introduction section is clear-cut, well-organized, and engaging. Now let's see what information elements should be included in the Introduction section.

1.1.2 Information Elements of the Introduction Section

The following are usually expected in the Introduction section of a thesis or dissertation:

- rationale for the research (or research background, reason/motivation of the study);
- aims and objectives;
- research questions;
- data;
- research method;
- theoretical framework;
- structure of the thesis or dissertation.

For relatively short essays, the following are worth including, in the following order:

- definitions of any terms in the title that are unclear;
- some background information;
- reference to other writers who have discussed this topic;
- the purpose of the writing and the importance of the subject;
- any limitations, e.g., geographical or chronological, that the writer sets;
- a summary of the main points the writer intends to cover.

1.1.3 Main Focus of Writing the Introduction Section

For the empirical study papers, John Swales (1990) proposed a Create-a-Research-Space (CARS) model: Three Moves in Research Paper Introduction, which includes: Move 1. Establishing a research territory; Move 2. Establishing a niche; Move 3. Occupying the niche. The linguistic realization of the three moves is as follows:

Move 1. Establishing a research territory:

- by showing that the general research area is essential, central, interesting, problematic, or relevant in some way (optional);
- by introducing and reviewing items of previous research in the area (obligatory).

Move 2. Establishing a niche:

- by indicating a gap in the previous research or by extending prior knowledge in some way (obligatory).

Move 3. Occupying the niche:

- by outlining purposes or stating the nature of the present research (obligatory);
- by listing research questions or hypotheses;
- by announcing principal findings;
- by stating the value of the present research;
- by indicating the structure of the research paper.

In summary, the information structure of the Introduction section is like an inverted triangular structure, as shown in Figure 1.1 below, making the statements from general to specific.

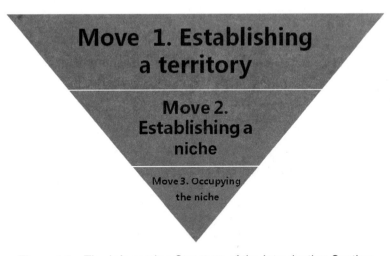

Figure 1.1 The Information Structure of the Introduction Section

1.2 Sample Analysis

Sample 1 (From the Field of Computer Science)

Sentences 1–5: **Move 1:** Establishing a research territory (by claiming centrality, making topic generalization(s)	1) Recently, because of the rise of deep learning, more and more people pay attention to the research and application of neural networks. 2) Various programming frameworks are developed, and a wide range of high-performance tasks such as visual and speech recognition, language modeling, object detection, and medical diagnosis are demonstrated. 3) Concurrently, neuromorphic computing aiming at mimicking brain intelligence has also experienced rapid development. 4) Many neuromorphic platforms supporting the bio-plausible spiking neural networks (SNNs) are reported, such as TrueNorth, SpiNNaker, and Loihi. 5) Besides various applications, the low power consumption benefit from the event-driven paradigm makes the neuromorphic chip quite promising for deployment on embedded devices.
Sentences 6–8: Introduction to the background and shortcomings of the previously adopted methods **Sentences 9–14:** **Move 2:** Establishing a niche (by indicating a gap in the previous research	6) Many-core architecture is widely adopted among the existing neural network chips due to the high parallelism via inter-core concurrency. 7) This architecture usually removes the off-chip global memory. 8) Instead, it pins the memory into every core for a better locality. 9) However, this memory partition makes the model-to-core mapping more complicated when deploying neural network models on the chip. 10) The scheme for mapping the logical cores describing the high-level model to the physical cores supporting low-level execution greatly influences the inter-core routing efficiency. 11) If the mapping is not appropriate, the transmission of data packets is liable to be blocked, the routing time will be significantly increased, and the entire system's efficiency will be reduced. 12) Therefore, it is necessary to optimize the mapping process.

	13) Furthermore, the interconnection topology of existing many-core architectures is mostly in a 2D mesh, which is very similar to conventional Network on Chip (NoC). 14) Similarly, there also exists a deadlock possibility under certain routing strategies, including point-to-point routing and multicast routing.
Sentences 15–18: Three ways to avoid the routing deadlock are specifically proposed	15) There are three possible ways to avoid the deadlock: (1) design large buffer in the router module to accommodate packets as many as possible; (2) design smart routing strategy to guarantee deadlock-free trajectories of data movement; (3) add extra constraints during core placement to destruct the deadlock condition. 16) Consider these three means in practice: First, the buffer size is usually a fixed value after chip fabrication which cannot always guarantee the non-full condition, so the first way is impractical; second, the deadlock-free routing strategy usually suffers from special constraints, which will cause an inefficient routing when the network becomes large. 17) Moreover, if a workload requires multicast routing, it is very difficult to design a routing strategy to avoid deadlock.
Sentence 18: Excluding the first two methods, and only considering the third method	18) Therefore, the third way of adding extra deadlock-free constraints during core placement seems the only promising solution that focuses on our work.
Sentences 19–30: **Move 3:** Occupying the niche (by outlining purposes and announcing principal findings)	19) In this paper, we formulate the model-to-core mapping towards low-latency and deadlock-free performance as a constrained optimization problem. 20) We use our developed Tianjic Chip as the objective mapping hardware, a coarse-grained multi-core neuromorphic chip. 21) The chip is composed of 2D-mesh arranged neuromorphic cores. 22) A core is the basic computing unit, including axon, synapse, dendrite, soma, and router modules. 23) The axon module acts as a data buffer to store the inputs and the outputs. 24) Synapses are designed to store on-chip weights and are pinned close to the dendrite for better memory localities. 25) The dendrite is an integration engine that contains multipliers and accumulators. 26) The soma is a computation unit for neuronal

	transformations. **27)** Intra-core and inter-core communications are realized by a router that supports arbitrary topology through packet transmission. **28)** Each core consists of 256 neurons, and multiple cores connection could perform larger network structures, e.g., a layer of a network or a whole network.
Sentences 29–30: Stating value or justification for carrying out the current study	**29)** Under the routing strategies with point-to-point and multicast paths, we incorporate two deadlock-free constraints and a simulated annealing algorithm to find a mapping scheme that minimizes the routing time, communication amount, and energy consumption for inter-core data movement. **30)** Then, we use multi-layer perceptron (MLP) and convolutional neural network (CNN) applications to evaluate our algorithm.
Sentences 31–36: Indicating paper structure	**31)** The rest of this paper is organized as follows. **32)** In Section 2, related works are briefly introduced. **33)** In Section 3, mapping preliminaries on the many-core architecture are provided, and the constrained optimization problem is formulated. **34)** Section 4 presents our mapping algorithm. **35)** Experimental results are shown in Section 5. **36)** Finally, we conclude the paper in Section 6. **Source:** Ma, C., Zhao, Q., Li, G., Deng, L. & Wang, G. 2020. A deadlock-free physical mapping method on the many-core neural network chip. *Neurocomputing, 401*: 327–337.

Sample 2 (From the Field of Public Management)

Sentences 1–3: **Move 1:** Establishing a research territory (from general to specific)	**1)** E-governance is the use of digital technologies by the government to improve how services are provided and transform government's overall functioning and effectiveness (Saxena, 2005; Torres, Pina & Acerete, 2006). **2)** Some scholars prefer e-governance rather than e-government to describe a similar range of government programs involving digital technology. **3)** Although the specific programs covered by both terms overlap, each term emphasizes a different way of organizing governmental authorities and institutions. **4)** E-government refers narrowly to public functions and

Sentence 4: Defining the term by distinguishing "e-government" from "e-governance"	institutions that have become digitized; e-governance is a broader concept that refers to the digitization of all the relationships and the governmental and non-governmental factors that contribute to the services and policy-making functions of public institutions (Coe, Paquet & Roy, 2001; Saxena, 2005).
Sentence 5: **Move 2:** Establishing a niche **Sentences 6–13:** **Move 3:** Occupying the niche (by stating value or justification for carrying out the current study) The core issues explored in the article Ideas and methods to address the issues	5) Despite the growing debate about the development and direction of e-governance, the extent of its influence on public organizations remains an open question. 6) In this article, we seek to add to this literature by adopting a global, evolutionary perspective to uncover patterns in trends at a historical and geographic level. For Torres et al. (2006), especially the city governments have posed interesting subjects for the study of e-governance. 7) They tend to have regular interactions with citizens in a localized geographic region, thereby providing a lens for the citizen-government relationships that characterize governance processes. 8) This study focused its attention on municipalities from around the world rather than the European Union cities studied by Torres et al. 9) Furthermore, the world's e-governance capacity is steadily rising, and the time is ripe for improving our scholarly understanding of why this is the case as well as uncovering stories from cities at the forefront of this truly global shift in public administration. 10) This article will answer three central questions concerning the evolution of global e-governance trends: (1) What e-governance features characterize the top e-governance performers? (2) Are cities steadily improving e-governance services, or is growth slowing over the time? (3) Are there any consistent patterns to e-governance development? 11) This paper provides a descriptive analysis of an original data source and an in-depth analysis of seven high-performing city websites to address the first and second questions. 12) To explore the third research question, we apply descriptive analyses and further conceptual analysis to assess different

Sentence 13: The significance of the research	global rates of change and e-governance achievements. 13) Through these analyses, we also create a typology of global e-government evolution. **Source:** Manoharan, A. P., Ingrams, A., Kang, D. & Zhao, H. 2021. Globalization and worldwide best practices in e-government. *International Journal of Public Administration, 44*(6): 465–476.

1.3 Linguistic Features of the Introduction Section

The Introduction is the first and also the key section for both the reader and the writer. It gives the first impression to the reader. For the writer, the Introduction section serves as a transition by moving the reader from the world outside of the paper to the world within. To some extent, a carefully crafted Introduction section acts as a springboard, establishing the order and direction for the entire paper. Whether short or long, Introduction sections should be intelligently structured with explicit language. In the following, we will analyze the language of the Introduction sections in terms of lexical features and syntactical features.

1.3.1 Lexical Features

There are some commonly used vocabularies and sentence structures corresponding to the three moves of the Introduction section. In the following, some frequently used words and sentence structures are provided to facilitate the writers in the writing process.

1. Commonly used verbs or phrases

The commonly used verbs or phrases for claiming centrality are: "is/are", "pay attention to", "concentrate on", "concern", "grow", "find", "pursue", "study", "develop", "improve", "use", "generate", "focus on", "turn to", "become", etc. For example:

- ✓ Recently, more and more people **pay attention to** the research and application of…
- ✓ Many recent studies **have focused on**…
- ✓ One major issue in early… research **concerned**…
- ✓ The issue **has grown** in importance in light of recent…
- ✓ The… **has been extensively studied** in recent years.
- ✓ The possibility of… **has generated** wide interest in…
- ✓ The study of… **has become** an important aspect of…

- ✓ Human beings **have pursued** well-being since ancient times.
- ✓ ... **is** one of the principal claims of a modern public management.
- ✓ ... **is** a popular way of specifying, designing, and verifying hardware systems.
- ✓ ... **are** some of the most widely used seismic structure forms at present.

The commonly used verbs for indicating gaps include: "neglect", "overlook", "underestimate", "challenge", "debate", "suffer", "limit", etc. For example:

- ✓ Previous research in this field **has neglected**...
- ✓ Previous research **has overlooked**...

The commonly used verbs for outlining purposes are: "specify", "report", "introduce", "provide", etc. For example:

- ✓ Related works **are briefly introduced**...
- ✓ ... **are provided**...

2. Commonly used transitional words and negative adjectives for establishing a niche

The commonly used transitional words for establishing a niche include: "however", "unfortunately", "yet", "nevertheless", "although", "despite", etc. For example:

- ✓ **However**, previous research in this field has been restricted to...
- ✓ **Unfortunately**, there is still no in vivo method available at present.
- ✓ **Yet**, the forces behind this reaction are still not fully understood.
- ✓ **Although** many colleges and universities have... courses and majors, few have attempted to include... perspectives in their general coursework.

Negative adjectives are also frequently used in indicating the gap, which may include: "controversial", "conflicting", "unconvincing", "questionable", "incomplete", "unsatisfactory", "disputed", "inconsistent", etc. For example:

- ✓ Nevertheless, these attempts to establish a link between secondary smoke and lung cancer are at present **unconvincing**.
- ✓ However, the literature provides **conflicting** evidence on the nature and extent of the earnings information contained in dividend announcements.
- ✓ The issue of... has been a **controversial** and much-**disputed** subject within the field of...
- ✓ Moreover, we find that these peer effects are **inconsistent** with rational responses to information flowing through the employee network.

3. Commonly used words or phrases for expressing needs/interests/desires

After the gap is indicated, the writer often tells the readers what needs to be done or should be done by using "need to be", "be of interest to", etc. For example:

- ✓ The differences **need to be** analyzed.
- ✓ It would thus **be of interest to** learn how…
- ✓ It **is desirable / of interest to** compare…
- ✓ It would seem, therefore, that further investigations **are needed** in order to…

4. Commonly used modal verbs for stating value or justification

Modal verbs such as "could", "may", "can", "might" are often used for stating value or justification for carrying the current study. For example:

- ✓ The model described here **could** serve as the basis for a study of automatic measurement systems.
- ✓ Both factors under investigation in this study **may** be of importance in explaining the irregular occurrence of this disease.
- ✓ As a move in this direction, I hope that the present small-scale study **could** serve as a starting point to later, possibly more sophisticated, research of a comparative nature.

1.3.2 Syntactical Features

There are also some syntactical features in writing the Introduction section, like using contrastive statements and descriptive sentences frequently. In the following, the usage of these sentences will be presented.

1. Making references

In Move 1 of the Introduction section, the writer often reviews some items or relevant studies of previous research in the area by making references. For example:

- ✓ Scholars have long debated the impact of… on…
- ✓ A much debated question is whether…
- ✓ One of the most significant current discussions in… is…
- ✓ Many researchers have found that in some countries…
- ✓ E-governance is the use of digital technologies by the government to improve how services are provided and transform government's overall functioning and effectiveness (Saxena, 2005; Torres, Pina & Acerete, 2006).

2. Statements for questions and challenges for establishing a niche

In Move 2, some writers establish a niche by raising questions. For example:

- ✓ However, **it remains unclear whether**…
- ✓ These findings suggest that this treatment **might not be so effective** when applied to…

- ✓ However, in all three cases, the methodologies used for analyzing self-citations **are flawed**.

3. The frequently used tenses

The present simple tense, the past simple tense and the present perfect tense are often used in writing an Introduction section.

1) The present simple tense + infinitives

The structure of "the present simple tense + infinitives" is used to make purpose statements in Move 3. For example:

- ✓ The aim of the present paper **is to** give…
- ✓ **It is** the purpose of the present paper **to** provide…
- ✓ The main purpose of the experiment reported here **is to**…
- ✓ This study **is designed to** evaluate…
- ✓ The aim of this investigation **is to** test…

2) The past simple tense

The past simple tense is often used in the Introduction section to review the past practice. For example:

- ✓ At the end of the 1980s and the beginning of the 1990s, many organizations **adopted** total quality management (TOM) in response to environmental changes.
- ✓ Similarly, Wagenheim and Reurink (1991) **called for** the adoption of customer service management in public administration because of the similarities with private enterprise, particularly in terms of customer expectations regarding information, responsiveness, and friendliness of the service provider.

3) The present perfect tense

The present perfect tense of the verbs is often used in the first sentence (opening sentence) in Move 1 to state the centrality of the paper. For example:

- ✓ Human beings **have pursued** well-being since ancient times.
- ✓ Many investigators **have recently turned to**…

4. Negative sentences

1) Negative sentences in general

Negative sentences are often used in Move 2 by showing that the research story so far is not yet complete (indicating a gap). For example:

- ✓ Previous studies of… **have not dealt with**…

- ✓ Researchers **have not treated**… in much detail.
- ✓ Such expositions **are unsatisfactory** because they…
- ✓ Most studies in the field of… **have not focused on**…

2) Negative subjects used for indicating gaps

Some writers also use negative subjects for indicating gaps in Move 2. For example:

- ✓ However, **little information** is about…
- ✓ **No attention** has been paid to…
- ✓ **No work** has been done/reported on…
- ✓ **Few/none of data/studies/investigations** are available on…
- ✓ **Few researches** have been devoted to…

5. Contrastive statements

A contrastive statement is often used to establish the motivation for the study by the end of Move 2. For example:

- ✓ The research has tended to focus on…, **rather than** on…
- ✓ These studies have emphasized…, **as opposed to**…
- ✓ Although considerable research has been devoted to…, **rather less attention has been paid to**…

6. Active voice and passive voice

When describing the structure of their paper step by step, some writers prefer to use the active voice. For example:

- ✓ The paper **proceeds** as follows: **Initially**, we review the e-commerce literature and illustrate the knowledge gap. We **then** discuss the research design, the measurement of the variables and data collection; we **present** the analysis and the results. **Finally**, we **conclude** with a discussion of the implications of the finding for theory and practice.

Other writers may prefer to use the passive voice. For example:

- ✓ The rest of this paper **is organized** as follows. In Section 2, related works **are briefly introduced**. In Section 3, mapping preliminaries on the many-core architecture **are provided**, and the constrained optimization problem **is formulated**. Section 4 **presents** our mapping algorithm. Experimental results **are shown** in Section 5.

There is a tendency to use the active voice instead of the passive voice for simplifying the language in scientific papers.

1.4 Useful Expressions for the Introduction Section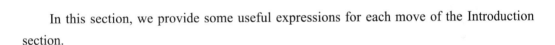

In this section, we provide some useful expressions for each move of the Introduction section.

1. Claiming centrality

- ✓ In recent years, applied researchers have become increasingly interested in…
- ✓ Chinese people today tend to believe that…
- ✓ Conventional wisdom has it that…
- ✓ Common sense seems to dictate that…
- ✓ The standard way of thinking about… is that…
- ✓ One implication of X's treatment of… is that…
- ✓ While they rarely admit as much, … often take for granted that…
- ✓ Recently, because of the rise of deep learning, more and more people pay attention to the research and application of…

2. Making topic generalization(s)

- ✓ In general, electronic government (e-government) means the use of new technologies in the public sector, especially to exchange information with external parties (Schmidt, 2003).
- ✓ Concurrently, neuromorphic computing aiming at mimicking brain intelligence has also experienced rapid development.
- ✓ An elementary precondition for an organization to be customer-oriented is to have knowledge about customer needs, or in terms of the private sector, to have market sensing capability (Day, 1994).

3. Reviewing items of previous research

- ✓ Many neuromorphic platforms supporting the bio-plausible spiking neural networks (SNNs) are reported, such as…, …, and…
- ✓ Initially, researchers had attributed this e-Gov divide to differences in IT and network infrastructure as well as a variety of national characteristics (e.g., Norris, 2001).

4. Establishing a niche

- ✓ However, the previous research in this field has concentrated on / disregarded / failed to consider / ignored…
- ✓ However, more recently some authors have persuasively argued that there is more to…

5. Making counter-claiming

- ✓ However, in all three cases, the methodologies used for analyzing self-citations are flawed.
- ✓ Recent arguments (e.g., Fowler & Aksnes, 2007) for excluding self-citations from performance assessments rest on a number of false assumptions.

6. Raising questions

- ✓ Doubts have been raised whether urban growth management is effective in…
- ✓ It would thus be of significance to learn how…
- ✓ It would seem that, therefore, further investigations are needed to…

7. Outlining purposes or stating the nature of the present research

- ✓ The aim of the present series of these studies was to investigate…
- ✓ With our study, we aim at providing scientific evidence on how…
- ✓ This study was designed to evaluate…
- ✓ The present work extends the use of the last model by…
- ✓ The primary focus of this investigation was to test…
- ✓ It is the purpose of the present paper to provide…
- ✓ We now report the interaction between…
- ✓ The primary focus of this paper is on…

8. Listing research questions or hypotheses

- ✓ A model for the discourse of genre analysis is then called for, which is rich in sociological, cultural, and institutional explanation in order to posit a correlation between language use and extra-linguistic situations.
- ✓ The underlying assumption is that there may be underlying recurrent features which are…

9. Announcing principal findings

- ✓ In this paper, we formulate the model-to-core mapping towards…
- ✓ We now report the interaction between…

10. Indicating the structure of the paper

- ✓ The remainder of this article is divided into two sections. Section 2 gives an overview of the literature. It identifies some gaps in the literature and issues of current concern. Section 3 suggests the way forward which in addition presents a framework for exploring theory and practice in LSP.
- ✓ After this opening introduction unit, Section 2 deals with abstract writing. The next

two sections deal in some detail with the many complexities surrounding the writing of a critical literature review. Section 5 then moves on to some… The final two sections switch attention to texts that are…

✓ The rest of this paper is organized as follows. In Section 2, related works are briefly introduced. In Section 3, mapping preliminaries on the many-core architecture are provided, and the constrained optimization problem is formulated. Section 4 presents our mapping algorithm. Experimental results are shown in Section 5. Finally, we conclude the paper in Section 6.

1.5 Reflections and Practice

❶ Answer the following questions.

1. What are the functions of the Introduction section?
2. What are the three moves of the Introduction section?
3. Is it necessary to indicate the overall structure of the paper in the Introduction section? Why?

❷ Analyze the information elements of the two Introduction sections. Text 1 is in the field of computer science and Text 2 in the field of urban management.

▶ Text 1

1) Recently, because of the rise of deep learning, more and more people pay attention to the research and application of neural networks. Various programming frameworks are developed, and a wide range of high-performance tasks such as visual and speech recognition, language modeling, object detection, and medical diagnosis are demonstrated. 2) Many neuromorphic platforms supporting the bio-plausible spiking neural networks (SNNs) are reported, such as TrueNorth, SpiNNaker, and Loihi. 3) Besides various applications, the low power consumption benefit from the event-driven paradigm makes the neuromorphic chip quite promising for deployment on embedded devices.

4) Many-core architecture is widely adopted among the existing neural network chips due to the high parallelism via inter-core concurrency. This architecture usually removes the off-chip global memory. Instead, it pins the memory into every core for a better locality. 5) However, this memory partition makes the model-to-core mapping more complicated when

deploying neural network models on the chip. The scheme for mapping the logical cores describing the high-level model to the physical cores supporting low-level execution greatly influences the inter-core routing efficiency. If the mapping is not appropriate, the transmission of data packets is liable to be blocked, the routing time will be significantly increased, and the entire system's efficiency will be reduced. Therefore, it is necessary to optimize the mapping process.

Furthermore, the interconnection topology of existing many-core architectures is mostly in a 2D mesh, which is very similar to conventional Network on Chip (NoC). Similarly, there also exists a deadlock possibility under certain routing strategies, including point-to-point routing and multicast routing. **6)** There are three possible ways to avoid the deadlock: (1) design large buffer in the router module to accommodate packets as many as possible; (2) design smart routing strategy to guarantee deadlock-free trajectories of data movement; (3) add extra constraints during core placement to destruct the deadlock condition. **7)** Consider these three means in practice: First, the buffer size is usually a fixed value after chip fabrication which cannot always guarantee the non-full condition, so the first way is impractical; second, the deadlock-free routing strategy usually suffers from special constraints, which will cause an inefficient routing when the network becomes large. Moreover, if a workload requires multicast routing, it is very difficult to design a routing strategy to avoid deadlock. Therefore, the third way of adding extra deadlock-free constraints during core placement seems the only promising solution that focuses on our work.

8) In this paper, we formulate the model-to-core mapping towards low-latency and deadlock-free performance as a constrained optimization problem. We use our developed Tianjic Chip as the objective mapping hardware, a coarse-grained multi-core neuromorphic chip. The chip is composed of 2D-mesh arranged neuromorphic cores. A core is the basic computing unit, including axon, synapse, dendrite, soma, and router modules. The axon module acts as a data buffer to store the inputs and the outputs. Synapses are designed to store on-chip weights and are pinned close to the dendrite for better memory locality. The dendrite is an integration engine that contains multipliers and accumulators. The soma is a computation unit for neuronal transformations. Intra-core and inter-core communications are realized by a router that supports arbitrary topology through packet transmission. Each core consists of 256 neurons, and multiple cores connection could perform larger network structures, e.g., a layer of a network or a whole network. Under the routing strategies with point-to-point and multicast paths, we incorporate two deadlock-free constraints and a simulated annealing algorithm to find a mapping scheme that minimizes the routing time, communication amount, and energy consumption for inter-core data movement. Then, we use multi-layer perception (MLP) and convolutional neural network (CNN) applications to evaluate our algorithm.

Unit 1 Introduction

9) The rest of this paper is organized as follows. In Section 2, related works are briefly introduced. In Section 3, mapping preliminaries on the many-core architecture are provided, and the constrained optimization problem is formulated. Section 4 presents our mapping algorithm. Experimental results are shown in Section 5. Finally, we conclude the paper in Section 6.

Sentence Number	Information Element
1)	
2)	
3)	
4)	
5)	
6)	
7)	
8)	
9)	

Text 2

1) Urban population growth over recent decades has created complications in the management of urban cities (Graham, 2010). To overcome such difficulties, the concept of Smart City was developed by employing smart sensing, computing, and communication technologies in urban management (Chourabi et al., 2012; Washburn et al., 2010). Applications of smart technologies in transportation infrastructure have been widely studied in the literature (Adeli & Jiang, 2009; Glancy, 2014; Xiong et al., 2012). Bridges, as key components of transportation networks, are prone to structural damage resulting in an irrecoverable financial and time loss (Ham et al., 2005). Many bridge structures in modern countries have reached their design life and need to be monitored and retrofitted to remain in service in a cost-effective manner. For example, according to the Canadian Infrastructural Report Card (CCA/CPWA/CSCE/FCM 2016), approximately 40% of bridges in Canada are in fair, poor, or deplorable conditions. The sustainability of transportation networks relies on appropriate monitoring and maintenance operations on bridges. Therefore, structural health monitoring (SHM) techniques were proposed as a critical component of viable transportation networks (Wenzel, 2008).

2) Traditionally, most of the proposed SHM methods required bridge instrumentation with fixed sensors installed on the bridge, for example, Catbas et al. (2008), Guan et al. (2019), Gül and Catbas (2009), Hoult et al. (2010), Hsieh et al. (2006), Ko and Ni (2005), and Wong (2004). The functionality and accuracy of these methods were demonstrated in those studies.

3) However, the feasibility of employing such direct SHM methods on a large number of bridges is a major concern. Instrumentation of each bridge with fixed sensors and creating a data collection network is costly and time-consuming and cannot be employed on all bridges.

4) Therefore, new SHM methods were suggested by focusing on sensors placed in passing vehicles as moving sensors, i.e., indirect monitoring of bridges.

The indirect bridge monitoring concept was first proposed by Yang et al. (2004). They performed dynamic analysis of vehicle-bridge interaction for a simple 2D beam model representing the bridge and a moving mass-spring system representing the vehicle. It was shown that the frequency of the bridge could be extracted from the vibration of the vehicle. Afterward, many studies followed indirect bridge monitoring (Malekjafarian et al., 2015), which are divided into analytical/numerical studies (Hattori et al., 2012; Hester & González, 2017; Keenahan et al., 2014; OBrien et al., 2017; Yang & Chen, 2016), lab-scale experiments (Cerda et al., 2014; Mei et al., 2019; Zhang et al., 2013), and real-life experiments (Kim & Lynch, 2012; Lin & Yang, 2005; Siringoringo & Fujino, 2012). All these studies corroborated the fact that bridge dynamic response exists in the vibration of the passing vehicle and can be extracted to assess the bridge condition.

5) Previously, many experiments studied the effect of car features on the frequency spectrum of the vehicle. Most of the past studies on indirect health monitoring of bridges were conducted using dedicated professional accelerometers placed in the vehicles to collect data from the car, while this study focuses on using smartphones as data-collecting devices in future smart cities. Li et al. (2019) studied the effect of speed on the frequency content recorded on the cars passing over the bridge using a lab-scale test. They concluded that lower speeds benefit the process of frequency identification. A similar conclusion was made in another study by Kim et al. (2011). However, the car models in both studies were not motorized, while the data in our experiments showed that the main effect of the change in the speed of the car on the spectrum was due to the change in the revolving speed of the motor, which is also expected in real-life practice. In another study, Mei et al. (2019) conducted laboratory experiments where both speed and suspension stiffness of the car were considered. However, the damage detection method employed in that study did not focus on the modal analysis of the acceleration data.

Unit 1 Introduction

Regarding large-scale indirect monitoring of populations of bridges in smart cities, where there are different vehicles with different features traveling at different speeds, it is vital to investigate the robustness of indirect monitoring methods using smartphones against vehicle features. **6)** Therefore, this study focused on the application of smartphones in different cars traveling at different speeds to capture the frequencies of the bridge. Several laboratory experiments were conducted using two experimental bridge models with different support conditions and a robot car model capable of changing suspension springs and traveling speeds. In total, three spring types and three speeds were applied to the car, resulting in nine combinations. The experiment consisted of three stages. First, vibration analysis of the bridge was conducted to extract the natural frequencies of the bridge. Then, robot car vibration was analyzed to study the frequency spectrum of the car while moving on a rigid non-vibrating surface. Finally, the vibration of the car while moving on the bridge was studied. Comparing the results of these three stages provided the possibility of investigating the robustness of using smartphones to capture bridge frequencies against vehicle features.

Sentence Number	Information Element
1)	
2)	
3)	
4)	
5)	
6)	

(II) Select two or three Introduction sections in your research field and complete the following tasks.

1. Identify the information elements in the Introduction sections of the articles you are reading.
2. Analyze the sequencing of the moves in the Introduction sections.
3. Highlight the verbs, references, and some other linguistic features of the Introduction sections, such as the use of tense, passive voice or active voice.

IV Match the three moves of the Introduction in Column A with the expressions in Column B.

Column A	Column B
Move 1: Establishing a territory **Move 2:** Establishing a niche **Move 3:** Occupying the niche	1) The paper attempts to address these gaps by presenting a new organization of the pathways linking the built environment to SWB and by providing an overview of the state of knowledge. 2) Improving the quality of life in cities is becoming an increasingly critical issue for urban planning. 3) Indeed, there appears to be an e-Gov differential developing among nations akin to the so-called digital divide. 4) Nevertheless, the whole range of ways through which the built environment may contribute to SWB—the personal evaluation of the quality of life—is still not sufficient. 5) However, more recently, some authors have persuasively argued that there is more to this e-Gov divide than technology infrastructure maturity and national culture.

V Below are the sentences from an Introduction section of a paper. Put the sentences into a proper order to work out the Introduction section. The Introduction section falls into four paragraphs. The first sentence is given for each paragraph. But the rest sentences of each paragraph are not yet in order. Rearrange the sentences in the order that you think the author originally wrote them.

Paragraph 1

____1____ A. Information technology is being developed and used by diverse groups of people. Reasons for this include the outsourcing of development activities, for example, from Europe to Asia, the emergence of globally available systems such as mobile phones and web-based applications, the increasing use of localized information technology by local-language populations across the world, and the emerging multi-culture dress of many countries in, for example, Europe.

_____ B. This is surprising because definitions of usability, and HCI in general, emphasize the importance of concepts such as the context of use, which includes users' cultural background.

_____ C. However, most research on usability valuation methods presupposes that usability evaluation is unaffected by cultural issues.

_____ D. For example, the cultural background of experimental participants is rarely reported, task scenarios are assumed to be culturally unbiased, interface heuristics are presented as universals, and disagreements between studies are rarely discussed in terms of cultural effects.

_____ E. In attempting to disentangle this diversity, culture has received increasing attention in software engineering, human-computer interaction (HCI), and usability evaluation.

Paragraph 2

__1__ A. This study examines differences in cultural cognition in the thinking-aloud method.

_____ B. In essence, TA consists of a user who thinks out loud while using a system, and an evaluator who observes the user and listens in on his or her thoughts.

_____ C. The presented arguments should be valid for the thinking-aloud method in general, but the context that is used to illustrate the arguments is usability evaluation.

_____ D. Usability evaluation based on the thinking-aloud method (henceforth, TA) is in widespread use and commonly considered the single most valuable method for usability evaluation.

_____ E. The research on TA is considerable and includes studies of the number of users needed for finding a specified proportion of the usability problems in an application, the potential of having users work in pairs, the evaluator's influence on the set of problems identified, and the validity of verbalization (Boren & Ramey, 2000).

_____ F. The aim of this study is to introduce the cultural psychology of Nisbett (2003) as a conceptual basis for thinking about TA and to analyze the influence of culture on TA.

_____ G. Recent work on the influence of culture on people's perception and thinking yields results that call into question whether our knowledge and assumptions about such essential characteristics of TA are valid outside of Europe and the U.S.

Paragraph 3

___1___ A. Culture is a complex concept. In this study, we follow Nisbett's (2003) use of the term culture to distinguish between regional differences in cognitive style, that is, empirically well defined differences in the perception and thinking of people with a background from majority cultures in different regions of the world.

_____ B. It is evident that stable cultural differences exist between numerous ethnic groups and countries, not just between Westerners and Easterners. For example, Nisbett's work may also be valid and vital for usability testing in India.

_____ C. Following Nisbett (2003), we focus on cultural differences between Westerners (people from Western Europe and U.S. citizens with European origins) and Easterners (people from China and the countries heavily influenced by its culture, such as Korea).

_____ D. Distinctions based on regional culture have contributed substantially to understanding differences in cultural cognition.

_____ E. We choose Nisbett's view of culture because we find its micro-level view of culture appropriate for an analysis of usability evaluation. In contrast to Hofstede (2001), which seems the more common approach to culture in HCI, Nisbett investigates how basic mental processes are culturally dependent.

Paragraph 4

___1___ A. This paper does not analyze cultural differences in what makes a good interface.

_____ B. In the next section, we introduce Nisbett's (2003) work on cultural cognition.

_____ C. Rather, we seek to provide a conceptual analysis of the influence of culture on various aspects of performing usability evaluations based on TA.

_____ D. Then, we provide a simplified overview of TA as a reference model for the subsequent analysis.

_____ E. In conclusion, we discuss implications for practical usability evaluation as well as for usability research.

_____ F. Our analysis in the subsequent section on the influence of culture on TA consists of applying the work on cultural cognition to four central elements of TA: (1) instructions and tasks, (2) the user's verbalizations, (3) the evaluator's reading of the user, and (4) the overall relationship between the user and the evaluator.

Unit 1 Introduction

Ⅵ Fill in each blank with the appropriate form of each verb given in the brackets.

The strong positive market reaction to announcements of dividend changes 1) _____ (be) one of the most robust empirical findings in corporate finance. Yet, the forces behind this reaction are still not fully 2) _____ (understand). Miller and Modigliani (1961) 3) _____ (suggest) that dividend changes 4) _____ (reveal) managers' information about the firm's future earnings prospects to investors. However, the literature 5) _____ (provide) conflicting evidence on the nature and extent of the earnings information 6) _____ (contain) in dividend announcements.

In surveys, managers 7) _____ (say) they 8) _____ (view) dividends as a persistent commitment to pay out cash and, therefore, change dividends only when 9) _____ (anticipate) a permanent change in earnings. Consistent with this intuition, several studies 10) _____ (find) that dividend changes 11) _____ (be) associated with greater persistence of past earnings changes and that higher dividend levels 12) _____ (be) associated with higher and more persistent earnings. These findings 13) _____ (seem) to suggest that dividend changes 14) _____ (be) useful for 15) _____ (predict) future unexpected earnings. However, the evidence on this question is decidedly 16) _____ (mix).

Ⅶ Select the appropriate word or phrase in the box to complete each sentence. Change the form where necessary.

examine	occur	be consistent with	include	show
be likely to be	address	be not necessarily	corroborate	identify

1. All these studies _____ the fact that bridge dynamic response exists in the vibration of the passing vehicle and can be extracted to assess the bridge condition.
2. The contribution of this paper is to _____ if these correlations emanate from a causal relation directly running from democratic development to loan pricing.
3. However, democratic development _____ always beneficial for loan rates.
4. Using a common classification, we can _____ two main classes of strategies: quasi steady-state methods and transient optimal methods.
5. Large magnitude earthquakes in densely populated regions do not _____ very frequently, but they can kill tens to hundreds of thousands of people.
6. To date, this _____ to be possible on dedicated smartphones but not on personal smartphones.

7. Although many colleges and universities have comparative literature courses and majors, few have attempted to _____ global perspectives in their general course work.

8. Moreover, we find that these peer effects _____ rational responses to information flowing through the employee network.

9. People's decisions _____ influenced by those with whom they interact.

10. To _____ this concern, we exploit a unique feature of our data relative to other samples of investor trading decisions used in prior research; namely, the inclusion of worker-firm matches.

VIII Rearrange the words and phrases in each group into clear and coherent sentences.

1. to build, is, the fastest and best, the main goal of, car racing teams, performing cars possible.

2. indicates, this result, that, provided, graphene, a hermetic seal for cells.

3. the special substrates, furthermore, to adapt to oil-immersion lenses, used in cryo-electron microscope and liquid enclosures, high-resolution optical microscopy methods, are difficult, for correlation with.

4. the best set-up, drivers and engineers work together to find, race line, and velocity profile, the time on a given track, minimizing.

5. the minimum-time problem, have been introduced, many computational strategies, in the literature to solve.

IX Translate the following sentences into English.

1. 铝是一个丰富的元素，它分布在人体的身体组织、器官和骨骼中，但是它确切的生物性功能还没有完全弄清楚。

2. 《美国肾病杂志》在1985年第6期用整个版面讨论了铝的毒性问题。

3. 近几十年来，城市人口的增长使城市管理变得复杂。为了克服这些困难，人们通过在城市管理中采用智能传感、计算和通信技术将"智能城市"的概念发展起来了。

4. 最近，一些研究小组提出了一种替代方法，即使用车辆中乘客智能手机的间接监视方法，如下所述。

5. 但是，两项研究中的汽车模型都不是电动的，而我们实验中的数据表明，汽车速度变化对频谱的主要影响是由于电动机转速的变化。

Unit 1 Introduction

✖ Translate the following paragraphs into Chinese.

Business scholars continue to document wide interest in the dynamics of business groups (BGs) and their affiliated firms. One growth strategy that BG-affiliated firms regularly implement is corporate diversification. Prior research has examined how diversification impacts profitability, company valuation, and other performance parameters of affiliated firms (Carney et al., 2011; Kedia et al., 2006; Lee et al., 2008). In enriching this research stream, previous studies have also examined how heterogeneous features of BG, such as interfirm relationships, social ties, group size, diversity, and shared ownership (George & Kabir, 2012), affect firm performance. These works are indeed insightful and increase our understanding of BG firms' diversification and subsequent implications. However, these studies implicitly assume that the relationships they examine are uniform across different industry sectors such as manufacturing and services.

Accordingly, in this study we explore two important issues relating to BG-affiliated firms: How does the industry sector influence (a) the corporate diversification-firm performance relationship and (b) the impact of BG heterogeneity (in size, diversity, and share ownership) on the corporate diversification-firm performance relationship? Drawing on strategy and marketing literature, we argue and empirically demonstrate that the aforesaid relationships vary depending on whether the local firm belongs to the manufacturing or serious sector. This study, therefore, contributes to the corporate diversification literature in general and BG scholarship in particular by shedding new light on the influence of industry sector. The section that follows provides the conceptual foundations of the study. The subsequent section develops hypotheses for empirical testing. We then provide details of data and statistical methods and present the results of data analysis of a sample of Indian BG-affiliated firms. The final section discusses the implications and limitations of the study and provides suggestions for future research.

Unit 2
Literature Review

Warm-up Questions

1. What is the purpose of the Literature Review section?

2. What information elements are included in the Literature Review section?

3. What are the salient linguistic features of the Literature Review section?

2.1 Overview

2.1.1 Purposes of the Literature Review Section

As an indispensable part in a paper, the Literature Review section serves the purposes of:
- summarizing the key research outcome from the previous work;
- classifying and synthesizing the work under review;
- providing a critical evaluation of the work under review;
- identifying research gaps in the literature for further study;
- laying a foundation for the writer's present work;
- relating the writer's present work to the selected literature;
- displaying the value of the writer's present gap-filling work.

In the Literature Review section, a writer introduces the development of the relevant research area, exhibiting its past, present and even future, and indicating the recent achievements and limitations in this area. The writer will also spare no efforts introducing his own comprehension and evaluation on the relevant research. This introduction demonstrates both the writer's knowledge of the related studies and his abilities of critical thinking, literature integration and literature evaluation. At the same time, this introduction reveals the research gaps to be filled. This gap-filling, furthermore, makes the importance and significance of the writer's present work clear.

On the other hand, many readers are very interested in the Literature Review section since it is a window on the research. The Literature Review section offers readers both global and local view of the research. This enables them to understand the research history and progress, as well as unsolved research problems and reasonable research prospects. It can also bring readers profound insight which may invest their own research with new meaning and new direction. Additionally, readers can also assess the writer's present research.

2.1.2 Information Elements of the Literature Review Section

1. The schema of the Literature Review section

How and what should a writer do in the Literature Review section? Based on the paper retrieval and critical reading, a writer should undertake the following tasks which are also indicated in Figure 2.1:
- generalize the research topic under consideration;
- synthesize and classify the work under review into categories;

- evaluate the work under review;
- identify the problems and limitations of the field;
- consolidate the importance of the writer's present work.

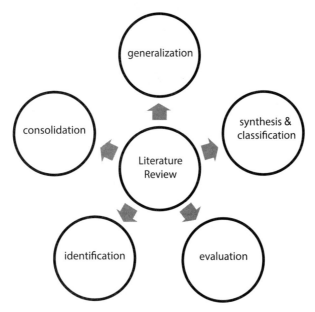

Figure 2.1 The Schema of the Literature Review Section

2. The main components in the Literature Review section

The Literature Review could be an independent section in a piece of paper or mingle with the Introduction section. Many papers are inclined to integrate the Literature Review section with the Introduction section. In both cases, the Literature Review section should, as indicated in Figure 2.2, include such information elements as:

- the field development of the seminal work related to a writer's research;
- the achievements of these studies;
- the methodology for conducting these studies;
- the present situations of these studies;
- the research tendency of these studies;
- the limitations of these studies;
- the research gaps from the limitations;
- the intention to fill the gap(s);
- the research point(s) about the present work and future work;
- the significance of the present study.

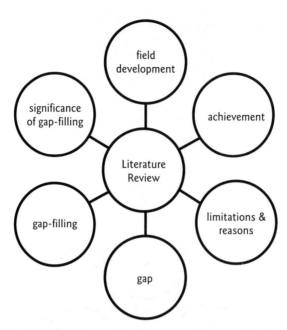

Figure 2.2　The Main Components in the Literature Review Section

2.1.3　Principles of Writing the Literature Review Section

To write a good literature review, writers should stick to the following principles:

- report the literature in a logical order;
- include the sufficient but relevant literature;
- focus on the typical and credible literature;
- synthesize the important literature in an all-round way;
- distinguish the ideas in the literature from the writer's evaluation;
- pinpoint the limitations of previous work in a polite manner;
- fill in the gap from a well-reasoned point of view;
- justify the novelty of the present work felicitously;
- emphasize the indispensable role of the present work;
- cite others' work in an appropriate way.

2.1.4　Citation Methods in the Literature Review

In a literature review, a writer should summarize and synthesize the previous research work in the relevant field. Therefore, the writer must refer to others' studies. Then how to cite others' research work? Generally speaking, there are two citation methods, namely information-prominent method and author-prominent method (Pang, 2008; Cargill &

O'Connor, 2013). The information-prominent method focuses on the information provided by the author while the author-prominent method highlights the name of the author who provides the information.

Usually a literature review begins in an information-prominent way when referring to general research developments and concentrating on the information from different perspectives. The review will, now and then, turn to the author-prominent method when laying stress on the specific author's work or when referring to some specific authors' studies closely related to the writer's research work.

1. Information-prominent citation method

Information-prominent citation method lists the information first, followed by source introduction. A writer can deploy the specific referencing style as per the instruction of a journal to which he intends to submit the research article. Referencing styles are elaborated in Unit 8. Look at the following examples:

- ✓ In the field of urban management, big data is also used in intelligent transportation, environmental monitoring, and urban planning (Jianshu, 2019).
- ✓ Genetic modification of plants is aimed to provide higher yielding crops in a sustainable way (Bongoni, 2016). As a result, food processing based on genetically modified organisms (GMOs) has been playing an increasingly important role in feeding the world's population, as evidenced by the approximately 100-fold rise in area planted with genetically modified (GM) crops in recent years (James, 2011).
- ✓ At the advanced level, the product approach to the teaching of writing "leads to practice in the structure and organization of different kinds of paragraphs and texts" (Richards, 1990: 106), as is used in the teaching of writing to native speakers.
- ✓ Since its inception, learning sciences has studied learning from a multidisciplinary perspective, involving anthropology, linguistics, philosophy, developmental psychology, computer science, neuroscience, and psychology disciplines (Bransford, 2013).
- ✓ Much attention has been paid to the possible negative effects of artificial intelligence on production and employment (Strulik et al., 2013; Goos et al., 2014), ethics (Zou & Schiebinger, 2018), social stability (Makridakis, 2017; Cisse, 2018) and the social attitude (Leavy, 2018; Yu & Cui, 2019).

2. Author-prominent citation method

Author-prominent citation method starts with either the specific author's name or the coreference of the author, followed by the introduction to the information. The listing of coreference of the author usually does not place the author's name "in the main part of the sentence" (Cargill & O'Connor, 2013: 48), so some researchers such as Cargill and O'Connor name this method "weak author-prominent" citation. Look at the following examples (the first one is the weak author-prominent citation while the rest ones are author-prominent citations):

- ✓ Many linguists and teachers (Littlewood, 1981; Brumfit, 1984; Rivers, 1983, 1987; Brooks & Grundy, 1990; etc.) advocate the creation of a natural linguistic environment where writing may well develop out of a relaxed linguistic interaction, not beset by anxiety.
- ✓ Richards (1990: 109) points out that "an undue concern with the formal aspects of writing" in the teaching of FL writing seems to "impede the development of efficient writing strategies".
- ✓ Keh (1990: 295–296) says that peer feedback is referred to by many names such as "peer response, peer editing, peer critiquing and peer evaluation", in light of its function in the writing processes.
- ✓ Lewis (1993) further suggests that teachers should be process-oriented rather than product-oriented. A change of the teacher's mindset from product to process is not only helpful but essential as well.
- ✓ Webb et al. (2011) found a positive association between improved perceptions of neighborhood and quality of life measured over a 4-year period.

2.1.5 Organizational Patterns of the Literature Review Section

The reference to other authors' studies usually depends on three organizational patterns which may, more or less, overlap in some cases. However, one of the patterns should largely dominate a literature report, knitting the information close together. To be brief, a literature review must observe its unity, clarity, and logicality; a haphazard literature review is doomed to failure.

1. Literature in a chronological order

One of the common organizational patterns is chronology summary. The literature is organized in order of publication years or developing stages. This pattern helps to trace the historical development of the related research work by following the underlying logical relation of time. On the other hand, a research progress may not keep pace with its chronology since it sometimes undergoes a spiraling process over a period of time that is a single line of no return. The extract below is a chronological literature:

- ✓ Knowledge of consumer attitudes towards novel food is a valuable source of information necessary for manufacturers when developing strategies related to the new product development and marketing (Frewer et al., 2004). Moreover, the topic of genetically modified foods evokes many controversies in both public opinion and scientific community (Domingo, 2016; Lopez et al., 2016; Cuevas, 2016; Sarno & Manzo, 2016)…

2. Literature in a general-to-specific order

Usually, a literature review begins with general introduction to the research topic and gradually moves to the specific information closely related to the writer's present work. This literature review could look at the parts in relation to the whole for the purpose of deep understanding of relevant research. This pattern enables readers to first catch a macro-level knowledge and then find a micro-level scholarship. The literature review in the extract below goes from general to specific:

- ✓ Due to many controversies evoked by the commercial application of biotechnology and in response to strong opposition of citizens to GM products, there are still many countries that have not decided to formally allow the cultivation of genetically modified plants (Weimer, 2015). The survey performed in European Union (EU) countries indicated that in the context of genetically modified foods, many Europeans remain distrustful (Boccia, 2016). Approximately 53% of people surveyed were opposed to GM foodstuffs. The lowest proportions of opponents of GM foods were in Portugal, Ireland, Spain, Finland. The highest, on the other hand, were noted in France and Denmark (65%), Austria, Norway and Hungary (70%) as well as in Cyprus (76%), Italy (77%), and Greece (81%) (Vlontzos & Duquenne, 2016)…

3. Literature in a point-by-point order

Very often, a literature review describes and synthesizes the background information from different perspectives, or based on different schools and approaches. This logical pattern can also ensure the information flow clear and compact. Moreover, the pattern would contrast the different points and penetrate their merits and demerits, which can facilitate the writer's gap-filling work. The following extract lists the methods of researching into the writing process in a point-by-point order:

- ✓ For the purpose of finding out how writers arrived at their final products, many researchers studied writers' procedures and strategies when they were engaged in writing. Some methodologists (Richards, 1990; Zamel, 1982; Brookes & Grundy, 1990; Arndt, 1987; etc.) listed several methods of researching into the writing process. They include:

    - Introspection: The researchers observe themselves at work writing, and afterwards note down what went on in their own minds during writing;
    - Observation: The researchers observe writers as they write and note down their outward signs when at work;
    - Interview: The researchers interview writers before and after writing to determine

how they cope with particular aspects of a writing task;
- Protocol technique: The researchers let writers talk through what is going on in their minds when they make decisions about writing;
- Reflection: The researchers examine writers' journal accounts of their writing progress.

2.1.6 Common Problems of Writing the Literature Review Section

When writing a literature review, a writer should avoid such common problems as follows:

- provide only a summary;
- include irrelevant literature;
- present insufficient and unreliable literature;
- lack classification and synthesis of the work under review;
- report the literature in a haphazard way;
- lack the evaluation of the previous work;
- lose clear exposition of research gaps;
- understate the relation between the gaps and the present work;
- neglect logical links between different paragraphs;
- use others' work without appropriate acknowledgment.

2.2 Sample Analysis

However short or long a literature review might be, the report of literature should follow a clear and coherent structure which entails sufficient but relevant information. Rigorous and well-organized, a literature review must illuminate the logic underlying the text and acknowledge the previous work in an appropriate way. Simultaneously, the literature review should also distinguish the description of the previous work from the writer's evaluation of the work. In other words, the writer must tell the viewpoints from the facts in his literature review.

Read the following samples. While doing this, identify the information elements and trace the underlying logic in each literature review. Comment on the writing strategies in these samples. The two samples use both the information-prominent method and the author-prominent method.

Unit 2 Literature Review

Sample 1 (From the Field of Medicine and Public Health)

Sentences 1–2: Description of others' studies	1) Cross-sectional studies have found safety concerns, street-level incivilities, and neighborhood disorder to be associated with depressive symptoms and anxiety (Ellaway et al., 2009; Steptoe & Feldman, 2001; Wilson-Genderson & Pruchno, 2013). 2) Both social cohesion and neighborhood climate have also been found to predict depressive symptoms over time (Brown et al., 2009; Stafford et al., 2011). 3) We are aware of only four studies to document an association between neighborhood perceptions and positive well-being. 4) Through the use of large population samples of older individuals living in England, neighborhood cohesion was found to show a positive association (Elliott et al., 2014; Gale et al., 2011) and neighborhood problems a negative association (Gale et al., 2011) with scores on the Warwick-Edinburgh Mental Well-being Scale, a measure of well-being which focuses exclusively on positive features of mental health such as positive affectivity and psychosocial functioning. 5) By using the same well-being scale with a general population sample, a greater sense of belonging to the neighborhood was found to be associated with higher positive well-being (Jones et al., 2014). 6) While these studies were cross-sectional, Webb et al. (2011) found a positive association between improved perceptions of neighborhood and quality of life measured over a 4-year period. 7) To the best of our knowledge, this is the only study to examine longitudinal associations between perceptions of neighborhood and positive well-being in older adults. 8) Thus, more evidence is needed in order to understand whether poor mental health leads to more negative perceptions of one's neighborhood or vice versa. 9) Additionally, as seen above, the majority of previous research has focused on depression with little attention paid to positive affective states. **Source:** Toma, A., Hamer, M. & Shankar, A. 2015. Associations between neighborhood perceptions and mental well-being among older adults. *Health & Place, 34*: 46–53.
Sentence 3: Synthesis of others' studies	
Sentences 4–5: Description of others' studies	
Sentence 6: Description and synthesis of others' studies	
Sentence 7: Evaluation of others' studies and gap 1	
Sentence 8: Gap-filling	
Sentence 9: Evaluation of gap 2	

35

Sample 2 (From the Field of Biomechanics)

Sentence 1: Overview statement	1) Arterial hemodynamics plays a decisive role in the study of artery diseases (especially atherosclerotic diseases) [1], and cardiac surgeons must also consider the dynamic factors of blood flow in the process of surgery and interventional therapy for cardiovascular diseases [2]. 2) At present, there are mainly three types of hemodynamics models [3].
Sentence 2: Classification statement	
Sentence 3: Classification 1	3) According to the spatial dimension, the first is the three-dimensional model, which introduces the blood viscosity and vascular mechanical properties, solves the incompressible Navier-Stokes (NS) equation and mass conservation continuity, and simulates the three-dimensional blood flow [4]. 4) But because of the massive computation required, the three-dimensional model can only simulate blood flow behavior in the range of a few centimeters to a few meters.
Sentence 4: Limitation of model 1	
Sentence 5: Classification 2	5) The second is the one-dimensional model, which simulates the pressure wave propagation behavior in a large range of vascular trees by using Euler equation according to the geometric features of one-dimensional cylindrical vessels [5, 6]. 6) However, the one-dimensional model is not applicable to the overall analysis of the blood vessel system.
Sentence 6: Limitation of model 2	
Sentence 7: Classification 3 **Sentences 8–11:** Achievements of model 3	7) The third widely used electrical model is Wind-kessel. 8) The model abstracts the functional circuit of the artery and studies the hemodynamic properties equivalent by means of the mechanical/electrical analogy method. 9) Wind-kessel model can be used for coupled analysis of the heart and vascular system, as well as to study the effects of vascular compliance and peripheral resistance on blood pressure [7]. 10) In clinical medicine, Wind-kessel model has also been used to predict dynamic atherosclerosis index [8], and describe the function of cardiac pump [9] and stability of cardiac output [10]. 11) Moreover, it has also been used to study the reliability of artificial heart load and artificial valve [11]. …

Sentence 12: Research gap	12) However, the above models only studied physical factors, ignoring the influence of vascular geometry on blood flow.
Sentences 13–15: Evaluation	13) In fact, arteries have multiple levels of structure: aorta, arterioles, and capillaries. 14) The three have different elasticity. 15) Different elasticity has different effects on blood flow.
Sentences 16–17: Gap-filling	16) Therefore, considering the differences between vessels of different levels, Goldwyn et al. processed the aorta and arterioles into two-stage elastic cavities, and established a lumped parameter model of four-element two-stage elastic cavities (Fig. 2a) [17]. 17) Furthermore, Liu et al. introduced blood micro circulation, processed the aorta, arterioles and capillaries into three-stage elastic cavities, and established a concentrated parameter model of three-stage elastic cavities (Fig. 2b) [18].

Source: extracted from student's authentic work, 2021.

2.3 Linguistic Features of the Literature Review Section

2.3.1 Lexical Features

1. Inanimate subjects

Inanimate subjects frequently emerge in the composition of a literature review. In other words, an abstract noun may serve as the subject in a sentence. Sentences with inanimate subjects lay more stress on objectivity, logicality, and accuracy of the information. At the same time, inanimate subjects may also perform one of the rhetoric functions, personification, and add beauty to a sentence. Sentences with inanimate subjects will also appear in other sections of a paper, such as the Results and Discussion sections. Below are some sentences selected from the Literature Review section of some papers. Inanimate subjects in these sentences are in bold.

✓ **Cross-sectional studies** have found safety concerns, street-level incivilities, and neighborhood disorder to be associated with depressive symptoms and anxiety.

✓ **Arterial hemodynamics** plays a decisive role in the study of artery diseases.

- ✓ **Different elasticity** has different effects on blood flow.
- ✓ **Trends** in public opinion about marriage and childbearing reflect the effectiveness of such policies.
- ✓ **No study** has looked specifically at attitudes towards marriage and children cross-nationally and over time.
- ✓ **The majority of previous research** has focused on depression with little attention paid to positive affective states.

2. Modal verbs and tentative verbs

Modal verbs may turn up in different sections of a research article while tentative language may also appear in such sections as Literature Review, Results and Discussion as well as Conclusion. In the Literature Review section, writers use modal verbs and tentative verbs to show their cautious and scrupulous attitude towards the literature or their own research topic, as illustrated in the following examples. Unit 6 will elaborate on tentative language.

- ✓ The assumption that FL rhetoric learners can transfer their intended thoughts into correct written form on paper, without committing many errors, **seems to be** over-optimistic.
- ✓ Peer feedback **may appear** at different phases in the composing process.
- ✓ Focusing on individual student characteristics **can be** problematic, as the emphasis is then placed on the individual behavior change process, with little attention to sociocultural and physical environmental influences on behavior.
- ✓ The teacher **could also serve as** classroom manager, being "responsible for grouping activities into lessons and for ensuring these are satisfactorily organized at the practical level" (Littlewood, 1981: 92).
- ✓ The written comments which are considered to be "brief and precise" by the teacher **may be seen as** "abrupt and unhelpful" by the student (Lewis, 1993).

3. Reporting verbs

When reviewing other researchers' studies, a writer will use reporting verbs to cite their ideas, viewpoints or stance. Likewise, a writer can also use reporting verbs to state the previous findings in the field and his own intended work. Usually it is critical to properly cite other scholars' research and, at the same time, to keep the writer's voice, which could be implied by reporting verbs. Table 2.1 lists some commonly used reporting verbs which could be divided into five categories: writer-neutral, writer-speculative, writer-positive, writer-critical, and other verbs suggesting the nature of cited idea as opinions.

Table 2.1 Reporting Verbs and Writers' Implied Attitudes

Attitudes Implied by the Reporting Verbs	Reporting Verbs
Writer-neutral	characterize, classify, define, describe, detail, discuss, document, echo, evoke, examine, explain, expound, formulate, illustrate, indicate, introduce, list, look at, mention, note, notice, outline, observe, point out, present, recount, refer, reiterate, report, review, specify, state, ...
Writer-speculative	advise, attempt, assume, doubt, intend, propose, speculate, suggest, wonder, ...
Writer-positive	advocate, agree, assert, confirm, detect, discover, emphasize, encourage, stress, support, underscore, maintain, propose, recommend, reinforce, ...
Writer-critical	criticize, deplore, declaim, against, disagree, be opposed to, refute...
Other verbs suggesting the nature of cited ideas as opinions	argue, believe, claim, consider, contend, comment, remark, think, ...

2.3.2 Syntactical Features

The syntactical features of the Literature Review section are listed from the perspectives of tense usage and point of view in person.

1. Tense usage

How to use the tense appropriately in a literature review? In broad outline, use the present simple tense to describe the scientific facts, use the past simple tense to introduce a particular piece of work in the past, and use the present perfect tense for situations continuing or related to the present and for generalizations of the previous achievement. However, a writer may also use the present simple tense for a work in the past when he thinks it is closely related to his present research or the work can be tenable. Below is a general orientation of tense usage which may have some exceptions.

1) In general introduction to the research topic

At the beginning of a literature review, the present perfect tense or the present simple tense is used to give a general introduction to the research topic, as shown in the following examples.

- ✓ This dynamic development of biotechnology, often seen as the future of food system, in recent years **has raised** serious public concerns about the possible risks arising from the uncontrolled discharge of hazardous transgenes into the environment, e.g., it may reduce the biodiversity or an increased resistance to parasites can make them stronger and harder to combat (Bongoni, 2016).
- ✓ Arterial hemodynamics **plays** a decisive role in the study of artery diseases (especially, atherosclerotic diseases)…

2) In integration of the research progression

From the information-prominent point of view, the present simple tense or the present perfect tense tends to be used in the integration of the research progression. Look at the following examples:

- ✓ Currently, the modifications **are mostly applied** in plants, with the aim to improve their resistance to disease and/or tolerance to herbicides (Domingo, 2016).
- ✓ In clinical medicine, Wind-kessel model **has also been used** to predict dynamic atherosclerosis index, and describe the function of cardiac pump and stability of cardiac output…

3) In author-prominent literature

When giving prominence to the author(s), a writer may take the author-prominent method, usually, in the past simple tense. Look at the following examples:

- ✓ Webb et al. (2011) **found** a positive association between improved perceptions of neighborhood and quality of life measured over a 4-year period.
- ✓ Gupta et al. (2010) **reported** that tendon collagen fibrils followed a double-stage exponential behavior by serially coupling a Voigt element with two Maxwell elements.

4) In literature closely related to the writer's present work

If the writer thinks the literature is very important or closely related to his present work, he may use the present simple tense (Pang, 2008) as the examples below:

- ✓ Feedback is an essential element of the process approach to writing. Keh (1990: 294) **defines** it as input from a reader to a writer with the effect of providing information to the writer for revision.
- ✓ Brookes & Grundy (1990) **define** a product as the end result of one's labor and process as the means by which one reaches such a product.

5) In evaluation of literature

The present simple tense or the present perfect tense is usually used in the evaluation of

literature. Look at the following examples:
- ✓ In fact, arteries **have** multiple levels of structure: aorta, arterioles, and arterioles. The three **have** different elasticity. Different elasticity **has** different effects on blood flow.
- ✓ Additionally, as seen above, the majority of previous research **has focused** on depression with little attention paid to positive affective states.

6) In introduction to the writer's work

The present simple tense is used in the introduction to the writer's work as the examples below:
- ✓ This study **intends** to establish a learning-teaching model integrating individuals, activities, concepts, and culture.
- ✓ In order to broaden our knowledge on this subject, the aim of this experimental study **is** to provide a greater understanding of fouling behavior by combined organic and inorganic fouling under more representative feed solutions and operating conditions.

2. Point of view in person

In most cases, the third person point of view could be used in writing a literature review. Below are some examples selected from the Literature Review section of some research articles:
- ✓ **The majority of previous research** has focused on depression with little attention paid to positive affective states.
- ✓ **Webb et al.** (2011) found a positive association between improved perceptions of neighborhood and quality of life measured over a 4-year period.
- ✓ **The objectivity of the research and a disclosure of the results to consumers** is essential for them to make conscious purchasing decisions (Saba & Vassallo, 2002).
- ✓ Since commercialization of GM crops in 1995, **no apparent adverse effects** have been identified. **No evident health effects** in the long-term studies have been detected either (Blancke et al., 2015; Davis, 2016; Qaim & Kouser, 2013).

2.4 Plagiarism and Paraphrase

2.4.1 Plagiarism

If a writer uses other people's ideas or words without appropriately acknowledging their sources or without acknowledgement at all, he is plagiarizing. Some people may make this mistake either intentionally or unintentionally. The knowledge of appropriate citations of others' information is a must. Then how to avoid plagiarism and cite others' ideas appropriately? Basically speaking, a writer should:

- use quotation marks when using others' original words and sentences;
- change the original key lexis and syntax of the sentences, that is, use one's own words and sentences to restate others' work;
- not imitate the original sentence patterns;
- not borrow the original key wording;
- acknowledge the source when the information is from others' work.

Plagiarism could be identified in the following examples:

Original:

Once the discussion circles have begun, the teacher's role reverts to one of quiet but attentive observation. It is up to the particular teacher to decide what he or she will be observing, and this may alter for each discussion. It may be desirable to observe individual role performance and interaction or each group as a whole. It may be that the teacher observes language usage, focuses on turn taking, or procedural concerns.

Source: Shelton-Strong, S. J. 2012. Literature circles in ELT. *ELT Journal. 66*(2): 214–223.

Mistake 1 (Intentional plagiarism without acknowledgement):

Once the discussion circles have begun, the teacher's role reverts to one of quiet but attentive observation. It is up to the particular teacher to decide what he or she will be observing, and this may alter for each discussion. It may be desirable to observe individual role performance and interaction or each group as a whole. It may be that the teacher observes language usage, focuses on turn taking, or procedural concerns.

Mistake 2 (Original wording without quotation marks):

When students begin their discussion, **the teacher's role reverts to one of quiet but attentive observation.** A teacher can decide what to observe, and **this may alter for each discussion**. A teacher can observe participants' **performance and interaction** or observe **language usage, turn taking, or procedural concerns**.

Mistake 3 (Imitated sentence structure and wording):

When students begin the discussion, the teacher will turn to a quiet but attentive observer. **It is up to the particular teacher to decide** what to observe, and this may be different in different discussions. **It may be desirable to observe individual role performance and interaction**. The teacher may also observe **language usage, turn taking, or procedural concerns**.

2.4.2 Paraphrase

When citing others' work, a writer prefers paraphrase to direct quotation since paraphrase could better blend others' studies with the writer's reviews. In other words, a writer would restate others' ideas in his own words. Paraphrasing can also exercise a writer's capacity of analytical generalization. To appropriately paraphrase other authors' work, a writer must:

- have a good command of the original ideas;
- change the syntax of the original sentences;
- avoid using the original key wording;
- introduce and integrate the original author(s) into the writer's interpretation sentences;
- acknowledge the source of information.

Take the original version of the paragraph on the previous page again as an example and let's see how we can paraphrase it.

The following is an example:

- ✓ Shelton-Strong (2012) reports that the teacher's role is changed into a quiet but careful observer when the discussion circles begin. The teacher may decide what to observe, with different purposes in each discussion. He may observe either the performance of a student or the behavior of the group, including the language used by the students, the turn taking between the students and the related discussion procedures.

2.5 Useful Expressions for the Literature Review Section

Below are some sentence patterns for a literature review describing the information elements at different stages.

1. Stating the background of the related field

- ✓ Driverless technology has been extensively studied in recent years.
- ✓ In recent years, researchers have become increasingly interested in technologies for…
- ✓ Spot welding is the most widely used joining method in the automobile manufacturing industry.
- ✓ Over the past three decades…
- ✓ It is noteworthy / well known that…

2. Stating the achievement of the related seminal works

- ✓ Recent experiments by… have suggested…

- ✓ The previous work on... has indicated that...
- ✓ Industrial applications of Robotics gained a paramount importance in the last century.
- ✓ This has stimulated many automakers to cultivate alternative energies, in order to deal with the energy crisis.
- ✓ The latest research on... has called attention to the need for further investigation into...
- ✓ Several researchers have theoretically investigated...
- ✓ A survey of... provides direct support for such a claim.

3. Stating the limitations of the related field

- ✓ Great progress has been made in this field, but...
- ✓ Until now no field experiments of... have been reported.
- ✓ As a result, a predefined process is likely to behave abnormally due to web services interacting incorrectly.
- ✓ Nevertheless, these attempts to establish a link between... and... are at present unconvincing.
- ✓ Although considerable research has been devoted to..., rather less attention has been paid to...
- ✓ Although much work has been done to date, more studies need to be conducted to...
- ✓ However, it appears that the results of these studies may not be applicable for second language educators...
- ✓ However, the experimental configuration was far from optimal.
- ✓ These studies have not taken... into account to provide the picture of...
- ✓ The above studies ignore an important aspect of the problem, namely...
- ✓ No clear advancement has so far been seen in...
- ✓ No direct outcome was then reported in...
- ✓ The data available in literature failed to prove that...
- ✓ Research about... needs to be further conducted from the perspective of...
- ✓ It is difficult to obtain satisfied reports about... from the relevant researches.
- ✓ The function of these proteins remains unclear.

4. Stating the present work

- ✓ This paper explores the possibility of teaching... based on Roach's theoretical framework.
- ✓ The purpose of this paper/study/thesis is to...
- ✓ The present work deals mainly with...
- ✓ The present study will therefore focus on...

- ✓ In this article, we shall focus both analytically and numerically on the following topics: (1)…; (2)…; (3)…
- ✓ In this paper, we propose an alternative approach which…
- ✓ This paper reports on…
- ✓ This study seeks to test empirically the relationship between… and…
- ✓ This paper suggests five useful techniques to…
- ✓ The primary goal of this research is…
- ✓ In this paper, I attempt to show how…
- ✓ In the current study, we attempt to address…
- ✓ In this paper, we aim at…

5. Stating the importance of the present work

- ✓ This study was identified as being of importance to…
- ✓ The model described in this article could serve as the basis for…
- ✓ This research will shed light on the nature of…
- ✓ This work may provide insight on…
- ✓ This study will deepen the understanding of…

2.6 Reflections and Practice

❶ Answer the following questions.

1. What are the functions of the Literature Review section?
2. What are the basic information elements in the Literature Review section?
3. How can you cite other researchers' work?

❷ Analyze the information elements and writing strategies of the two Literature Review sections. Text 1 is in the field of engineering mechanics and Text 2 in the field of software engineering.

▶ Text 1

1) Several studies have been carried out to explain bio-fibre mechanical behaviors from its structural characteristics. 2) A tension-shear chain model was proposed by Ji and Gao

(Ji & Gao, 2004) to investigate the mechanics of protein-mineral nanocomposite biomaterials. **3)** Gupta et al. (2010) reported that tendon collagen fibrils followed a double-stage exponential behavior by serially coupling a Voigt element with two Maxwell elements. **4)** According to Gautieri et al. (2012), multiple Kelvin-Voigt elements have been staggered in series-parallel connection to provide a bottom-up description of bio-fibres visco-elastic properties. **5)** So far, the majority of studies have been seeking for the phenomenological characterization of a specific kind of bio-fibres, whereas the uniform description of self-similarity among various bio-fibres remains untackled to depict the mathematical and geometrical principles after their gross behavior.

Sentence Number	Information Element
1)	
2)	
3)	
4)	
5)	

› Text 2

1) Trusted execution as offered by the Intel Software Guard Extensions (SGX) protects execution from unauthorized access by privileged users and software, even including some forms of physical attacks. **2)** Accordingly, it has been identified as a promising means to guard all kinds of outsourced workloads against tampering of execution and data extraction.

3) Securing an application and its associated data using SGX as a readily available form of trusted execution environment (TEE) in commodity systems poses the fundamental question of how to apply this technology. **4)** In particular, a number of systems [2] propose to secure legacy applications by manually placing sensitive code and data under the protection of an enclave, the latter resembling a trusted execution context when utilizing SGX.

5) However, not all applications can be easily secured by separating sensitive code and data into a trusted execution context. **6)** Particularly applications which perform complex data processing are difficult to partition by hand, especially if the implementation language provides weak memory isolation mechanisms such as C/C++. **7)** Nevertheless, Glamdring [7] proposes a semi-automated support for splitting complex applications into a trusted and untrusted parts. **8)** This is achieved by annotating sensitive data and performing dataflow analysis. **9)** An alternative direction is to not partition an application, but simply putting it as a whole under the protection of trusted execution [1, 13]. **10)** This seems convenient as no analysis of the application is necessary and transparent protection can be achieved. **11)** Nevertheless, this approach comes attached with a rather large trusted computing base, not only including the application itself, but also an execution substrate that can be as large as an operating system [13].

12) Both of these approaches only perform a separation into a trusted and untrusted part, assuming that the code in the trusted execution context is flawless and cannot be attacked. **13)** This seems to be a strong assumption, especially when whole applications are placed in a trusted execution context. **14)** As a consequence, other approaches propose to apply additional isolation techniques to partition applications within a single enclave [8, 11], yet this adds complexity and additionally increases the trusted computing base. **15)** SGX does not limit the partitioning to a single trusted context and a remaining untrusted application but is capable of splitting an application into multiple enclaves. **16)** This was first investigated in Panoply [12] and EActors [9], which proposed a system abstraction and the use of the actor programming model as a flexible means to distribute an application over multiple trusted execution contexts respectively. **17)** However, neither the in-enclave partitioning approaches [8, 11] nor the multi-enclave approaches provide a metric-driven guidance on how an application should be partitioned. **18)** For brevity, we will refer to partitioning into multiple trusted contexts simply as partitioning from now on…

Sentence Number	Information Element
1)	
2)	
3)	
4)	
5)	
6)	
7)	
8)	
9)	

(Continued)

Sentence Number	Information Element
10)	
11)	
12)	
13)	
14)	
15)	
16)	
17)	
18)	

III **Select two or three Literature Review sections in your research field and complete the following tasks.**

1. Identify the information elements in these Literature Review sections.
2. Analyze the logic underlying the text in these Literature Review sections.
3. Comment on the strong points and weak points of these Literature Review sections.

IV **Match the organizational patterns of the Literature Review section in Column A with the excerpts in Column B.**

Column A	Column B
Chronological order	1) Mental well-being is a human aspiration and an increasingly valued indicator of societal progress (Stiglitz et al., 2009). There is also a considerable body of research indicating that higher levels of well-being in old age are associated with improved health outcomes, including better physical and cognitive function, decreased levels of frailty and disability, and lower mortality (Gale et al., 2014; Ostir et

	al., 2000; Steptoe et al., 2014a, 2014b; Steptoe & Wardle, 2011, 2012). In the UK, there are currently more than 11 million individuals aged 65 years and over, and this number is expected to increase by nearly 50% by 2030 (Age UK, 2014). Therefore, understanding the factors that affect mental and physical well-being in older age is of primary social and economic significance. Qualitative work with older adults suggests that optimism, contentment and adaptation are more relevant than absence of disabilities and disease when thinking about "optimal aging" (Reichstadt et al., 2007), further reinforcing the need to understand what factors are associated with positive well-being in this group.
General-to-specific order	2) Research Methodology in the above studies can be divided into two categories: literature-review-based studies and bibliometric-based studies, where most of them belong to qualitative research. Researchers such as Jian Zhao and Jianli Jiao have reviewed the existing research in learning sciences and summarized the core themes of this field, which is to bring together and integrate the studies on the brain and learning such as implicit learning, informal learning, and formal learning. Other researchers, such as Nanchang Yang and Haifeng Li, through content analysis, have revealed the characteristics and development of research in learning sciences, while Jiagang Chen summarized the increase in learning sciences' focus on practice and context, based on an interview with Professor Keith Sawyer. Besides, the related quantitative research focused on two types of databases: CNKI and *Journal of the Learning Sciences*. However, neither of these two types of databases can fully reveal the development of learning sciences due to its complexity and looseness. Most of these studies do not directly mention "learning sciences" in the title, keywords, and abstracts. Therefore, it is difficult to obtain comprehensive results by directly searching through CNKI with "learning sciences" as the keyword.

Point-by-point order	3) While scholars have tried to understand and articulate what constitutes a "good life" for many centuries, the scientific study of emotional well-being only started in the 1960s (Campbell et al.,1976) and since then has grown rapidly (Diener et al., 1985). A conceptual distinction has been proposed between the hedonic (Kahneman et al., 1999; Diener, 2000) and the eudaimonic traditions (Ryan & Deci, 2001; Ryff & Singer, 2006, 2008). The hedonic approach is characterized by an affective component based on feelings of joy and pleasure and absence of negative affectivity, and by a cognitive component based on one's evaluation of one's own life satisfaction. The cognitive component has also been termed as evaluative well-being in some conceptualizations (Dolan et al., 2011).

Ⅴ Fill in each blank with the appropriate form of each verb given in the brackets.

In 2013, approximately 40% of the world population 1) _____ (have) access to the Internet. There is evidence that the rate of adoption of the Internet 2) _____ (double) every 100 days (Department of Commerce, 1998). A recent search of prior literature also 3) _____ (reveal) over 30 different types of offenses that fall under the umbrella of cyber crime 4) _____ (include) hacking, malware, identity theft, online fraud, credit card fraud, spamming, web and email spoofing, cyber bullying, harassment and stalking, and distributed denial of service attacks. Accordingly, as the number of people worldwide using the Internet to socialize, access information, and conduct business increases, cyber crime 5) _____ (present) significant and increasing threats to Internet users, consumers, businesses, financial institutions, and governments all over the world. Additionally, as a global criminal phenomenon, cyber crime 6) _____ (pose) issues and challenges for law enforcement officials and prosecutors who 7) _____ (task) with investigating, apprehending, and prosecuting cyber criminals.

The financial consequences of cyber crime 8) _____ (be) also substantial and dire. According to a report by Symantec Corporation, a security software manufacturer, cyber crime 9) _____ (cost) the global market an estimate of $110 billion each year. Still, another security software manufacturer, McAfee Incorporated, 10) _____ (claim) that the true annual cost worldwide from cyber crime 11) _____ (be) much higher, at around $1 trillion (Hyman, 2013). Although the precise magnitude of the financial cost of cyber crime 12) _____ (remain) unknown, what is known is that cyber crime 13) _____ (increase) at a rapid pace (Winmill et al., 2000).

VI Select the appropriate word or phrase in the box to complete each sentence. Change the form where necessary.

| suppress | be subject to | detect | implement | squander |
| apply | attempt to | witness | breed | conduct |

1. Results should always _____ challenge from experiment.
2. Currently, the genetic modifications are mostly _____ in plants, with the aim to improve their resistance to disease and tolerance to herbicides.
3. Flawed research _____ money and efforts of some of the world's best minds.
4. Since the commercialization of GM crops in 1995, no apparent adverse effects have been _____ .
5. In 2015, a face-to-face survey was _____ to obtain the empirical data.
6. The sub-district offices can go deep into the grassroots level and effectively _____ the policies to the communities and families.
7. Recent two decades have _____ a swift transforming of human and social landscape due to the pervasive use of digital networks.
8. A legal and regulatory system has been taking shape to _____ the spread of cyber crime of multiple forms in cyber space.
9. This paper _____ provide some new information on dynamic compressive stress failure through the use of an ultrafast camera.
10. Unemployment is bound to _____ resentment and resistance.

VII Rearrange the words and phrases in each group into clear and coherent sentences.

1. top-down policy implementation, and, is, China's micro public management system, bottom-up communication mechanism, characteristic of.
2. healthy, the ability, appropriately, people, who, have, to, emotions, are, express, mentally.
3. a major cause, military conquest, foreign cultures, of language change, is, the influence of, often, and, as a result of, interaction with.
4. women, at the same time, because, usually, their brains, think more intuitively, they, use, both sides of, seem to.

5. be classified, state schools, the pupils' ages, in Britain, can, according to, and, the types of education.

VIII Rearrange the following sentences into a coherent paragraph.

1. Big Data is the vast quantities of information amenable to large-scale collection, storage, and analysis.
2. Using such data, companies and researchers can deploy complex algorithms and artificial intelligence technologies to reveal otherwise unascertained patterns, links, behaviors, trends, identities, and practical knowledge.
3. "Big Data" are two small words with enormous societal meaning.
4. Individuals invisibly contribute to Big Data whenever they live digital lifestyles or otherwise participate in the digital economy, such as shopping with a credit card, researching a topic on Google, or posting on Facebook.
5. The words signify a complex phenomenon that has come to define the second decade of the 21 century.
6. The information that comprises Big Data arises from government and business practices, consumer transactions, and the digital applications sometimes referred to as the "Internet of Things".

IX Translate the following sentences into English.

1. 直到20世纪末期我们才开始真正重视环境问题。
2. 这个预测后期通过实验得以证实，为此，他获得了1973年的诺贝尔物理学奖。
3. 虽然电子出版物给读者和出版社都带来很多好处，但是它们不可能取代纸质读物。
4. 究竟是什么原因让希特勒决定暂时把英国搁置一旁，转而向东攻打苏联？
5. 一篇高质量的文献综述可以引发读者持续深入的思考。

X Translate the following paragraph into Chinese.

Interests in cyber crime over the last two decades have culminated in a sizable and growing body of literature. However, there are research gaps in the extant body of knowledge. For instance, there is a lack of reliable and valid statistics on the prevalence, nature, and trends of cyber crime. There is also a dearth of research on the best practices related to combating and preventing cyber crime. In this article, we outline and propose five salient and pertinent areas of inquiry relating to cyber crime for researchers, scholars, and practitioners interested in understanding, combating, and preventing this type of crime. Although our list of suggested topics by no means represents a comprehensive research agenda, we feel these five areas of inquiry constitute a sufficient basis to advance our knowledge and the scholarship on cyber crime.

Unit 3
Methods

📝 Warm-up Questions

1. What is the purpose of the Methods section?

2. What are the information elements in the Methods section?

3. What are the salient linguistic features of the Methods section?

3.1 Overview

3.1.1 Purpose of the Methods Section

Before we turn to the purpose of the Methods section, it is worth mentioning here that the naming of this section varies in different disciplines and journals. Generally speaking, the naming can be classified into those named with "Method" (e.g., Methods, Methods and Materials, Materials and Methods, Methodology), with "Experiment" (e.g., Experiments, Experimental Procedure, Experimental Setup, Experimental Section, Experimental Setting), with "Research" or "Study" (e.g., Research Design, The Present Study, The Study), and with topical names, i.e., subheadings closely related to the content of the study.

The Methods section aims to answer the question, "What did you do/use in your research?" It is generally accepted that the purposes of writing the Methods section are two-fold, concerning the replicability and credibility of the research. Firstly, the Methods section should provide sufficient information for another competent scientist to replicate the work done and obtain similar results (Glasman-Deal, 2010; Cargill & O'Connor, 2013). Secondly, the Methods section should provide information that will let readers judge the appropriateness of the methods and establish credibility for the results for readers to decide for themselves whether the results mean what the authors claim they mean (Cargill & O'Connor, 2013; Gastel & Day, 2016).

Therefore, a well-written Methods section should be able to "communicate information about a new procedure, a new method, or a new approach so that everyone reading it can not only carry it out and obtain similar results, but also understand and accept your procedure" (Glasman-Deal, 2010: 44).

3.1.2 Information Elements of the Methods Section

Research approaches, research designs, and research methods are three key terms that represent a perspective about research that presents information in a successive way from broad constructions of research to the narrow procedures of methods.

Qualitative, quantitative, and mixed methods are three approaches to research. Unquestionably, the three approaches are not as discrete as they first appear. Qualitative and quantitative approaches should not be viewed as rigid, distinct categories, polar opposites, or dichotomies. Instead, they represent different ends on a continuum (Newman & Benz, 1998). A study tends to be more qualitative than quantitative or vice versa. Mixed methods research resides in the middle of this continuum because it incorporates elements of both qualitative and quantitative approaches.

Often the distinction between qualitative research and quantitative research is framed in terms of using words (qualitative) rather than numbers (quantitative), or using closed-ended questions (quantitative hypotheses) rather than open-ended questions (qualitative interview questions). A more complete way to view the gradations of differences between them is in the basic philosophical assumptions researchers bring to the study, the types of research strategies used in the research (e.g., quantitative experiments or qualitative case studies), and the specific methods employed in conducting these strategies (e.g., collecting data quantitatively on instruments versus collecting qualitative data through observing a setting). Moreover, there is a historical evolution to both approaches with the quantitative approaches dominating the forms of research in the social sciences from the late 19th century up until the mid-20th century. During the latter half of the 20th century, interest in qualitative research increased and along with it, the development of mixed methods research.

Qualitative research is an approach for exploring and understanding the meaning individuals or groups ascribe to a social or human problem. The research process involves data collection in the participant's setting, inductive data analysis, building from particulars to general themes, and interpretations of the meaning of the data. The final written report has a flexible structure. Those who engage in this form of inquiry support a way of looking at research that honors an inductive style, a focus on individual meaning, and the importance of rendering the complexity of a situation.

Quantitative research is an approach for testing objective theories by examining the relationship among variables. These variables, in turn, can be measured, typically on instruments, so that numbered data can be analyzed using statistical procedures. The final written report has a set structure consisting of introduction, literature and theory, methods, results, and discussion. Like qualitative researchers, those who engage in this form of inquiry have assumptions about testing theories deductively, building in protections against bias, controlling for alternative explanations, and being able to generalize and replicate the findings.

Mixed methods research is an approach to inquiry involving collecting both quantitative and qualitative data, integrating the two forms of data, and using distinct designs that may involve philosophical assumptions and theoretical frameworks. The core assumption of this form of inquiry is that the combination of qualitative and quantitative approaches provides a more complete understanding of a research problem than either approach alone (Creswell, 2014).

In some research fields, there is a standard set of subheadings for presenting the Methods section, such as data collection, participants, measuring instruments, data analysis, or sampling procedure, experimental setup, model testing. It is highly recommended to check analogous papers in your target journal (Cargill & O'Connor, 2013; Gastel & Day, 2016).

If the Methods section is short and does not require subheadings, you can organize it in the following order (Glasman-Deal, 2010; Wallwork, 2016):

(1) provide a general overview of the methods chosen;

(2) provide specific and precise details about materials and methods (i.e., quantities, temperatures, duration, sequence, conditions, locations, sizes);

(3) point out any precautions / appropriate care taken (this helps you gain credibility as a researcher who carries out his/her work accurately and thoroughly);

(4) highlight the benefits of your methods in comparison with other authors' approaches;

(5) discuss any limitations in your methods or problems you encountered.

In most journal articles, the Methods section follows the Introduction section or the Literature Review section; in others, it follows the Conclusion section. For instance, in the biochemical field, the Methods section is becoming increasingly de-emphasized and may be downgraded by being physically relocated towards the end of the paper.

3.1.3 Principles of Writing the Methods Section

Careful writing of the Methods section is critical because "the cornerstone of the scientific method requires that your results, to be of scientific merit, must be reproducible" (Gastel & Day, 2016: 66). To write a good Methods section, writers should make sure:

- the descriptions are complete and yet are also as concise as possible;
- to write extremely clearly, with generally no more than two steps described in one sentence and in a logical order;
- to cover every step required. Do not leave out essential information either thinking that it is implicit (and thus not worth mentioning) or simply because you forgot (Wallwork, 2016).

3.2 Sample Analysis

Sample 1 (A Methods Section with Subheadings)

Data collection	Data collection
	Data were collected through three versions of self-report, web-based questionnaires. Undergraduate and graduate student

	versions were completed by EL1 students at the undergraduate and graduate levels respectively, and the faculty version was completed by faculty members who teach undergraduate and graduate students. A letter of invitation to complete the survey was emailed to individuals belonging to each of the three participant groups, following the university's ethical guidelines (Protocol Number 07378). Taking into account the number of respondents from each group that accessed its respective questionnaires and the number of respondents who then completed them, completion rates for graduate and undergraduate students were 66 percent and 60 percent respectively, and the completion rate for instructors was 75 percent.
Respondents	**Respondents** A total of 458 respondents voluntarily and anonymously completed the web-based questionnaires: 370 EL1 students (295 undergraduate and 75 graduate) and 88 instructors (58 teaching at the undergraduate level and 30 at the graduate level). The questionnaires asked those who responded to provide importance ratings for academic language skills, to assess their own or their students' skill status, and to respond to open-ended questions. Table 1 presents the demographic characteristics of the respondents.
Measuring instruments (Questionnaire)	**Questionnaire instruments** To facilitate comparisons of EAL and EL1 students' needs and self- and instructor-assessments of skill status at the institution, the same set of questionnaires, adapted and modified from Rosenfeld, Leung and Oltman (2001), as reported in Huang (2010), was used for all participant groups. Briefly, the questionnaire for graduate students included 45 ratable skill statements; 11 each were related to the reading, writing, and listening domains, and 12 were related to the speaking domain. For undergraduate students, the questionnaire included 43 ratable skill statements, with 11 each related to the reading, listening, and speaking domains, and 10 related to the writing domain. The two additional items included in the survey completed by graduate students were discipline-

	specific writing (e.g., proposal writing, thesis/dissertation writing) in the writing domain and conference presentations in the speaking domain.
Data analysis	**Data analysis** Quantitative analyses were conducted using SPSS Version 16.0 for multiple levels of analysis: (a) analyses by groups (i.e., undergraduate students, graduate students, and instructors), which were followed by (b) subgroup analyses that included divisions (i.e., humanities, social sciences, physical sciences, and life sciences), (c) language-skill domains analyses (i.e., reading, writing, speaking, and listening), and (d) analyses of individual skill items within each of the four skill domains. **Source:** Huang, L. S. 2013. Academic English is no one's mother tongue: Graduate and undergraduate students' academic English language-learning needs from students' and instructors' perspectives. *Journal of Perspectives in Applied Academic Practice, 1*(2): 17–29.

Sample 2 (A Methods Section Without Subheadings)

Data collection	Manuscripts submitted to *Headache* from January 1, 2014 through December 31, 2016 were considered in this retrospective review of peer reviewer comments. Only initially submitted manuscripts rejected by the Journal after associate editor or peer review were included in the study. Papers that had been immediately rejected by the editor-in-chief were excluded because there were usually no comments available about the reasons for rejection. Research submissions (i.e., manuscripts reporting the collection and analysis of new data or the secondary analysis of an existing dataset) and review articles (systematic or narrative reviews of the literature) were included. The data were made available to the research team by the Journal's executive editor. All manuscripts had been categorized as research or review manuscripts by the Journal at the time of submission. Manuscripts were further categorized as clinical medical, behavioral, or basic science at the time of submission.

Data analysis	Because there are no standard criteria of reasons for manuscript rejection, prior to the beginning of the full study, one author (DT) piloted a system for coding reviewer comments. Themes in reasons for rejection that emerged during piloting of the coding system were used to guide categorization during the full study. Next, two authors (CS and CH) independently coded reviews from the same ten papers. The two authors had a 73% rate of concordance for major categories at that step, but further refined the categories and discussed interpretation of each to maximize concordance to ensure consistency and similarity of approach. The remaining papers were then split equally, and each was reviewed by either CH or CS, with discussion as needed. Unlimited reasons for rejection from the following list were noted for each manuscript: **General** Topic more appropriate for another journal Overlaps with previous publications Low addition to the literature **Background/Purpose** Insufficient literature review / prior papers misrepresented Question/purpose of study unclear/faulty **Ethical Concerns** Unclear ethics board approval Conflict of interest / unclear disclosures **Definitions of Cases, Controls, and Comorbidities** Did not use standardized diagnostic criteria, such as International Classification of Headache Disorders (ICHD) Problems with covariates/outcomes Problems with control or case group **Methodological Problems** Poor methods / study design Poor reporting of methods

	Statistical Problems
	Poor approach or analysis
	Results
	Data collection problems—poor response rate, high rate lost to follow-up, etc.
	Results illogical/questionable
	Conclusions/Discussion
	Conclusions not supported
	Insufficient discussion
	Writing
	Organization/clarity problem, major problems with grammar/fluency
	Comments from prior peer review (in another journal) not addressed
Research ethics	The project was considered nonhuman subjects research, and therefore was exempt from IRB review.
Tools for statistical analysis	Statistical Methods—Data were collected in a shared REDCap25 project housed at Children's Hospital of Philadelphia, and analyzed using STATA 12.
	Results were summarized by standard descriptive statistics, including proportions for binary and categorical variables, and medians for continuous variables with nonparametric distribution.
	Source: Adapted from Hesterman, C. M., Szperka, C. L. & Turner, D. P. 2018. Reasons for manuscript rejection after peer review from the journal *Headache*. *Headache, 58*: 1511–1518.

3.3 Linguistic Features of the Methods Section

3.3.1 Lexical Features

The Methods section features the use of rich verbs and verbal phrases and sequence words.

1. Using verbs and verbal phrases

Commonly used verbs and verbal phrases in writing the Methods section of research articles include: "normalize", "obtain", "administer", "generate", "approve", "collect", "run", "complete", "set", "identify", "gather", "code", "conduct", "search", "carry out", "undertake", "repeat", etc. Listed below are several example sentences with the verbs used in the passive form.

- ✓ The data **were normalized** using…
- ✓ Drugs **were administered** by ICV injection…
- ✓ The procedures of this study **were approved** by…
- ✓ Data **were collected** using semi-structured interviews in…
- ✓ Two sets of anonymized questionnaires **were completed** by…
- ✓ Significance levels **were set** at the 1% level using the student t-test.

2. Using sequence words

Sequence words are essential for the Methods section to introduce research procedures. Commonly used sequence words are listed below in the order of time sequence:

- ✓ **The first step in this process** was to…
- ✓ **After** (the appliance was fitted, the patients attended X every four weeks.)
- ✓ **On** (completion of X, the process of parameter estimation was carried out.)
- ✓ **Following** (this treatment, the samples were recovered and stored overnight.)
- ✓ **Finally**, questions were asked as to the role of…
- ✓ The **final** stage of the study comprised a semi-structured interview with participants who…

3.3.2 Syntactical Features

Novice writers often wonder what voices (active or passive) and tenses they should use in writing the Methods section. Hopefully, you will find your answer after reading the following section.

1. Using the active or passive voice

The passive voice is one of the most well-known features of scientific writing to create an impersonal scientific text (Ding, 2002). However, researchers are often advised to minimize the use of the passive voice and use the active voice as much as possible to make the writing more direct and less wordy. Nevertheless, when it comes to writing the Methods section, the passive voice can often be validly used, for the emphasis is on the action, whereas the doer of the action is often irrelevant (Cargill & O'Connor, 2013; Gastel & Day, 2016). Cargill and O'Connor put forward three factors influencing the choice of an active or passive voice in writing the Methods section (2013: 46–47).

First, does the reader need to know who carried out the action? If this information is unimportant or irrelevant, you may choose to use a passive verb. Thus, for instance, it might be better to write "Mice were injected with…" than "I / A student / A technician injected the mice with…"

Second, does it sound repetitive (or immodest) to use a personal pronoun subject? Please look at the following example selected from the Experimental Procedures section of one research article published in *Cell* (Weixlbaumer et al., 2013). The need to avoid repetition can explain the complete absence of active voice sentences in the example. If we rewrite the paragraph in the active voice, the subject of every sentence would be "we", even if a single member of the team did that part of the work. One point worth mentioning here is that although "belief persists that journals prohibit the use of first person, many journals permit the use of 'I' and 'we'" (Gastel & Day, 2016: 70).

- ✓ Tth core RNAP with C-terminally His_{10}-tagged $B'0$ subunit **was purified** from a Tth HB8rpoC::10H strain (Sevostyanova et al., 2007). The RNAP **was initially purified** by polyethyleneimine fractionation, ammonium sulfate precipitation, Ni2+-chelating chromatography, anion exchange chromatography, and gel filtration. Contaminating RNases **were removed** in subsequent purifications by a reverse-phase chromatography step before the gel filtration step. The purified RNAP **was dialyzed** into storage buffer (TGED: 10 mM Tris-HCl [pH 8.0], 5% glycerol, 0.1 mM EDTA, and 1 mM DTT, plus 0.15 M NaCl and 15% glycerol and flash frozen. Aliquots **were thawed**, **dialyzed** into crystallization buffer (10 mM Tris-HCl [pH 7.7], 0.15 M NaCl, and 1% glycerol; Tagami et al., 2010), and **concentrated** by centrifugal filtration to about 30 mg/ml for crystallization. Endogenous Taq RNAP **was purified** as previously described (Zhang et al., 1999), dialyzed into TGED + 0.15 M NaCl, and **concentrated** to about 30 mg/ml for crystallization. Tth and Taq nusA **were subcloned** into pET-based expression vectors and purified using standard methods.

Third, does it help the information flow to choose either the active or passive voice? A unit of information is the tension between what is already known (the Given) and what is new (the New). In the idealized form, each information unit consists of a Given element accompanied by a New element (Halliday & Matthiessen, 2004: 89). In English sentences, effective writers generally put the old information (the Given), which the reader already knows, before the new information (the New) to make the passage easy to follow (Cargill & O'Connor, 2013: 56). Thus, writers may choose to use the passive voice to realize information flow. Please read the following two versions (the active and passive voices are identified in square brackets). Which version do you think is better in terms of realizing information flow?

Version 1:

- ✓ We used [active] the results of these analyses to inform the construction of mechanistic candidate functions for the relationship between propagule input, space availability and recruitment. We compared [active] these candidate functions using differences in the Akaike information criteria (AIC differences) (Burnham & Anderson, 2002). We then used model averaging [active]...

Version 2:

✓ We used [active] the results of these analyses to inform the construction of mechanistic **candidate functions** for the relationship between propagule input, space availability and recruitment. **These candidate functions** were compared [passive] using differences in the Akaike information criteria (AIC differences) (Burnham & Anderson 2002). We then used [active] model averaging...

We can tell from the example above that in Version 2 "candidate functions" introduced in the first sentence became old information in the second, and "using differences in the Akaike information criteria" is new information. Thus, Version 2 might be considered better in terms of realizing information flow and avoiding repetitiveness.

Next, we turn to one common problem frequently found in writing passive sentences. Let's read the original version of two examples and try to identify the problem.

✓ Wheat and barley, collected from the Virginia field site, as well as sorghum and millet, collected at Loxton, **were used**.

✓ Actual evapotranspiration (T) for each crop, defined as the amount of precipitation for the period between sowing and harvesting the particular crop plus or minus the change in soil water storage in the 2m soil profile, **was computed** by the soil water balance equation (Xin, 1986; Zhu & Niu, 1987).

There is one common problem in the two examples above that makes them difficult for readers to follow, that is, top-heavy sentences. Top-heavy sentences are those with "very long subjects and a short passive verb right at the end" (Cargill & O'Connor, 2013: 41). As suggested by Cargill and O'Connor (2013: 41), "try to get both the subject and the verb within the first nine words of the sentence, and make sure any list of items is at the end of the sentence." Accordingly, the above sentences could be revised as follows:

✓ **Four kinds of cereal were used:** wheat and barley, collected from the Virginia field site; sorghum and millet, collected at Loxton.

✓ **The soil water balance equation** (Xin, 1986; Zhu & Niu, 1987) **was used** to compute actual evapotranspiration (T) for each crop, defined as the amount of precipitation for the period between sowing and harvesting the particular crop plus or minus the change in soil water storage in the 2m soil profile.

2. Using past or present simple tenses

Different tenses are required in the Methods section to differentiate what you did from what others did in the literature, thus making sure that your own contribution is clear and easy to identify. The past simple tense is required to describe what you did yourself, while the present simple tense is commonly used to describe a standard method or refer to methods reported in the literature, i.e., not one you invented yourself for the specific purpose of the research that you are reporting in your paper (Wallwork, 2016). Below is an example of the Methods section (named Research Approaches) with the use of both past simple and present simple tenses.

- ✓ **Research Approaches**

    This research **was grounded** in the combination of action research (AR) strategy (Wood-Harper, 1985), participatory design (PD) (Greenbaum & Kyng, 1991), and situation-awareness (SA) oriented design (Endsley et al., 2003). Because **AR refers to** a class of research approaches rather than a single, monolithic research method, our work particularly emphasized the participatory form of action research and followed the design science build-and-evaluate approach (Dang et al., 2011) and the life cycle of software systems development requirements-prototyping development-deployment-evaluation. The cycle is repeated until the expected results are produced. **PD relies on** domain experts and the direct involvement of practitioners from relevant disciplines. Consequently, the development of the design focus is part of the ongoing work of the project group and not something specified beforehand. PD has been used in designing emergency medical service for future practice (Kristensen et al., 2006). The basis of **SA is** an awareness of what is happening around you and understanding what that information means to you now and in the near future. This awareness is important to first responders and the fire commanders in emergency response because they need to be adequately aware of the real situation if they are to have confidence in making what could be life-and-death decisions. SA has been used in graphic user interface design of emergency response systems in the work of Yang et al. (2009a).

When the authors describe what they did in the research, past simple tense was used (e.g., "This research was grounded in the combination of..."). We can tell from the text that their approach draws on a combination of three different approaches (AR, PD, SA) that have been reported in the literature. Thus, in the rest of the Methods section, the authors give the details of those three published approaches, using the present simple tense and the citation to the original source ("AR refers to…"; "PD relies on…"; "The basis of SA is…")

However, the choice of tenses often depends on disciplinary variations and your target journal. Below is an example of the Methods section (named Methodology) from a research article in the field of computer science and technology.

- ✓ **Methodology**

    To comprehensively measure the performance of the three popular smart APs (during Mar. 1–22, 2015), we randomly sample 1,000 real offline downloading requests issued by Unicom users in the workload trace of Xuanfeng (refer to §3). These sampled requests (which we refer to as the sampled workload) are restricted to Unicom users because our benchmark experiments are conducted by replaying the sampled workload with smart APs on Unicom network connections. On the other hand, the data sources of these sampled requests are located across various ISPs in China. For every request record, we ignore its user ID, IP address, and request time (since these factors cannot be reproduced in our benchmarks), but reuse the user's access bandwidth, as well as the file type, file size, link to the original data source, and file transfer protocol.

    To replay the sampled workload using the three smart APs, we utilize three independent residential ADSL links provided by the Unicom ISP, each of which was used exclusively by one smart AP, as depicted in Figure 12. Each link has 20 Mbps (= 2.5 MBps) of Internet access bandwidth. When replaying an individual offline downloading request, we restrict the smart AP's pre-downloading speed within the recorded user access bandwidth, so as to approximate the real network connection status. We sequentially replay around 333 requests (request i + 1 is replayed after request i completes or fails) on each smart AP and record the performance data.

    HiWiFi uses an embedded 8-GB SD card (Max Write/Read Speed: 15 MBps / 30 MBps) as the storage device. The SD card can only be formatted as FAT (otherwise, HiWiFi does not work). Newifi uses an external 8-GB USB flash drive (Max Write/Read Speed: 10 MBps / 20 MBps) via a USB 2.0 interface. The USB flash drive is formatted as NTFS. Since both HiWiFi and Newifi have a small storage capacity, we remove requested files from the storage device after they are completely downloaded or the corresponding pre-downloading task failures (refer to §4.1). At the same time, the performance data is aggregated into a storage server. MiWiFi uses its internal 1-TB SATA hard disk drive (5,400 RPM, Max Write/Read Speed: 30 MBps / 70 MBps). This hard disk drive has been formatted as EXT4 by the manufacturer, and it cannot be re-formatted to any other file system.

It is obvious that the authors use only one tense (the present simple tense) in the Methods section, no matter in describing their own research methodology or those previously published in literature. Therefore, remember to always look at your target journal and check what tense other scholars use in the Methods section.

3.4 Useful Expressions for the Methods Section

In this section, you will find some useful expressions for each information element in the Methods section (Glasman-Deal, 2010).

1. Providing specific and precise details about materials and methods

- ✓ The impact tests used in this work were a modified version of…
- ✓ All cell lines were generated as previously described in…
- ✓ Both experiments were performed in a greenhouse so that…
- ✓ The cylindrical lens was obtained from Newport USA and is shown in Figure 3.
- ✓ The material investigated was a standard aluminum alloy; all melts were modified with sodium.
- ✓ Topographical examination was carried out using a 3D stylus instrument.
- ✓ Porosity was measured at the near end and at the far end of the polished surface.
- ✓ The compression axis is aligned with the rolling direction…
- ✓ The source light was polarized horizontally and the sample beam can be scanned laterally.
- ✓ The mirrors are positioned near the focal plane.
- ✓ Electrodes comprised a 4 mm diam disk of substrate material embedded in a Teflon disk of 15 mm diam.
- ✓ The intercooler was mounted on top of the engine…
- ✓ The concentration of barium decreases towards the edge…
- ✓ Similar loads were applied to the front and side of the box…
- ✓ A laminar flow element was located downstream of the test section of the wind tunnel…

2. Pointing out any precautions / appropriate care taken

- ✓ The resulting solution was gently mixed at room temperature for…
- ✓ A sample of the concentrate was then carefully injected into…
- ✓ The soil was then placed in a furnace and gradually heated up to…
- ✓ The vials were shaken manually to allow the soil to mix well with the water.
- ✓ The medium was then aseptically transferred to a conical flask.
- ✓ The tubes were accurately reweighed to six decimal places using…
- ✓ A mechanical fixture was employed to hold the sonic horn firmly in place.

- ✓ After being removed, the mouse lungs were frozen and thawed at least three times.
- ✓ The specimen was monitored constantly for a period of 24 hours.
- ✓ They were then placed on ice for immediate FACS analysis.
- ✓ Frequent transducer readings were taken to update the stress conditions smoothly.

3. Highlighting the benefits of the writer's methods in comparison with other authors' approaches

1) Referring to the literature to justify a method or approach
- ✓ In a recent article, Smith (2009) argues that case studies offer…
- ✓ Smith et al. (1994) identify several advantages of the case study…
- ✓ Jones (2012) argues that case studies are useful when the conditions of the research…
- ✓ According to Smith (2011), semi-structured interviews have a widespread popularity in…
- ✓ The sensitivity of the X technique has been demonstrated in a report by Smith et al. (2011).
- ✓ Jones (2006) points out that there is a role for both qualitative and quantitative approaches in…

2) Indicating the use of an established method
- ✓ The solution was then assayed for X using the Y method.
- ✓ X was prepared according to the procedure used by Jones et al. (1957).
- ✓ The synthesis of X was done according to the procedure of Smith (1973).
- ✓ X was synthesized using the same method that was detailed for Y, using…
- ✓ Samples were analyzed for X as previously reported by Smith et al. (2012).
- ✓ Analysis was based on the conceptual framework proposed by Smith et al. (2002).
- ✓ This compound was prepared by adapting the procedure used by Jones et al. (1990).

3) Giving reasons why a particular method was adopted
- ✓ A major advantage of X is that…
- ✓ The benefit of this approach is that…
- ✓ X based methods provide a means of…
- ✓ X was selected for its reliability and validity.
- ✓ This method is particularly useful in studying…
- ✓ Qualitative methods offer an effective way of…
- ✓ The X method is one of the more practical ways of…
- ✓ The X approach has a number of attractive features: …
- ✓ The second advantage of using the multivariate method is…

- ✓ The study uses qualitative analysis in order to gain insights into…
- ✓ One advantage of the X analysis is that it avoids the problem of…
- ✓ Another advantage of using computer simulations is that it allows…
- ✓ Continuous sampling methods have a number of advantages over…
- ✓ The collaborative nature of the focus group offers another advantage…
- ✓ Qualitative methods can be more useful for identifying and characterizing…
- ✓ The advantage of this particular method is that it allows us to make predictions about…
- ✓ Many of the distributions were not normal so non-parametric signed rank tests were run.
- ✓ It was considered that quantitative measures would usefully supplement and extend…

3.5 Reflections and Practice

❶ Answer the following questions.

1. Where is the Methods section commonly located in journal articles in your research field? (after the Introduction section? Or at the end of the article?) Why?

2. What type of method is commonly used in your research field? Qualitative? Quantitative? Or mixed?

❷ Analyze the information elements of the two Methods sections.

> **Text 1**

1) This study contains a contrastive study of two corpora: scientific and poetic language to explore how scientific use of English is different from literary use of English. 2) Poetic language has been compared with scientific use of language. 3) In order to carry out this research, ten scientific research articles drawn from scientific journals such as *The Lancet*, *BMJ* and *Down to Earth* have been analyzed. 4) These journals are based on research findings of medical and natural sciences. 5) On the other hand, poems drawn from classical English poets such as Milton, Spenser, John Keats, Hopkins, etc. have been taken up for general linguistic survey. 6) The aim of this contrast is to make the linguistic features of scientific texts clearer and understandable. 7) So the critical analysis of linguistic features in scientific texts has been substantiated by contrastive analysis. 8) The scientific research articles have been analyzed in the light of Swale's (1990) model in order to explore how scientific facts and findings are intrinsically formulated and what kinds of linguistic features govern varied

segments of scientific research articles. **9)** Those scientific research articles were written by native users of English and published in scientific research journals. **10)** Examples from scientific research articles have been given in the present study to consolidate established notions about linguistic features used in scientific texts. **11)** Frequency of occurrence of the passive voice in the Methods section of scientific research articles has been analyzed by tables and figures. **12)** Exact data deduced from tables and figures about the frequency of the passive voice determine the reliability of this study. **13)** Grammatical components such as structure of sentences, vocabulary and discourse features used in the organization of scientific research articles have been analyzed thoroughly in this study.

Sentence Number	Information Element
1)	
2)	
3)	
4)	
5)	
6)	
7)	
8)	
9)	
10)	
11)	
12)	
13)	

Text 2

1) The current investigation involved sampling and analyzing six sites to measure changes in groundwater chemistry. **2)** The sites were selected from the London Basin area, which is located in the southeast of England and has been frequently used to interpret groundwater evolution. **3)** A total of 18 samples was collected and then analyzed for the isotopes mentioned earlier. **4)** Samples 19 were collected in thoroughly-rinsed 25 ml brown glass bottles which were filled to the top and then sealed tightly to prevent contamination.

5) The filled bottles were shipped directly to two separate laboratories at Reading University, where they were analyzed using standard methods suitably miniaturized to handle small quantities of water. **6)** Samples 1018 were prepared in our laboratory using a revised version of the precipitation method established by the ISF Institute in Germany. **7)** This method obtains a precipitate through the addition of $BaCl_2 \cdot 2H_2O$; the resulting precipitate can be washed and stored easily. **8)** The samples were subsequently shipped to ISF for analysis by accelerator mass spectrometry (AMS). **9)** All tubing used was stainless steel, and although two samples were at risk of CFC contamination as a result of brief contact with plastic, variation among samples was negligible.

Sentence Number	Information Element
1)	
2)	
3)	
4)	
5)	
6)	
7)	
8)	
9)	

(III) Select one journal article in your research field and fill in the following table about the analysis of the Methods section.

Title	
Journal	
Name of the Methods section	
Passive or active verbs	
Tenses (past simple / present simple)	
Are there any in-text citations?	
In-text citation style (information-prominent / author-prominent / weak author-prominent)	

Unit 3 Methods

IV Match the corresponding information elements in Column A with the phrases in Column B.

Column A	Column B
Providing specific and precise details about materials and methods	1) In this investigation, there are several sources for error. The main error is…
Giving reasons why a particular method was adopted	2) The vials were shaken manually to allow the soil to mix well with the water.
Pointing out any precautions / appropriate care taken	3) All reactions were performed in a 27 ml glass reactor…
Indicating the use of an established method	4) The semi-structured approach was chosen because…
Discussing any limitations in the method or problems the writer encountered	5) The sensitivity of the X technique has been demonstrated in a report by Smith et al. (2011).
Referring to the literature to justify a method or approach	6) Samples were analyzed for X as previously reported by Smith et al. (2012).

V Select the appropriate word in the box to complete each sentence. Change the form where necessary.

| modify | validate | qualitative | partition | consist |
| construct | material | follow | adapt | negligible |

1. To _____ the results from the metroscale model, samples were collected from all groups.
2. By _____ the array, all the multipaths could be identified.
3. The cylinder was _____ from steel, which avoided problems of water absorption.
4. In our implementation we _____ Smith et al. (2010) by using a discrete kernel size.
5. Although centrifugation could not remove all the excess solid drug, the amount remaining was _____.
6. The centrifuge is a slightly _____ commercially available model, the Beckman J6-HC.
7. The _____ investigated was a standard aluminium alloy; all melts were

modified with sodium.

8. This study employed a case study of _____ design.

9. The questionnaire was _____ from Horwitz, Horwitz and Cope (1986), Cheng (2004), and _____ of two parts: Part A addressed the general learning atmosphere during the learning process and Part B addressed writing competency of the learners.

VI Fill in each blank with the appropriate form of each verb given in the brackets.

1. Significance levels _____ at the 1% level using the student t-test. (set)
2. Data management and analysis _____ using SPSS 16.0 (2010). (perform)
3. The pilot interviews _____ informally by the trained interviewer. (conduct)
4. This experiment _____ under conditions in which the poor signal/noise ratio was improved. (repeat)
5. Blood samples _____ with consent, from 256 Caucasian male patients. (obtain)
6. The specimen _____ constantly for a period of 24 hours. (monitor)

VII Rearrange the words and phrases in each group into clear and coherent sentences.

1. were broken, as, ultrasonic treatment, cells, previously, by, described.
2. was adopted, an explorative research approach, using, on, a seven-page survey, opinions and religious background.
3. outlined, two minor modifications, our methods, followed, Tian and Zhang (2020), in, with, the procedures.
4. can be found, full, our previous paper, the methods, details, of, used, in, (Liu & Li, 2019).
5. once, the bacteria, the study, were, had been completed, no further interest, of.

VIII Rearrange the following clauses into a coherent paragraph.

1. The study was conducted just before the start of the school year,
2. we conducted a field study at a metropolitan zoo in North America.
3. The parents were solicited to participate in a short survey about the zoo in exchange for the possibility of winning a prize for one of their children.
4. Participants were 52 parents (29 women; M_{age} = 35.14, SD = 8.13, ranging 24–61 years) who were visiting the zoo with children of each sex ($M_{child\ age}$ = 7.05).

5. so parents were asked to choose whether they wanted to win a girl's or a boy's back-to-school pack (Appendix).
6. To test whether the same pattern emerged with actual parents when real economic consequences were at stake,

IX Translate the following sentences into English.

1. 注射溶液（injection solutions）由一位同事编码，以减少实验者的偏见。
2. 本研究为所有变量生成了描述性数据。
3. 样本间差异可忽略不计。
4. 分析是基于 Smith 等人（2002）提出的概念框架。
5. 为了验证这一假设，本研究从《美国科学院院报》（*Proceedings of the National Academy of Sciences of the United States of America*）中随机选取了 15 篇生物科学的研究论文。

X Translate the following paragraphs into Chinese.

Two experiments were carried out using different combinations of seasoning and varying cooking temperatures. A 4.5 kg frozen organic chicken was purchased from Buyrite Supermarket. Buyrite only sells grade "A" chickens approved by the Organic Farmers Association, thus ensuring both the homogeneity of the sample and the quality of the product. Seasonings were obtained from Season Inc UK and were used as supplied.

According to the method described by Hanks et al. (1998), the chicken was first immersed in freshly boiled water cooled to a temperature of 20°C and was subsequently rinsed thoroughly in a salt solution so as to reduce the level of bacteria on the surface of the chicken. In order to obtain two samples of equal size and weight for testing, the chicken was first skinned using a standard BS1709 Skinomatic; the flesh was then removed from the bone with a 4 cm steel Sabatier knife, after which it was cut into 3 cm-cubes, each weighing 100g.

Unit 4
Results

 Warm-up Questions

1. What is the purpose of the Results section?

2. What information elements are included in the Results section?

3. What are the salient linguistic features of the Results section?

4.1 Overview

4.1.1 Purpose of the Results Section

The purpose of the Results section is to present the key results of the experiment without interpreting their meaning. In the majority of the research papers, the Results section provides the investigation results described in the Methods section separately and leaves the discussions of the result in the Discussion section. In a few of other research papers, results are combined with discussion; while still others may be combined with methods and discussion in body sections within an AIBC (Abstract, Introduction, body sections, Conclusions) (Cargill & O'Connor, 2013: 33).

The Results section is where visual, numerical, and textual display attracts the reader's attention to the contributions and the merits of the work. If the separate style is used, it is generally important to highlight the main points of the findings and confine any comments in the Results section to saying what the numbers show, without comparing them with other research, or suggesting explanations. However, writers sometimes include comparisons with previous work in the Results section where the point being made relates to a component of the results that will not be discussed in detail in the Discussion section. In the following, we will discuss the information elements of the separate style only for the convenience.

4.1.2 Information Elements of the Results Section

The list in Table 4.1 is typical and provides us with a good information model of the Results section of the empirical research papers (Weissberg & Buker, 1990).

Table 4.1 Moves of the Results Section

Move 1	Location of the results: showing where the results can be found
Move 2	Findings: presenting the most important findings

Move 3	Brief comment: commenting on the results, which may include:
	  Step 1: Generalizing from the results
	  Step 2: Explaining possible reasons for the results
	  Step 3: Comparing the results with what was expected or with results from other studies

The information is usually given in the form of tables, charts, graphs, diagrams, lists, etc. Accompanying each table, chart, or graph is a description or an explanation. The visual and verbal elements complement one another to assist readers to acquire a clearer picture or a better grasp of the findings.

4.1.3 Sequential Structure of the Results Section

Since the results of the thesis have two goals: to describe and interpret the obtained data as objectively as possible in the form of a narrative stream, and to convey key information based on these data, the sequential structure should be carefully created.

The main structure of the Results section is as shown in Figure 4.1:

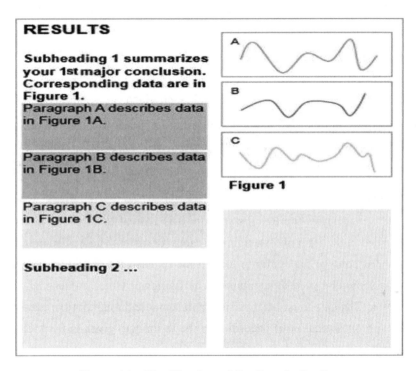

Figure 4.1   The Structure of the Results Section

After the results are listed, a writer should undertake a brief review. There are two types of organizational patterns.

1. Sequential pattern (See Sample 1 on Pages 82–87):

All of the results + A brief comment

2. Alternating pattern (See Sample 2 on Pages 87–94):

Result 1 + Comment 1

Result 2 + Comment 2

Result 3 + Comment 3

Nowadays, an increasing number of researchers use computers to prepare tables, charts, diagrams, etc. Sigmaplot, Origin, and Graphpad are the most often used tools. Each piece of the software has a unique feature that writers can combine to make greater use.

4.1.4 Principles of Results Presentation

In most cases, the Results section should have sub-parts specified by tables, charts or paragraph headings to help the reader understand the findings. Writers should look at the Results sections of published papers to better understand how the results are presented by figures, charts, and texts.

The general presentation principle of the figures and tables is that: figures and tables are consecutively numbered in the same order as they are mentioned in the text. It is often located appropriately within the text of the Results section. And the specific presentation principles of the figures and tables are listed as follows:

- A heading for each figure and table should be provided.
- Depending on the journal, the table titles and figure legends should be listed individually or above the table / below the figure.
- Each figure and table must be complete enough to stand alone, separate from the text.
- Details appearing in the figure captions and table headings are not repeated in the text.

When the writer writes the Results section, it is critical to consider whether the data should be provided in the form of text, figures, graphs, or tables. The writer should summarize the findings and encourage the reader to look at the relevant data in the text, figures, and/or tables. The text should be used to supplement the figures or tables, rather than to repeat the same information. The data must be consistent and accurate throughout the manuscript. They are arranged in chronological order according to the techniques given in the Methods section, or in an importance order.

It is also essential to present the results selectively. In this section, the writer should state the outcomes of statistical studies but not go into depth about every detail he obtained or observed. The relevance to the major question(s) or hypothesis(es) given in the Introduction section determines which outcomes to offer. The rules for selection of outcomes presentation are as follows:

- Writers should make sure that the readers and reviewers are able to identify which specific hypotheses were supported, which were only partially supported, and which were not supported.
- Non-significant findings should not be ignored. They should be mentioned briefly in relation to the hypothesis.
- Results of minor variations on the principal experiment should be summarized rather than included.

In a well-written empirical paper, the Results section is generally the shortest.

4.1.5 Common Mistakes in Writing a Results Section

There are three common mistakes in writing a Results section.

1. Redundancy

Writers often present their findings in a table before restating everything in the text. This is redundant. Text should be used to clarify figures and tables, not to repeat them.

2. Methods/Materials reported

Writers may write something like this in the Results section: "We found that Sample A contained pyroxene, therefore we ground Sample B to a powder and repeated the experiment again. With Sample B, we discovered pyroxene again."

The information "therefore we ground Sample B to a powder and repeated the experiment again" belongs to the Methods section, not to the Results section. Writers should only report results in the Results section.

3. No figures or tables

In general, the Results section should have at least one table. The writer should provide data regardless of the discipline. Some papers in humanities are notable exceptions.

4.1.6 Criteria for Judging a Results Section

Different journals might use different criteria to judge Results sections, but the following criteria, as shown in Table 4.2, cover the basics:

Table 4.2 Results Section Review Criteria

Results exposition	Sufficient detail: enough to understand the key results of the study
	Appropriate detail: no superfluous information
	Appropriate presentation: numbers and results are tabulated, not listed
Experimentation / Number of trials	Sufficient to test the hypothesis
Statistical tests	Performed when appropriate
Data	Believable: not an artifact of a poor experimental setup
Results section overall	Succinct: not verbose
	Clear: easy to read and understand
	Balanced: all the significant topics covered
	Focused: no superfluous information included

4.2 Sample Analysis

Sample 1 (From the Field of Psychology)

Subtitle for Result 1 **Move 1:** Location of the results	**Correlations Among Emotions** Figure 2 (presented in the Methods section) displays the correlations of the nine emotions studied. The emotions correlate as high as the 0.6 range for the pairs anxiety/fear and excitement/happiness. 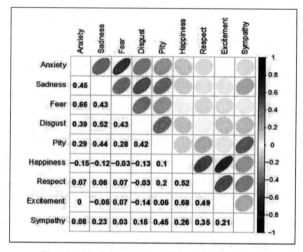 Figure 2 Correlations Among Emotions Note: The lower triangle shows correlations among the nine emotions; the upper triangle color-codes the size and sign of the correlations (deeper narrower = more positive, deeper rounder = more negative). The ellipses are not actual scatterplots, but represent the general shape of the scatterplot, calculated mathematically from the correlation coefficient.
Move 2: Findings: a result presented by a figure	Figure 2 displays the correlations of the nine emotions studied. The emotions correlate as high as the 0.6 range for the pairs anxiety/fear and excitement/happiness. As noted earlier, the fact that distinct conditions are often correlated limits the strength of conditions that can be drawn from any study that measures only one or a few emotions. Negative emotions (the first five listed) tend to cluster together, as do the four positive emotions; correlations between positive and negative emotions are generally near 0 rather than strongly negative. As previously stated, the fact that several emotions are frequently associated restricts the strength of conclusions that can be drawn from any study that just assesses one or a few emotions. Negative

emotions (the first five listed) tend to cluster together, as do the four positive emotions; correlations between positive and negative emotions are often close to zero rather than highly negative.

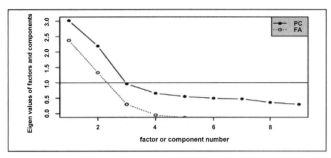

Figure 3　Scree Plot of Factor Analysis of Nine Discrete Emotions

Explaining Willingness to Interact with Emotion Groups

Move 3: Brief comment: results exposition

Step 1: Generalizing from the results and commenting

Our first analysis focuses on the impact of different emotion groups (e.g., positive, negative) on willingness to interact with robots. As emotion groups, we examined positive and negative emotions as emotion groups first, and then distinguished anxiety-related emotions from other negative emotions based on empirical findings and theoretical reasoning.

Table 2　Factor Analysis Results for Nine Discrete Emotions

Principal Component Analysis	Component 1	Component 2
Anxiety	0.68	−0.24
Sadness	0.76	−0.01
Fear	0.69	−0.19
Disgust	0.74	−0.08
Pity	0.71	0.33
Happiness	−0.18	0.80
Respect	0.08	0.75
Excitement	−0.22	0.74
Sympathy	0.40	0.65
Proportion of variance	33.49%	33.49%
Cumulative proportion	33.49%	57.84%

Note: Oblimin rotation.

Positive and Negative Emotions

Step 2: Explaining for some specific findings

To validate the distinction between positive and negative emotions, we first conducted an exploratory factor analysis (principal components analysis with oblimin rotation) on the nine emotions. The scree plot (Figure 3) revealed a clear two-factor solution that accounted for 58% of the total variance in the emotion items. Table 2 shows that the first factor represents negative emotions (33% of the total variance), with anxiety, disgust, fear, pity, and sadness having strong positive loadings onto the factor. The second factor, positive emotions (24% of the total variance), included high positive loadings for happiness, respect, excitement, and sympathy. Importantly, the correlation between these two factors was relatively low ($r = -0.10$), indicating a clear distinction between them. We then centered each emotion measure in each condition (Brauer & Curtin, 2017). Based on the unstandardized emotion measures, we computed unit-weighted composite scores for negative and positive emotions, with scale alpha reliabilities of 0.77 and 0.72, respectively. The means were 2.29 (95% confidence interval [CI] = [2.23, 2.35]) for negative and 3.89 (95% CI = [3.81, 3.97]) for positive; positive emotions were reported with much higher intensity than negative. The core analysis is the previously published Bayesian multilevel model, with negative and positive emotions as fixed effects and willingness to interact with robots as the outcome. Diagnostic checks (Muth et al., 2018) found that R-hat never exceeded 1.01, indicating satisfactory convergence. There were no divergent transitions, the Monte Carlo standard error (MCSE) was small relative to the posterior standard deviations, and effective posterior sample size had a mean of 3,395 which was greater than 940 for all parameters of interest. Results are shown in Table 3. Negative emotions related to willingness to interact ($b = -0.21$, 95% CI = [−0.28, −0.12]), as did positive emotions ($b = 0.36$, CI = [0.29, 0.42]). Both posterior credible intervals excluded 0. In absolute terms, the coefficient for good emotion (0.36) is greater than the coefficient for negative emotion (−0.21). To formally test the difference, we used the posterior distribution from the model estimation process. Each step includes estimates of all model parameters including the coefficients for positive and negative emotions. For each of the 4,000 steps, we computed the difference between the absolute value of the positive coefficient and the absolute value of the negative coefficient, for example, $|0.36| - |-0.21|$. Finally, we examined the distribution of these differences. They are positive in 3,986 cases (99.6%). Their median is 0.151 and the 95% posterior interval is [0.050, 0.254], demonstrating that the coefficient for positive emotions is consistently larger in absolute value than the coefficient for negative emotions. An increase of 1 scale point in positive emotions is associated with a larger increase in willingness to interact, compared with a decrease of 1 scale point in negative emotions.

Table 3 Multilevel Regression Investigating Positive and Negative Emotions as Predictors of Willingness to Interact with Robots

Predictors	Willingness to Interact		
	Estimates	SE	CI (95%)
(Intercept)	3.427	0.059	[3.286, 3.564]
Positive emotions	0.358	0.030	[0.288, 0.415]
Negative emotions	−0.207	0.037	[−0.284, −0.119]
Random effects			
σ^2	0.56		
τ_{00} Cond Study	0.03		
τ_{00} Study	0.01		
τ_{11} Cond Study, Em2Pos	0.00		
τ_{11} Cond Study, Em2Neg	0.00		
τ_{11} Study Em2Pos	0.00		
τ_{11} Study Em2Neg	0.00		
ICC	0.10		
N_{Cond}	25		
N_{Study}	5		
Observations	1,014		
Marginal R^2 / Conditional R^2	0.272 / 0.343		

Note: Under random effects, σ^2 is the residual variance of the model. τ_{00} parameters are the random intercept variances for (Condition within Study) and Study, and τ_{11} are the random slope variances for the predictors. CI = confidence interval; ICC = intraclass correlation.

	We ran the Bayesian multilevel model with negative emotions, anxious emotions, and positive emotions as fixed effects and behavioral willingness to interact with robots as the outcome. As this model has more parameters, a total of 8,000 steps were used to attain an adequate effective sample size. Diagnostic checks found that R-hat never exceeded 1.01, indicating satisfactory convergence, and there were no divergent transitions. The MCSE was small relative to the posterior standard deviations, and the effective posterior sample size had a mean of 6,783 and was greater than 1,390 for all parameters of interest. Results are shown in Table 4 (see the Discussion). Anxious emotions ($b = -0.09$, 95% CI = [−0.15, −0.02]), other negative emotions ($b = -0.11$, 95% CI = [−0.19, −0.04]), and positive emotions ($b = 0.36$, 95% CI = [0.29, 0.42]) were all significantly related to willingness to interact. We used the posterior distribution to see if the coefficient for positive emotions was bigger in absolute value than the coefficients for anxious and negative emotions. For negative emotions, the difference is positive in 7,998/8,000 cases (99.9%). It has a median of 0.24, and a 95% posterior interval of [0.15, 0.33]. For anxious emotions, the difference is always positive. It has a median of 0.27, and the 95% posterior interval is [0.18, 0.36]. Thus, positive emotions consistently relate more strongly to willingness to interact than either negative or anxious emotions. **Specific Emotions**
Step 3: Comparing the results with what was expected or with results from other studies	Finally, rather than looking at groups of emotions, we looked at the variance explained by nine specific emotions. Diagnostic checks, once again, revealed no issues with model convergence or estimations. Results of our analysis (Table 5 and Figure 4 [See the Discussion]) indicate that two positive emotions—excitement ($b = 0.186$, 95% CI = [0.137, 0.235]) and happiness ($b = 0.072$, 95% CI = [0.019, 0.124])—had posterior intervals that excluded 0. Two negative emotions, fear ($b = -0.056$, 95% CI = [−0.107, −0.005]) and disgust ($b = -0.100$, 95% CI = [−0.160, −0.040]), had negative coefficients and intervals that excluded 0. Like the previous analyses using scales of positive emotions and negative emotions, these results demonstrate that specific positive and negative

	emotions contribute to people's willingness to interact with robots. **Source:** Eliot, R. S., Steven, S., Marlena, R. F. & Selma, S. 2020. Positive emotions, more than anxiety or other negative emotions, predict willingness to interact with robots, *Personality and Social Psychology Bulletin, 1–14*: 234.

Sample 2 (From the Field of Public Management)

Move 2: Presenting the first part of the results: the most important findings	The first part of the results answers the questions "which municipalities practice customer orientation" and "which municipalities are interested in customer needs". One-third evaluate user statistics of their websites, nearly 10% conduct customer and/or citizen surveys, and 18% integrate customers in e-government projects or new process developments. 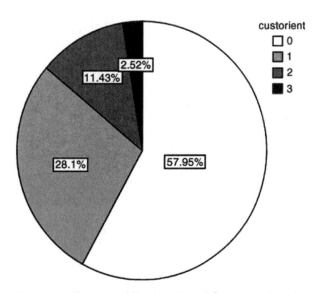 Figure 1 Degree of Exploration of Customer Needs Note: Phi coefficient, Cramer's V, or Tau and Lambda measures indicate the strength of correlation.
Move 1: Location of the results: Figure 1	The three approaches to customer orientation are depicted in Figure 1. Only around 2.5% of all towns in the survey use all three strategies to investigate customer demands. Almost 60% do not investigate consumer demands using any of the three ways. (Figure 1 appeared in the original article's Methods section).

Testing Hypotheses 1, 2, and 3	The first two hypotheses relate to the impact of structural factors of municipalities on their customer orientation. Hypothesis 1 concerns wealth, Hypothesis 2 concerns the size of the evaluation of user statistics, customer/citizen surveys, and customer integration. Both are tested by using discriminant analyses. Hypothesis 3 focuses on the cultural aspect of pragmatism versus etatism, indicated by the language spoken. It uses contingency analysis.
	Table 6 Structural and Cultural Factors Fostering the Exploration of Customer Needs
			Evaluation of User Statistics	Customer/ Citizen Surveys	Customer Integration
	|---|---|---|---
		Wilks' Lambda			
		Tax burden (wealth)	0.997	0.988	0.999
		Inhabitants (size)	0.929**	0.984**	0.979**
		Cramer's V			
		Language (political culture)	0.142**	0.164**	0.182**
	* Significance < 0.05; ** Significance < 0.01.
	Table 6 presents the results of the analyses. Two general characteristics significantly influence the adoption of methods to explore customer needs: the number of inhabitants with a high rate of explanation and the spoken language with low impact (Table 6). They both have an effect on all three methods. The level of the tax burden as an indicator of the financial situation of a municipality has no significant impact on the use of evaluation methods.
Testing Hypotheses 4 and 5	Hypotheses 4 and 5 suggest that the motives of municipalities to implement electronic government have an impact on their customer orientation. Hypothesis 4 covers cost reduction as an essential motive, and Hypothesis 5 covers image improvement. As it shows, only the latter factor correlates significantly with

	customer orientation, whereas cost reduction does not seem to have an impact (Table 7).
	Table 7 Motives for E-government Fostering the Exploration of Customer Needs
			Evaluation of User Statistics	Customer/ Citizen Surveys	Customer Integration
	|---|---|---|---
		Wilks' Lambda			
		Cost reduction	0.995	0.997	1.000
		Improving the image	0.990*	0.978**	0.998
	* Significance < 0.05; ** Significance < 0.01.
Testing Hypotheses 6 and 7	Hypothesis 6 suggests that political support leads to higher customer orientation, and Hypothesis 7 advocates a relation between the importance of electronic government for public managers and the customer orientation of the municipality. In short, both are looking at the leaders' attitudes towards e-government. Results seem to demonstrate that political support highly correlates with user statistics and customer integration, but not significantly with customer surveys. In contrast, there is only low correlation for the importance of electronic government for public managers, although highly significant (Table 8).
	Table 8 Leaders' Attitudes Towards E-government Fostering the Exploration of Customer Needs
			Evaluation of User Statistics	Customer/ Citizen Surveys	Customer Integration
	|---|---|---|---
		Wilks' Lambda			
		Political support	0.977**	0.994	0.983**
		Kendall's Taub			
		Importance for the management	0.142**	0.164**	0.182**
	* Significance < 0.05; ** Significance < 0.01.

In the following, hypotheses about the effect of customer orientation on the provision of electronic public services are tested. Figure 2 shows the number of usability features on websites of municipalities. Nearly one-third of municipalities provide none of the four prompted usability features on their websites or did not answer the question. About 12% have three of the four features, and less than 2% provide all four features on their websites.

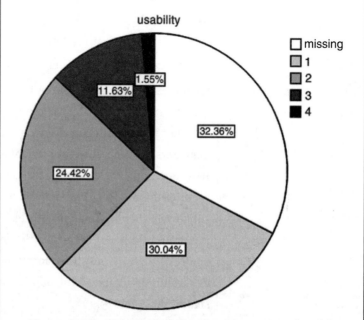

Figure 2　Number of Usability Features on the Website

> Transition: Introducing the effect of the result; testing Hypotheses 8 and 9

Hypothesis 8 supposes that there is a correlation between customer orientation and the provision of usability features. Correlation coefficients of the hypotheses test in Table 9 indicate a significant link between customer orientation, measured by the number of methods used to explore customer needs, and the availability of usability features on municipal websites.

Hypotheses 9 proposes that municipalities with customer-oriented features will provide a set of public services that differ from non-customer-oriented municipalities. To test that, the supply in 35 different topics (e.g., taxes, unemployment, public transport) was surveyed. The results ranked four times:

two times for customer-oriented municipalities and two times for non-customer-oriented municipalities. Municipalities are considered customer-oriented, if the value of the variable "custorient" is two or higher.

Table 9 Customer Orientation and Provision of Usability Features

	Correlations			
			Custorient	Usability
Spearman's Rho	Custorient	Correlation coefficient	1.000	0.222 (*)
		Significance (one-tailed)	–	0.000
		N	516	349
	Usability	Correlation coefficient	0.222 (*)	1.000
		Significance (one-tailed)	0.000	–
		N	349	349

*Correlation is significant at the 0.01 level (one-tailed).

Presenting the results by tables and figures and explaining possible reasons for the results

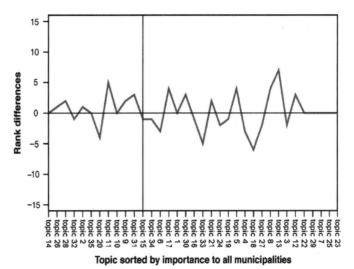

Figure 3 Rank Differences of the Topics at Least Between Customer-oriented and Non-customer-oriented Municipalities with at Least Information Online

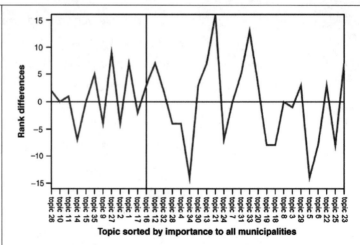

Figure 4　Rank Differences of the Topics Between Customer-oriented and Non-customer-oriented Municipalities with at Least Downloadable Forms Online

If the value is 0, the municipality is rated as non-customer-oriented. The first ranking of the topics is based on the number of municipalities that provide at least information on a particular topic. The second ranking applies to the number of municipalities providing at least downloadable forms on a certain topic. All four rankings are presented in Appendix A.

Figure 3 shows the differences in the ranks of topics between customer-oriented and non-customer-oriented municipalities. Rank orders are based on the number of municipalities, which provide to a certain topic at least information online. Differences range from minus 6 (Topic 18) to plus 7 (Topic 13). Topics are sorted on the x-axis based on the number of all municipalities that have at least information online. So, for example, more municipalities provide at least information on Topic 14 than on Topic 26. Therefore, in general, Topic 14 is more important to municipalities than Topic 26. For Topic 14, there is no difference in the rankings between customer-oriented and non-customer-oriented municipalities. It is the most important topic for both groups. In contrast, Topic 26 is more critical to customer-oriented municipalities than to non-customer-oriented municipalities.

	Although there seems to be an obvious difference between the two groups, Spearman's Rho's correlation coefficient is at 0.965**. This demonstrates a tight correlation between the two rankings. Thus, correlation is highly significant at the 0.01 level (two-tailed), so that we must assume that there is no systematic difference between the two rankings.
	Figure 4 presents the differences in the ranks of topics to which municipalities provide at least downloadable forms online. Levels differ from minus 14 (Topics 5 and 34) to plus 16 (Topic 21). It is evident that differences between the rankings based on the availability of downloadable forms (Figure 4) are much bigger than differences based on the availability of information (Figure 3).
	The correlation coefficient is at 0.763**, which is lower than before, so they confirm the observation of more enormous differences. However, the correlation is still statistically significant. That means there is no systematic difference in the topic rankings between customer-oriented and non-customer-oriented municipalities.
Explaining possible reasons for the result	In both figures, but particularly in Figure 4, significant differences do not occur on top-ranked topics. However, differences seem to occur for lower-ranked topics. A new hypothesis can be deduced from these results.
A new hypothesis (H10) is deduced	**H10** Municipalities investigating customer needs provide the same top-ranked electronic public services as others but different lower-ranked electronic public services.
Explaining the new hypothesis	To verify this hypothesis, the same correlations as before are calculated, but the first third of the top-ranked topics are excluded. Correlations of the rankings based on the online availability of information are still extremely significant; although the correlation coefficient is lower.
	A different result can be observed for rankings based on the online availability of downloadable forms: They no longer correlate statistically significant (0.356). Thus, it can be

	expected that there are systematic differences in the rankings of lower-ranked topics with downloadable forms or more between customer-oriented and non-customer-oriented municipalities.
	Source: Schedler, K. & Summermatter, L. 2007. Customer orientation in electronic government: Motives and effects. *Government Information Quarterly*, *24*(2): 291–231.

4.3 Linguistic Features of the Results Section

4.3.1 Lexical Features

1. Reporting verbs

To report the results, writers frequently use reporting verbs. The most commonly used reporting verbs are "show", "indicate", "suggest", "reveal", "report", "propose", "provide", "display", "demonstrate", "describe", "explain", "present", etc. For example:

- ✓ The following tables **show**…
- ✓ The analysis **shows** that…
- ✓ Hypothesis 6 **suggests** that…
- ✓ Table 6 **presents** the results of…
- ✓ We **demonstrate** super-resolution imaging at depths of up to 66 μm for cells.
- ✓ Yet, the illumination used is still not optimal for deep imaging and **provides** limited capabilities for optical sectioning.
- ✓ Here we **report** obSTORM, a light-sheet SMLM approach that works with any sample type mounted on regular coverslips.

2. Definition words

Definition words are often used to define or redefine, estimate or re-estimate some technical terms or equations. For example:

- ✓ Statistically, we **define** the conditional transition probability Pr (Hf + |Hf, f|), where Hf means the system being in the H state for the current congestion rate f.
- ✓ At the same time, Hf + **refers to** the system remaining in the H state if the congestion rate increases by Δf (here, we set $\Delta f = 0.01$).
- ✓ A similar **definition** can be made for the system's likelihood of staying in the L state

as the current congestion rate f is decreased and is indicated by Pr (Lf − |Lf, f|).

- ✓ "Business occupations" **are defined as** finance and marketing jobs, and "high-information occupations" **are defined as** jobs in finance, accounting, engineering, etc.
- ✓ We then **re-estimate** equation (1) on the remaining sample.

3. Modal words

Modal words are frequently used in the explanation of the results. For example:

- ✓ They **can** sometimes be more costly to the power of our analysis.
- ✓ The instruments **can** be interpreted as…
- ✓ Hypothesis 8 supposes that there **would** be a correlation between… and…
- ✓ The language used during a TA session **may** have an impact on the outcome.

4.3.2 Syntactical Features

In the following, we examine the syntactical features of the Results section from the use of tenses and agents of the predictive verbs.

1. Use of tenses

1) The present simple tense

The present simple tense is the most frequently used tense in the Results section. For example:

- ✓ Table 1 **presents** descriptive statistics of the sample and the primary population.
- ✓ The sample **covers** about 30% of the population of Switzerland.
- ✓ The following table **contains** variables describing general characteristics of municipalities; the number of inhabitants, tax burden, and spoken language in the municipality.

2) The present perfect tense

The present perfect tense is often used in the first sentence of the Results section. For example:

- ✓ Our datasets **have been collected** from real-time traffic in the (directed) road network of different cities.
- ✓ Data for these variables **have not been gathered** by questionnaire but **have been taken** from statistics of the federal government (Table 3; Steuerverwaltung, 2003; Bundesamt & Statistik, 2003).

3) The past simple tense

Past tense forms are also used in some cases where there is a reference to the results of previous research. For example:

- ✓ With the addition of the language model, our model **achieved** the lowest word mistake rate among all available models.
- ✓ Ji et al. (2004) **discovered** that whether the test language was Chinese or English mattered for bilingual Chinese who grew up in an environment dominated by one language and culture and only afterwards learned the other language and culture.
- ✓ When participants **were assessed** in Chinese, their responses **were more in line with** a Chinese manner of thinking than when they **were examined** in English.
- ✓ For bilingual Chinese who grew up in a mixed linguistic and cultural environment, the test language **did not influence** their responses.

2. Agents of the predictive verbs

In the Results section, three types of agents (subjects) of the reporting verbs are frequently used, namely, "we", "things/materials", and "it". For example:

- ✓ **We** further achieved 3D obSTORM by adding a third dimension (zo) of localization normal to the 45° oblique plane using astigmatic PSFs22 with a section thickness of 1μm.
- ✓ **The experimental results** show that the method can effectively estimate the pose and velocity of non-cooperative targets.
- ✓ Moreover, **the system** can adapt to the sporadic space illumination conditions and provide a pose measurement and motion estimation method with good robustness and high estimation accuracy for space non-cooperative targets.
- ✓ **Part of the nano tubes** shows the projected coiling shape of the helix, while **part** displays the stretched zigzag shape with a node at the cross region.
- ✓ **This** indicates that the catalysis particles were initially involved in the nucleation of the carbon tubes, but they may not be directly involved in the growth because their catalytic activity had been terminated.
- ✓ **It** can be observed that when two types of constraints are used, the performance is not as good as using only one constraint.

3) The passive voice

When the agent (subject) is not "we", the passive voice is used. For example:

- ✓ A careful search **was conducted** to see if there are catalysis particles with sizes significantly larger than the diameter of the nano tubes, but we found none.
- ✓ As more graphitic layers **are built up**, a node close to a spherical shape **is formed**.
- ✓ For thick tissues, larger spatial variations **were noted**, primarily owing to non-uniform

illumination and increased background fluorescence.
- ✓ Two adjacent microtubules at a center-to-center distance of 128 nm **were clearly resolved** with an apparent width of ~ 69 nm for each microtubule.
- ✓ In principle, smaller regions of interest **can be isolated** for SMLM imaging if they **can be identified**, but such approaches may be inconvenient and lead to sample damage.

4.4 Useful Expressions for the Results Section

Below are some useful expressions for each information element in the Results section.

1. Locating the results
- ✓ Table 9 reports the accuracy of our methods and existing methods.
- ✓ Figure 3 illustrates urban growth in Shenzhen during the three planning periods.
- ✓ The results of the policy evaluation can be found in Table 4.
- ✓ The hierarchical controller was tested in simulation and on-track with the full-size autonomous racing vehicle, shown in Figure 1.

2. Presenting the most important findings
- ✓ The results suggest that public pension funds do not earn systematically different returns from other types of investors.
- ✓ The experimental results show that the method can effectively estimate the pose and velocity of non-cooperative targets.
- ✓ A different result can be observed for rankings based on…
- ✓ We further achieved 3D obSTORM by adding a third dimension (zo) of localization normal to the 45° oblique plane…
- ✓ We next acquired a stack of ~10 oblique sections by…

3. Making brief comment

1) Generalizing from the result
- ✓ These results in Table 4 suggest the advantage of placing the convolution module after the self-attention module in the Conformer block.
- ✓ Based on the experimental results, the average position error is less than 6.1367 mm, and the average attitude error is less than 2.415°. In addition, the proposed VSV method uses two monocular cameras to measure two different measurement objects; the amounts of computation are reduced by half in the process of image recognition

and pose calculation.

- ✓ Traditional stereo-vision-based methods are susceptible to illumination conditions, incomplete feature extraction, and low contrast. This paper proposes a measurement system that combines stereo-vision information with 3D laser radar information and estimates the pose and velocity of the target through the EKF algorithm.

2) Explaining possible reasons for the result

- ✓ An alternative explanation for these results is that LPs have different risk preferences.
- ✓ We determined the noise floor (17) of the accelerometers on numerous Android phones by placing them in a basement and enabling them to record for one month to better understand which earthquakes we can record on smartphones.

3) Comparing the results with what was expected or with results from other studies

- ✓ On comparing the second decimal in dev WER, we find kernel size 32 to perform better than the rest.
- ✓ Conversely, when the conditions satisfy the 3D reconstruction, the point cloud information reconstructed by the stereo-vision is merged with the point cloud information acquired by the laser radar, thereby obtaining the target point cloud data.
- ✓ It comes out that only 2.5% of all municipalities in the sample apply all three methods to explore customer needs.

4.5 Reflections and Practice

❶ Answer the following questions.

1. What are the functions of the Results section?
2. What information elements are included in the Results section?
3. Is it necessary to interpret data or reach a conclusion in the Results section? Why?

❷ Analyze the information elements of the two Results sections. Text 1 is in the field of machine intelligence, and Text 2 in the field of computer science.

> **Text 1**

Quantitative Results

Results on MS-COCO. 1) Quantitative results for MS-COCO are reported in Table 1.

2) We compare our methods with state-of-the-art methods, including CNN-RNN, RNN Attention, ML-ZSL, SRN, ResNet101-ACfs, Multi-Evidence, etc. **3)** From the table, it is apparent to see that both C-GCN and P-GCN observe consistent improvements over comparing methods on all the evaluation metrics, especially on mAP (+5%), CF1/top1 (+3%), OF1/top1 (+2%), CF1/top3 (+4%) and OF1/top3 (+2%). Regarding the proposed two methods, P-GCN works slightly better. **4)** The results for VOC 2007 are presented in Table 2. Because the results of many previous works on VOC 2007 are based on the VGG model, for fair comparisons, we also report the results using VGG models as the backbone. **5)** As shown in Table 2, our proposed methods achieve better performance than comparing methods. Concretely, the proposed C-GCN obtains 94.0% mAP, and P-GCN obtains 94.3% mAP, which outperforms state of the art by 2% and 2.3%, respectively. **6)** Particularly, even RNN-Attention and Atten-Reinforce perform tenview evaluation across different scales, which is not directly comparable to our methods, we can still achieve better results (+0.8% for C-GCN and +0.7% for P-GCN) by using VGG model as the base model. Note that the improvements over existing methods are not as significant as that in MS-COCO, where part of the reason lies in that the performance for VOC 2007 has almost been saturated.

Sentence Number	Information Element
1)	
2)	
3)	
4)	
5)	
6)	

> **Text 2**

Results

Learning architecture: 1) Figure 5 shows the main differences regarding the learning architecture in training DNNs using BWN and DST methods. **2)** In the forward pass of BWN, the full-precision weights have to be read from the external memory and converted to binary values $\{-1, 1\}$, termed as a binarization step which can be based on either a stochastic sampling or just a deterministic sign operation. At the same time, DST only consumes a much smaller memory cell for each weight element (only $[N + 1]$ bits). **3)** As a result, the external full-precision memory device (regarded as off-chip memory) can be replaced by an internal buffer (regarded as on-chip memory) to enable fast data exchange within the ALU (Arithmetic

Logical Unit). In addition, the binarization step is unnecessary in the forward pass in DST. **4)** In the backward pass, the case becomes a bit more complicated. In summary, the major differences are listed as follows: (a) Due to the requirement of binary weights at computation time while full-precision weights at updating time, the BWN has to frequently switch between the external CWS and internal BWS and buffer the full-precision weights for the following updating operation. Unlike this, DST can load the discrete weights from the internal buffer for all computations. (b) Although DST introduces a gradient-based probabilistic projection operator to transform the real-valued weight to discrete states, this simplifies the design of the adder for weight updating. In particular, the BWN requires a floating-point and full-precision adder to generate the new weights based on the old weights and weight increments at each iteration. **5)** While the discrete transition in DST indicates that the state variable n in (1) is only possible to be integers, which significantly simplifies the floating-point adder in BWN into an integer version.

Cost comparisons: 6) The cost comparisons of DST and BWN are shown in Tables 1 and 2. As seen in Table 1, in the forward pass, BWN requires a full-precision external memory cell (usually 32 bits), one external read operation CR, one space switching step CS (binarization). Thus, the total computation cost is (CR + CS) for BWN methods. While DST only requires an (N + 1)-bit internal buffer cell, and the on-chip read cost is negligible compared with the mentioned off-chip memory operation. Space switching is no longer necessary. Therefore, the total computational cost in DST forward pass can be ignored compared with the BWN scheme. We conduct a similar analysis for the backward pass case in Table 2. The cost for BWN appears with the same external memory cell (32 bits) and (CR + CW + CS + float weight adder) computing resources; while for DST, only an (N + 1)-bit internal buffer and (CS + fixed-point weight adder) are consumed. In general, under the framework of DST, algorithms could be designed for online training of DNNs without external memory read and write cost. As well, the adder cost for updating weights in the backward pass can also be significantly reduced. **7)** Thus, the DST greatly improves memory and resulting computing resources, providing top-down theoretical guidance toward the on-chip training of large-scale DNN in the near future.

Sentence Number	Information Element
1)	
2)	
3)	
4)	
5)	

Unit 4 Results

(Continued)

Sentence Number	Information Element
6)	
7)	

III Select two Results sections in your research field and complete the following tasks.

1. Identify the information elements in these Results sections.
2. Underline the reporting verbs and clauses used in the Results sections.
3. Take a closer look and think about how the tables and figures in the Results sections help present the experiment results.

IV Match the organizational patterns of the Results section in Column A with the sentences in Column B.

Column A	Column B
Move 1: Location of the results **Move 2:** Findings **Move 3:** Brief comment Step 1: Generalizing from the results Step 2: Explaining possible reasons for the results Step 3: Comparing the results with what was expected or with results from other studies	1) Time course for respective nitrogen concentrations in the reactor at different phases is shown in Figure 1. 2) The results of the performances mean that the anammox culture in our reactor could hydrolyze urea and produce ammonium, which was then used with nitrite for anammox to carry out the Anammox reaction. 3) The phenomena in phase III might be due to the increase of urease hydrolyzing urea, and it requires further study. 4) The change of the three kinds of nitrogen charge was approximately consistent with the Anammox stoichiometry, demonstrating the Anammox reaction has taken place well in phase I. 5) According to the reports by Sliekers et al. (2004), the Anammox bacteria in their study were not able to hydrolyze urea, and a question whether or not other kinds of Anammox bacteria are capable of hydrolyzing urea exist was raised. However, in phase II, although ammonium concentration was hardly measured, the urea removal was increased all the time. 6) As a result of the possible existing of other bacteria in Anammox culture, the conclusion that Anammox can hydrolyze urea could not be obtained by the above experiments.

V Below are the sentences from a Results section. Put the sentences into a proper order to work out the Result section. The Results section falls into three paragraphs. The first sentence is given for each paragraph. But the rest sentences in each paragraph are not yet in order. Rearrange the sentences in the order that you think the author originally wrote them.

Paragraph 1

____1____ A. Our datasets have been collected from real-time traffic in the (directed) road network of different cities, among which Beijing includes over 27,000 nodes and 52,000 links (within the 5th Ring Road).

_____ B. The velocity data are also recorded with the same resolution, covering five working days in October 2018.

_____ C. The velocity dataset covered real-time velocity records of roads in Beijing for 17 working days in October 2015 and 9 working days in October 2018.

_____ D. Road velocity is obtained from global positioning system (GPS) data recorded in floating cars with 1-min resolution.

_____ E. Ji'nan, a comparatively small city in China, has around 12,000 nodes and 22,000 links.

_____ F. The dataset of Shanghai, which is composed of over 26,000 nodes and 51,000 links, has the same temporal resolution as Beijing and covers five working days in October 2015 and 17 working days in October 2017.

Paragraph 2

____1____ A. By applying percolation analysis for each city, we first determine the service level of each road in the city.

_____ B. Then, we normalize the velocities of each road at each instant by dividing them by their standard maximal velocity on that day.

_____ C. Here we use the relative velocity derived from real-time data to indicate the road operation level.

_____ D. We sort in increasing order the velocity measured at a given day and choose the 95th percentile as the standard maximal velocity for a given road.

_____ E. In this way, we obtain the relative velocity of each road at every minute, $r_{ij}(t) = v_{ij}(t)/v^m_{ij}$.

_____ F. Here, vij(t) is the real-time velocity of the road connecting node i to node j at time t, v m ij is the standard maximal velocity of this road for that day, and rij(t) is the relative velocity.

_____ G. The congestion rate, f, is therefore defined as the fraction of failed roads concerning the total number of roads.

_____ H. For a given relative velocity threshold, q, the road with rij(t) < q is considered failed.

Paragraph 3

__1__ A. Here, we mainly focus on the transportation system of Beijing in China as an ideal system for our study.

_____ B. This regime shift suggests that urban traffic may undergo a sharp transition between alternative network states.

_____ C. In Beijing, with the central area covering over 700 km² and a population of over 20 million inhabitants, passengers usually spend almost twice as much time for commuters during rush hours, compared to non-rush hours, which causes huge economic losses and other social risks.

_____ D. For instance, for a given fraction (i.e., f = 0.25) of congested roads, at 7:41 a.m. of 27 October 2015, the traffic network breaks into several fragmented parts; however, a few minutes later, with the same fraction of congested roads, at 7:48 a.m., these small traffic clusters merge into a sizeable functional cluster spanning almost the whole city of Beijing.

_____ E. We study data from October, which is one of the busiest months in Beijing.

_____ F. As shown in Figure 1, we observe that the urban traffic can have multiple network states describing the global performance at the scale of the entire city.

_____ G. In fact, during most morning hours in a typical day, the dynamic state of the traffic system in Figure 1 shifts back and forth frequently between these two states (more demonstrations are shown in SI Appendix, Figure S2-2).

Ⅶ Fill in each blank with the appropriate form of the verb given in the brackets.

As 1) _____ (show) in Table 4, the number of total routing cycles after optimization 2) _____ (be) much less than before the optimization. Specifically, the addition of periodic constraints 3) _____ (result) in a decrease in routing cycles by 80.3% and 38.1% respectively, when 4) _____ (compare) to the zigzag mapping method, and a decrease of 83.2% and 38.4% compared to the neighbor mapping method, respectively. Furthermore, when we 5) _____ (add) cyclic and turning constraints simultaneously, the reduction 6) _____ (be) 74.9% and 34.4% respectively compared to zigzag mapping method and 78.5% and 34.8% respectively compared to neighbor mapping method. Table 5 7) _____ (reveal) the effectiveness of various mapping methods in terms of routing power for two CNNs configurations. Random mapping 8) _____ (result in) deadlock occurrences in 25% of the experimental cases for configuration 1 and 100% for configuration 2.

Ⅶ Select the appropriate word or phrase in the box to complete each sentence. Change the form where necessary.

| susceptible | demonstrate | lead to | achieve | conduct |
| observe | round up to | make | replace | draw |

1. In Figure 4, we _____ that the red curve is higher than the black dashed one, which implies that the defender always gets more benefit by knowing the presence of the insider.

2. The electronic and catalytic properties of the single supported atoms are highly _____ to their local chemical environment.

3. All our evaluation results _____ 1 digit after decimal point.

4. This clearly _____ the effectiveness of combining transformer and convolution in a single neural network.

5. Using swish activations _____ faster convergence in the conformer models.

6. We found that this worsens the performance when _____ our proposed architecture.

7. With the language model added, our model _____ the lowest word error rate among all the existing models.

8. As a result, the external full-precision memory device (regarded as off-chip memory) _____ by an internal buffer (regarded as on-chip memory) to enable fast data exchange within the ALU (Arithmetic Logical Unit).

9. We _____ a similar analysis for the backward pass case in Table 2.

10. From the results in Figure 6, we _____ two key conclusions as follows.

Ⅷ Rearrange the words and phrases in each group into clear and coherent sentences.

1. are among the best-performed method, as reported, both of our methods, the previous competing methods, compared with.

2. whose names contain multiple words, for the categories, we, for all words, obtain the label representation as an average of embeddings.
3. are reported, quantitative results, the partial label setting, in Table 5 and Table 6, for.
4. can also demonstrate, those observations, the practicality of, for multi-label classification, the proposed schemes, in real-world applications.
5. between worker and worker, there is alienation, by virtue of their incessant struggle, limited employment opportunities, for the fruits of.

IX Translate the following sentences into English.

1. 总体而言，我们发现，在大多数情况下，国家治理体制的大气候（climate）对电子政务发展提供了强有力的支持（详细信息见表2的第四列）。
2. 我们可以发现，无论采用何种映射方式，随机XY路由策略的路由周期转数总是比XY路由的转数多一点。(the random XY routing strategy, the XY routing)
3. 我们通过方程（1）中包含的职业固定效应来解决这个问题，结果发现它是由未观察到的职业角色差异所驱动。
4. 分析结果表明，我们设计的女性主义行为量化表（FBS）具有内在的一致性。
5. 在研究过程中已经确定，运动员的人体测量指标（体长和质量）（body length and mass）略有不同。

X Translate the following paragraph into Chinese.

Nisbett's results show that culture affects individual experiences on a very basic perceptual level. It appears, however, that two limitations must be kept in mind in discussing Nisbett's work. First, it is based on studies of college and university students. Students are generally young, well educated, and unlikely to be representative of the entire population. It is unclear how this may affect the results. Second, some studies suggest that analytic and holistic thinking can be induced by dynamic, situational factors (Briley et al., 2000; Hong & Mallorie, 2004). Thus, analytic and holistic thinking may either be intrinsic to participants' cultural background or be two cognitive styles that are available across cultures and may be triggered by situational factors or even used knowingly in situation-dependent ways.

Unit 5
Discussion

📝 Warm-up Questions

1. What is the purpose of the Discussion section?

2. What information elements are included in the Discussion section?

3. What are the salient linguistic features of the Discussion section?

5.1 Overview

5.1.1 Purpose of the Discussion Section

The purpose of the Discussion section is to interpret the results and relate them to previous studies that the writer and other writers have done. If we say the Results section deals with facts, then the Discussion section deals with points. Facts are descriptive, while points are interpretive. The writers interpret the experimental results and make speculations about the findings. Furthermore, they have some flexibilities in deciding which of their possible points to include and then which to highlight in the Discussion section.

Overall, the function of the Discussion section is interpretation + discussion. It is more than summaries. They should go beyond the results. They should be:

- more theoretical or more abstract;
- more general;
- more integrated with the field;
- more connected to the real world;
- more concerned with implications or application.

5.1.2 Information Elements of the Discussion Section

The information elements commonly included in the Discussion section are given below:

- A reference to the main purpose or hypothesis of the study, or a summary of the main activity of the study.
- A restatement or review of the most important findings, generally in order of their significance, including
  - whether they support the original hypothesis, or how they contribute to the main activity of the study, to answering the research questions, or to meeting the research objectives; and
  - whether they agree with the findings of other researchers.
- Explanations for the findings, supported by references to relevant literature, and/or speculations about the findings, also supported by literature citation.
- Limitations of the study that restrict the extent to which the findings can be generalized beyond the study conditions.
- Implications of the study (generalizations from the results: What the results mean in the context of the broader field).

- Recommendations for future research and/or practical applications.

The above list can form a checklist for you as you write. You may not have something to say under every point in the list for every result you discuss, but it is worthwhile thinking about each element in turn as you draft the section.

These elements, except the first one and the last one, are often repeated for each group of results that is discussed.

When you draft this section, you can think about the main points you want your readers to understand by addressing the following series of questions:

- Did the results provide answers to the (testable) hypothesis?
- If so, what does this mean for the hypothesis?
- If not, do the results suggest an alternative hypothesis? What is it? Why do the results suggest it? What further results might solidify this hypothesis? Have others proposed it before?
- Do these results agree with what others have shown? If so, do other writers suggest an alternative explanation to explain the results? If not, how does this experiment differ from others? Is there a design flaw in this experiment?
- How do these results fit in with results from other studies? Do results from related studies affect the way these results are being interpreted?

In addition to interpreting the results, the writer should discuss the following questions (the order may vary):

- What factors or sources of error might have influenced these results?
- What anomalous data turned up and how can it be explained? Is it explained by the writer's theory or someone else's theory? Is it right?
- Is this experiment the most effective way to test this hypothesis? (Obviously the writer thought so at the beginning, but does he or she still think so? How could the experiment be improved to gain further insight?
- How have the results and conclusions of this study influenced our knowledge or understanding of the problem being examined?
- What would be the next step in this study?
- What experiments could be run (or what data could be found) that would lend further support to the writer's hypothesis? (Either the original hypothesis, or the new one designed to explain the results.) What experiments could be run (or what data could be found) that would disprove the writer's hypothesis?

5.1.3 Principles of Writing the Discussion Section

To write a good Discussion section, writers should stick to the following principles:

- Generally, the Results and Discussion sections cannot be combined. They have two different purposes. The Results section is for fact while the Discussion section is for interpretation.
- A new result should not be included in the Discussion section. All results must be reported in the Results section. New results can be restated in the Discussion section, but they must appear in the Results.
- Writers must answer all the questions you can think of. Never miss any information such as re-state hypothesis and motivation, the ties of the work in the larger field of research, comparison analysis of their work to others, the discussion of the sources of error, etc.
- The Discussion section must be conclusive. The writer needs to draw conclusions, and then suggest how the experiment should be changed to properly test the hypothesis.
- Always be clear with whose study is being discussed: this study or the results of other studies. Never be ambiguous about the data sources when the writers talk about the results.

Table 5.1 is the basic criteria of peer review for the Discussion section. (Besides this, different journals might use different standards to judge the manuscript of the section.)

Table 5.1 Discussion Section Review Criteria

Motivation for study	Clearly restated
Interpretation of results	Sufficient interpretation of results Logical interpretation of results
Possible limitations and sources of error	Adequate discussion Acceptable errors: the sources of error do not lower confidence in the results
Ramifications	Clear and adequate discussion Realistic
Discussion section overall	Succinct: not verbose Clear: easy to read and understand Balanced: all the major topics are covered Focused: no superfluous information is included

5.1.4 Organizational Pattern of the Discussion Section

Typically, the organizational pattern of the Discussion section falls into four moves as shown in Table 5.2:

Table 5.2   Moves of the Discussion Section

Move 1	Points to consolidate the research space (obligatory) Step 1: A reference to the purpose or hypothesis of the study Step 2: A review of the most important findings Step 3: Explanations for or speculations about the findings
Move 2	Points to indicate the limitations of your study (optional but common)
Move 3	Implications of the study (optional)
Move 4	Recommendations for further research and practical applications (optional and only common in some areas)

5.2 Sample Analysis

Sample 1 (From the Field of Public Management)

Sentences 1–4: **Move 1:** Points to consolidate the research space Step 1: A reference to the purpose or hypothesis of the study	1) Using a theoretical framework which focuses on the significance of national governance institutions and the associated country indicators from several global databases, we have provided a fresh perspective on why the institutions of governance can shape e-Gov development and serve as an explanation for the e-Gov divide. 2) Our analysis provides evidence that indeed a more sophisticated national governance institutional climate positively influences the development and diffusion of e-Gov. 3) In particular, the analysis shows that national governance institutions represented via democratic practices, transparency of corporate governance, corruption perception, and press freedom tend to positively shape the adoption and diffusion of e-Gov, all else being equal. 4) Overall, we surmise that our formulation of the national governance institutions—as forces which can facilitate or impede

Sentences 5–7: Step 2: A review of the most important findings	e-Gov development—is a credible framework for analyzing and explaining the e-Gov diffusion differentials among countries. **5)** The e-Gov researchers have established that indeed there is a sort of a "divide" in the e-Gov diffusion worldwide (e.g., Helbig et al., 2009). **6)** That is, e-Gov as an ensemble of techniques, processes and systems to improve government has become popular among governments both in the industrialized as well as developing and transition economies (Mayer-Schönberger & Lazer, 2007). **7)** However, the examination of e-Gov penetration beyond the initial adoption in different countries reveals a pattern whereby the diffusion among the industrialized countries appears to be greater than within the developing and transition nations.
Sentences 8–20: Step 3: Explanations for or speculations about the findings	**8)** This difference among the two groups of industrial and developing/transition economies has been the subject of research and more specifically a search for the key drivers that can explain the difference (e.g., Boyer-Wright & Kotterman, 2008). **9)** Indeed, the prior research has revealed useful factors including the level of economic development, availability of broadband, cost of telecommunications, and website design which may explain some of the differences in diffusion rates (e.g., West, 2007). **10)** However, persistence of this difference over the last decade begs for additional theoretical insights to augment our knowledge of existing factors and drivers (e.g., Heeks & Bailur, 2007). **11)** Our research, following in the footsteps of institutional economics researchers (North, 1990, 1994) has pointed to the national governance institutions as important shaping mechanisms that can largely enable or constrain e-Gov diffusion. **12)** In particular, we started with Wilson's (2003, 2004) qualitative framework and analysis (of Brazil, China, and Ghana) on the importance of national governance institutional forces (private sector, public sector, and NGO sector) for the diffusion of ICT and Internet. **13)** We then adapted this framework in order to analyze the influence of these governance institutions on e-Gov development across a wide range of countries globally via our four alternative hypotheses and quantitative indicators. **14)** Thus, one contribution

Unit 5 Discussion

	of our research is that it complements the prior inventory of drivers and factors of e-Gov development by adding the distinctive role of governance institutional climate as a fundamental consideration. **15)** That is, we provide preliminary evidence that the national governance institutions play a significant role in the diffusion of e-Gov systems. **16)** The extant research has documented that e-Gov adoption is on the rise while at the same time pointing to the difficulties some countries face in moving beyond providing simple website and information catalogue functions (e.g., Coursey & Norris, 2008; Helbig et al., 2009). **17)** Indeed, the importance of institutional factors as opposed to traditional metrics to explain these difficulties is alluded to in related research (e.g., Tolbert, Mossberger & McNeal, 2008). **18)** Our research affirms this difficulty but then goes a step further. **19)** We extend the three country qualitative study and framework of Wilson (2004) by adapting it to address e-Gov diffusion quantitatively and globally. **20)** We demonstrated the distinctive influences of national governance institutional climate captured as democratic practices (H3), transparency of corporate governance (H4) and corruption perception (H5), and the free press (H6). **21)** A major thrust of e-Gov in practice and the associated research has been the push towards enhanced accountability via the use of focal systems "simplifying the institutional structure of government, making it more transparent" (Dunleavy, 2007: 422). **22)** Our research, though preliminary and exploratory, proposes to reverse this causality. **23)** That is, in fact such institutions may be pre-requisites for diffusion of e-Gov beyond the simple adoption of systems. **24)** It is indeed the theoretical argument of our research that national governance institutions provide the underpinning on which foundational e-Gov systems are designed, developed and implemented. **25)** A corollary of this is that e-Gov systems may be adopted initially. **26)** However, if the national governance institutions within the three sectors (private sector, NGO and government) are lacking and/or underdeveloped, then further development and assimilation of e-Gov systems may be negatively influenced
Sentences 21–23: Further explanations for the findings	
Sentences 24–28: Significance about the findings	

Sentences 29–36: Explaining for the unexpected result	or slowed down or simply stalled. 27) Our data in all the national governance institutional categories, namely, democratic practices, transparency of corporate governance and corruption perception, and press freedom support such reasoning. 28) Thus, our research has extended the literature by providing initial evidence of the supportive role of national governance institutions in shaping the development of e-Gov beyond the simple adoption stage. 29) However, a counter-intuitive and unexpected result of our proposed model was the lack of a significant relation between economic level of development and e-Gov development and diffusion (i.e., H1 in the Proposed Model). 30) The methodological and secondary data problems notwithstanding, there appears to be an interesting mechanism at work. Although, it is only a conjecture at this stage, we surmise that, our Proposed Model is not equipped to account for the so called symbolic adoption and institutional decoupling phenomena (Meyer & Rowan, 1977). 31) That is, although countries are adopting e-Gov systems in large numbers (e.g., Boyer-Wright & Kotterman, 2008), some are not moving beyond the adoption stage. 32) In particular, only those that have fairly developed national governance institutions may be able to actually exploit the underlying technologies in their operations to move towards the assimilation stages of e-Gov. 33) This phenomenon is referred to as "symbolic adoption" or "decoupling" by neo-institutionalist researchers (Meyer & Rowan, 1977; Di Maggio & Powell, 1983; Strang & Meyer, 1993). 34) More recent empirical analysis (Meyer, Boli, Thomas & Ramirez, 1997; Lee & Strang, 2006; Dobbin, Simmons & Garrett, 2007) has shed additional light on this institutional decoupling mechanism. 35) These researchers argue that, there is a trend in global adoption of "rational systems" (e.g., be they organizational forms or policies, or computer systems) among nation states. 36) However, underpinning this trend, there can be a pattern of action at work whereby the adoption of "rational systems" is decoupled from the follow-up implementation and assimilation. 37) In essence, some polities in the "world society

Sentences 37–39: Criticism for some politics to enact "rational systems" by challenging the definition of it	of nation states" appear to enact the so-called rational systems only symbolically as a means to gain legitimation but often do not (or are not able to) follow up the adoption stage with actual implementation (Dobbin et al., 2007). **38)** Some e-Gov researchers have gone so far as characterizing this trend as "Potemkin e-Villages" in reference to the Soviet officials who in the Stalin era used to create fake settings to impress visiting government dignitaries (Katchanovski & La Porte, 2005). **39)** It is beyond the scope of our research to ascertain whether such mechanisms are at work within the focal countries, a point that can be taken up in future research.
Sentences 40–49: **Move 2 and Move 4:** Points to indicate the limitations of the study and recommendations for further research and practical applications	**40)** Our research has limitations which can be addressed through further research. **41)** First, the data elements that are missing can be worked on and rectified to increase the pool of countries in the sample (e.g., to increase the number of nations in the sample). **42)** This will require rectification and reconstruction of missing data from diverse sources—a challenge we could not attempt to meet in this paper due to resource constraints. **43)** Second, as additional data are obtained, we can increase the pool of countries to 100–150 cases, then Structural Equation Modeling can be utilized to perform confirmatory analysis and produce more robust test of our Proposed Model. **44)** Third, more recently researchers have documented and theoretically accounted for the potential of e-Gov systems to initiate changes in the underlying institutional environment, e.g., reducing corruption (Kim & Lee, 2009). **45)** On the surface, this type of theoretical argument and evidence runs counter to the logic of the model specification we have presented—e.g., low perception of corruption as a pre-requisite. **46)** However, by expanding the framework into a structurational model (Wilson, 2004; Jones & Karsten, 2008), changes in underlying institutional environment can be allowed to vary. **47)** Furthermore, they can be represented as co-evolutionary phenomena in parallel to the technology-based changes introduced via e-Gov systems. **48)** As a result, national governance institutional climate becomes a set of dynamic social norms and patterns rather than static givens which

	then can also be allowed to co-evolve with the technology. **49)** This is a noteworthy research direction to explore which can build on the current paper's theoretical and empirical horizon.
	Source: Azad, B., Faraj, L. S., Goh, J. M. & Feghali, T. 2009. What shapes global diffusion of e-Government: Comparing the influence of national governance institution. JGIM Final Manuscript ref. Paper 2009-1006-a, *Forthcoming in *Journal of Global Information Management*.

Sample 2 (From the Field of Computer Science)

The discussion falls into several parts, each part with a subject title	**Necessity and Challenges of Modeling Low-level Resources** Recall from §2 that modeling of resources at a fine granularity is necessary, as it allows for better performance without overprovisioning. It is difficult to model the dependence between low-level resource requirements and quantifiable performance gain while dealing with uncertain and noisy measurements. FIRM addresses the issue by modeling that dependency in an RL-based feedback loop, which automatically explores the action space to generate optimal policies without human intervention. **Why a Multilevel ML Framework?** A model of the states of all microservices that is fed as the input to a single large ML model leads to (i) state-action space explosion issues that grow with the number of microservices, thus increasing the training time; and (ii) dependence between the microservice architecture and the ML-model, which sacrifices the generality. FIRM addresses those problems by incorporating a two-level ML framework. The first level ML model uses SVM to filter the microservice instances responsible for SLO violations, thereby reducing the number of microservices that need to be considered in mitigating SLO violations. That enables the second level ML model, the RL agent, to be trained faster and removes dependence on the application architecture. That, in turn, helps avoid RL model reconstruction/retraining.

	Lower Bounds on Manageable SLO Violation Duration for FIRM
A figure helps explain	Table 6 Avg. Latency for Resource Management Operations

Operation	Partition (Scale Up/Down)					Container Start	
	CPU	Mem	LLC	I/O	Net	Warm	Cold
Mean (ms)	2.1	42.4	39.8	2.3	12.3	45.7	2050.8
Std Dev (ms)	0.3	11.0	9.2	0.4	1.1	6.9	291.4

As shown in Table 6, the operations to scale resources for microservice instances take 2.1–45.7 ms. Thus, that is the minimum duration of latency spikes that any RM approach can handle. For transient SLO violations, which last shorter than the minimum duration, the action generated by FIRM will always miss the mitigation deadline and can potentially harm overall system performance. Worse, it may lead to oscillations between scaling operations. Predicting the spikes before they happen, and proactively taking mitigation actions can be a solution. However, it is a generally-acknowledged difficult problem, as microservices are dynamically evolving, in terms of both load and architectural design, which is subject to our future work.

Limitations

Limitation

Recommendation for further study

FIRM has several limitations that we plan to address in future work. First, FIRM currently focuses on resource interference caused by real workload demands. However, FIRM lacks the ability to detect application bugs or misconfigurations, which may lead to failures such as memory leak. Allocating more resources to such microservice instances may harm the overall resource efficiency. Other sources of SLO violations, including global resource sharing (e.g., network switches or global file systems) and hardware causes (e.g., power-saving energy management), are also beyond FIRM's scope. Second, the scalability of FIRM is limited by the maximum scalability of the centralized graph database, and the boundary caused by the network traffic telemetry overhead. (Recall the lower bound on the SLO violation duration.) Third, we plan to implement FIRM's tracing module

	based on side-car proxies (i.e., service meshes) that minimizes application instrumentation and has wider support of programming languages. **Source:** Qiu, H., Banerjee, S. S., Jha, S., Kalbarczyk., Z. T. & Iyer, R. K. 2020. FIRM: An intelligent fine-grained resource management framework for SLO-oriented microservices. *Computer Science, 1–20*: 805–825.

5.3 Linguistic Features of the Discussion Section

5.3.1 Lexical Features

In the Discussion section, writers need to pay particular attention to the verbs they use to comment on the results. The following introductory verbs, thinking verbs, reporting verbs and modal verbs carry much of the meaning about attitude towards findings and strength of claim. In addition, the using of modal verbs, modal adverbs, modal adjectives, modal nouns, evaluative adjectives, evaluative adverbs, adverbs of frequency, as well as certain signaling words are also the features of this section.

1. Introductory verbs

Introductory verbs such as "seem", "indicate" and "suggest" are frequently used to introduce the discussion topic. For example:

- ✓ Only promotion-related strategies **seemed** to have a higher and more consistent association in more than one test.
- ✓ In their introduction to the manual for the present tests, Arlin and Hills (1976) **indicate** that "assessment of students' attitudes is an exceedingly complex task".

2. Thinking verbs

Thinking verbs like "believe", "assume", "suggest" and "hope" are used to indicate the writer's opinion. For example:

- ✓ In line with this hypothesis, we **assumed** that older workers in speed jobs would have poorer performance than younger workers.
- ✓ From a policy point of view, this **suggests** that one important channel through which better rule of law and judicial enforcement may reduce informality is by making market interactions more efficient.

✓ We sincerely **hope** this study inspires scholars to undertake similar research in the future that examines the influence of sector on other BG dynamics.

3. Reporting verbs

Reporting verbs such as "claim", "find", "confirm" and "assert" are also commonly used to review the results in the first move of the Discussion. For example:

✓ In other words, we **find** that substantive responsiveness exists in an authoritarian system.

4. Modals

1) Modal verbs

Modal verbs like "may" and "should" are frequently used to indicate the writer's attitude. For example:

✓ The characteristics of practice-based research **may** create difficulties in that high-ranking journals.

✓ The strategies presented here **can** be further elaborated with more detailed actions.

✓ Future research **should** conduct similar analysis for firms from other nations such as China, Russia, Japan, South Korea, and so forth.

2) Modal adverbs

Model adverbs such as "certainly" "definitely" are frequently used in the Discussion section to emphasize the writer's attitude. For example:

✓ We've **certainly** improved the figures of Table 1.

3) Modal adjectives

Modal adjectives such as "certain" "definite" are frequently used in the Discussion section. For example:

✓ The system has **definite** extend value for electric power industry.

4) Modal nouns

Modal nouns such as "assumption" and "possibility" are frequently used in the Discussion section. For example:

✓ The only safe **assumption** is that the world's financial markets will have to find solutions themselves.

5. Evaluative words

1) Evaluative adjectives

Evaluative adjectives such as "important", "actual", "just", "misguided", "wrong" "inaccurate" and "incorrect" are often used to make the writer's voice louder. For example:

- ✓ Thus, to analyze the content of the articles examined, it is **important** to highlight which are the most popular aspects studied in relation with group interventions with adolescents and youth.
- ✓ In some articles the **actual** intervention is described in detail (i.e., Streng, 2002; Villalba, Ivers & Ohlms, 2010; Westergaard, 2012), whereas in others it is just explained in a simple paragraph to give more importance to research aspects.

2) Evaluative adverbs

Evaluative adverbs such as "accurately", "generally" and "unsatisfactorily" are frequently used to indicate the writer's judgement. For example:

- ✓ What many people mean by the word "power" could be more **accurately** described as "control".
- ✓ As for benefit, they are **generally** considered as resulting from enhanced access to public good.
- ✓ FBG, serum lipid and blood pressure were controlled **unsatisfactorily** in patients with type 2 diabetes mellitus in Beijing urban community.

6. Adverbs of frequency

Adverbs of frequency are often used to make the writer's voice stronger or weaker. For example:

- ✓ In essence, some polities in the "world society of nation states" appear to enact the so-called rational systems only symbolically as a means to gain legitimation but **often** do not (or are not able to) follow up the adoption stage with actual implementation.
- ✓ In **some** articles the actual intervention is described in detail, whereas in others it is just explained in a simple paragraph to give more importance to research aspects.

7. Signaling words

In addition, some signaling words are also frequently used to strengthen the claim, whatever the part of speech they are.

Signaling words such as "rather", "instead", "furthermore", "moreover", "thus", "even", "similarly" and "neither…nor…" are commonly used to make the writer's voice stronger. For example:

- ✓ **Rather**, there is an association with the possibilities of change and social involvement participants can experience.
- ✓ **Moreover**, the choice of aspects to analyze could be considered arbitrary to an extent.
- ✓ **Even** when articles do not take intervention methods as their principal focus, they refer to them as a key aspect.

✓ In other words, monitoring and guidance from non-financial corporations will **neither** add to **nor** diminish the benefits they can generate for their firms by pursuing diversification independently.

5.3.2 Syntactical Features

Some sentences are also commonly used to indicate the writer's attitude or show the writer's position or stance.

1. Sentences with "it" as the formal subject

Sentences with "it" as the formal subject are frequently used in this section, as indicated in the following examples:

✓ **It is worth mentioning** the use of terms related to ethnic background to identify the target population.

✓ **It seems that** customer needs are more important for those services, which are not so widespread and rather complex and expensive to implement.

2. Sentences with "there is / there are" as the formal subject

✓ **There is also a strong tendency** to define the target population in relation to the problem or adverse situation participants are facing.

✓ **There are not clear patterns regarding** the kind of problem or situation, so it can be deduced that social group workers address a wide array of problems.

✓ **Moreover, there is some presence of** community and social action purposes such as social action, citizenship, or activism.

3. Emphatic sentences

Emphatic sentences are frequently used to emphasize the writer's viewpoints. For example:

✓ However, the research conducted shows that certain journals, such as *Social Work with Groups*, **do** have a high publication rate concerning articles relating to SWGA (Social Workers Group Association).

✓ **Nor** can we confirm whether researchers consider it would be useful to include this aspect in the report of their research.

4. Comparatives and superlatives

Comparatives and superlatives are frequently used to emphasize the writer's attitude. For example:

✓ This lack of impact may discourage researchers from conducting research in this area, as their findings **are less likely** to be published or cited.

- ✓ Additionally, bibliometrics may not be **the most suitable** tool to find the cause of this uneven distribution.
- ✓ Hence, the online offering of information is **much more widespread** on local government websites **than** the provision of forms or transactions.

5. Adverbial clause of concession introduced by "although"

Writers often use the adverbial clause of concession introduced by "although" to make a judgement. For example:

- ✓ **Although** some of the results are not as clear as expected, **it seems that** using measures of customer orientation is both well motivated and fruitful to a municipality.

6. Conditional statements

Conditional statements are often seen in the Discussion section, as indicated in the following example:

- ✓ However, this is only true **if** the municipality has the preconditions to really adjust its services to customer needs.

5.4 Useful Expressions for the Discussion Section

Below are some useful expressions for each information element in the Discussion section.

1. Points to consolidate one's research space

- ✓ As previously described, there are comparable results showing the importance of…
- ✓ In particular, the analysis shows that…
- ✓ Our research affirms…
- ✓ Our analysis provides evidence that…
- ✓ Our research affirms this difficulty but then goes a step further.
- ✓ Our research, though preliminary and exploratory, proposes to reverse this causality.
- ✓ The result indicated that our approach is practicable for…

2. Contributions and explanations for findings

- ✓ Therefore, a more detailed investigation is needed in adjusting these parameters.
- ✓ Thus, one contribution of our research is that…
- ✓ Thus, our research has extended the literature by providing initial evidence of…
- ✓ Indeed, the prior research has revealed…

- ✓ Furthermore, they can be represented as…
- ✓ It seems possible to interpret… as…
- ✓ To harness the full potential of crowdsourcing, scientists must use sensors that are…
- ✓ In the future, existing EEW systems that use traditional seismic and geodetic networks could benefit from MyShake just as MyShake could benefit from…
- ✓ The data could also potentially be used to…
- ✓ The defender should ensure effective practices to prevent its happening.
- ✓ But those two methods could be affected by actions such as…

3. Indicating limitations

- ✓ It is difficult to…
- ✓ It is a generally-acknowledged difficult problem.
- ✓ It is indeed the theoretical argument of our research that…
- ✓ It is beyond the scope of our research to ascertain whether…
- ✓ Our research has limitations which can be addressed through further research.
- ✓ In contrast to the two-player game, the defender obtains more benefit with smaller CD in three-player game.
- ✓ We also discussed the limitation of current methods and the possible future research directions.

4. Implications and recommendations

- ✓ This is a noteworthy research direction to explore…
- ✓ These findings are in line with the result…
- ✓ All three methods found that…
- ✓ The findings largely correspond to the results provided here except for…
- ✓ Different reasons might be responsible for this difference.
- ✓ What is key to this study is that…
- ✓ As previously described, there are comparable results showing the importance of…
- ✓ It remains to be seen if customer orientation on the long hand improves electronic public services.
- ✓ Further research comparing human interracial interaction and HRI in the same paradigm will be required to establish whether…
- ✓ It is beyond the scope of our research to ascertain whether such mechanisms are at work within the focal countries, a point that can be taken up in future research.

5.5 Reflections and Practice

❶ Answer the following questions.

1. What are the functions of the Discussion section?
2. What are the basic information elements in the Discussion section?
3. In which ways can the writer's position or voice be represented and inferred?

❷ Analyze the information elements of the two Discussion sections. Text 1 is in the field of cultural psychology, and Text 2 in the field of earth sciences.

▶ Text 1

1) Our analysis of the TA (thinking-aloud) method by use of Nisbett's cultural psychology suggests that culture influences how instructions are acted upon by users, how users verbalize, how evaluators read users, and how the overall relationship between evaluators and users develops. These influences have implications for practitioners and for researchers, in particular those wishing to do cross-cultural work. Below we discuss these implications.

2) Table 1 summarizes our advice for practitioners who do TA tests, in particular for Western evaluators intending to test in Eastern cultural contexts. Compared to existing guidelines on international use of TA tests (e.g., del Galdo & Nielsen, 1996) our advice is grounded in principles of cultural psychology. Some of the advice is related to common recommendations for how to do TA tests, for instance those of Rubin (1994), but again the advice differs by providing a psychological motivation.

3) With respect to the overall relationship between user and evaluator, several subtle effects are at play. As a result of conversational indirectness, expressions from Eastern users may seem vague or unclear with respect to preference. Practitioners should not conclude that an Eastern user is satisfied just because no open critique is voiced. Similarly, fewer attempts should be made to find a middle way. Practitioners should not just focus on the test and what needs to be done, but take into account that Eastern users will be oriented toward the development of a harmonic socio-emotional relationship with the evaluator.

4) The ways in which culture may influence TA testing also raise issues relating to research. In the following discussion we stay within the context of usability evaluation, but the arguments may hold also for the use of TA in other contexts. One implication of our analysis is that it may not be possible to compare or easily transfer the findings of research based on thinking aloud in one cultural setting to another setting.

5) Our paper has identified a number of areas that need further research so as to characterize more completely the pitfalls and possibilities of cross-cultural TA. First, priming appears a strong mechanism for engendering culture-specific cognition. It is not clear, however, whether and how this could be used in TA to dispense with the need for testing with multiple cultures. Second, more research is needed on the effect of thinking aloud on users' task performance during usability tests. To remove differences in users' ability to think aloud while performing tasks, Hall et al. (2004) had participants think aloud after the full set of tasks had been completed. Another possibility is to have users think aloud after the completion of each task. It is currently unknown how such variations of TA are influenced by differences in cultural background. Third, the relative benefits of testing with evaluators and users who share or do not share cultural background are largely unknown. Yeo (2001) provides some initial data on this question but other cultures and other combinations of evaluators and users must also be investigated. Fourth, it would be interesting to instrument an interface with issues identified by users with one cultural background but not by users with another cultural background. If user satisfaction with that interface increases for both cultures, then what appeared to be cultural differences in the usability of systems could instead be a difference in the extent to which users are able to describe the usability issues they experience. Knowledge about whether cultural differences in the results of TA sessions indicate different usability issues, different ability to describe such issues, or both would be very useful to TA evaluators.

Paragraph Number	Information Element
1)	
2)	
3)	
4)	
5)	

Text 2

1) The MyShake project to date demonstrates proof of concept for a smartphone-based seismic network that provides instrumental recordings of ground shaking in damaging earthquakes and potentially delivering EEW. **2)** What is key to this study is that the system has been designed for and tested on privately-owned smartphones, of which there are billions. To harness the full potential of crowdsourcing, scientists must use sensors that are already being used by consumers, develop systems that can harness the data from these sensors with minimal impact to the owners, and provide the owners with real benefits to participating.

3) MyShake uses the accelerometers on common smartphones, which is freely available from the Google Play store for easy installation and automatic update, and uses minimal power, meaning phones only need to be recharged daily as commonly practiced, and participation leads to delivery of earthquake hazard information and could include the delivery of earthquake-shaking alerts.

4) In the future, existing EEW systems that use traditional seismic and geodetic networks could benefit from MyShake just as MyShake could benefit from integration of data from traditional networks. As described above, observations from even one traditional seismic station could help reduce uncertainties in MyShake earthquake estimates. Likewise, a handful MyShake phone triggers could be used to confirm a preliminary earthquake detection from one or two traditional network station triggers; most traditional EEW systems require several stations to trigger before issuing an alert. Finally, and perhaps most importantly, MyShake could deliver alerts in regions that have little in the way of traditional seismic networks.

5) The data could also potentially be used to image shallow Earth structure beneath our cities and perhaps even to image the earthquake rupture process itself.

Sentence Number	Information Element
1)	
2)	
3)	
4)	
5)	

III **Select two or three Discussion sections in your research field and complete the following tasks.**

1. Identify the information elements in these Discussion sections.
2. Analyze the sequencing of the moves in these Discussion sections.
3. Highlight the useful expressions that can represent the writer's posture.

IV **Match the moves of the Discussion section in Column A with the sentences in Column B.**

Column A	Column B
Move 1: Points to consolidate the research space	1) Revealed fundamental differences should be used in the process of athletes' technical preparation. 2) At the

Step 1: A reference of the purpose or hypothesis of the study Step 2: A review of the most important findings Step 3: Explanations for or speculations about the findings **Move 2:** Points to indicate the limitations of the study **Move 3:** Implications of the study **Move 4:** Recommendations for further research and practical applications	same time, a legitimate question arises as to whether disproportion should be eliminated and insufficiently developed parameters of athletes' technical skills should be improved, or it would be better to rely on their advantages. **3)** The coach often tries to increase those capacities of athletes that are largely limited genetically or are constrained by exceptionally high level of development of other qualities. In this case, a sports training not only fails to produce results, but often suppresses the fitness strongest points, smooths out those individual traits that would be the cornerstone of success in realizing the technical skills of a particular athlete. **4)** Similar conclusion was reached by specialists, who compared the indices of the developed multifunctional models with individual biomechanical characteristics of the long jump technique of the outstanding Ukrainian female jumper (world record holder in the triple jump) Inessa Kravets and considered the competitive activity modelling as the basis for individualizing the design of long-term preparation in track and field all around. **5)** There is reason to believe that it is necessary to focus on those individual characteristics of technical skills of long jumpers, which ultimately provide the achievement of high sports results.

Ⅴ Fill in each blank with the appropriate form of the verb given in the brackets.

Urban traffic, as a nonequilibrium complex system, 1) _____ (undergo) in megacities critical transitions almost every day. 2) _____ (face) with the challenge of increasing uncertainty, and various perturbations from extreme climate to collision accidents, it 3) _____ (be) essential to understand and explore the nature of the system's adaptation and recovery. Here, we 4) _____ (identify) multiple states in functional traffic networks under the same perturbation at the scale of the entire city. These phenomena may 5) _____ (be) due to the existence of long-range correlations. Based on real data, the emergence of long-range correlations in traffic congestion 6) _____ (find) during the rush hours. Indeed, it 7) _____ (suggest) that long-range connections can determine the overall flow conductance of the network. This long-range correlation, combined with the dynamical fluctuations of commute traffic in the megacity, may 8) _____ (generate) the multiple macroscopic states, which can 9) _____ (identify) by our percolation method. Moreover, the long-range correlation 10) _____ (propose) a statistical approach to accurately locate the critical point separating the region where a single state exists and the region of multiple states. We 11) _____ (find) that the multiple states of the system and the transitions between them 12) _____ (be) highly parallel to the hysteresis phenomenon from statistical physics. Precisely, we 13) _____ (observe) that the system experiences strong persistence in the metastable regime. For adiabatic changes (small changes) in f, the system's state is highly dependent on its previous state with the system 14) _____ (be) more likely to remain in the same state. Nonetheless, we 15) _____ (refer) to this phenomenon as "hysteresis-like" since the mechanisms behind this pattern require further study in the future. Even still, the parallels are remarkable and strongly justify the applications of statistical physics to complex systems such as urban traffic.

Ⅵ Select the appropriate word or phrase in the box to complete each sentence. Change the form where necessary.

| cause | suggest | there be | potential | provide |
| address | compare | challenge | insight | room |

1. FIRM has several limitations that we plan to _____ in future work.
2. First, FIRM currently focuses on resource interference _____ by real workload demands.
3. Our simulations _____ that the difference between the tracks is in the order of 1.5s.
4. _____ the frequency contents of this section with those of the off-bridge experiment in the previous section makes it possible to identify the effect of bridge vibration on the recorded acceleration on the car.
5. In real-life situations, _____ many sources of excitation acting simultaneously on the bridge, e.g., many cars moving in multiple lanes in similar or opposite directions, or the effects of winds, which result in larger vibration of the bridge.
6. At this point, the main _____ is the damage detection capability of these types of signals.
7. To investigate the _____ of the framework presented in this paper for damage detection of bridges, analysis results presented in the previous sections are compared in Figure 15.

8. The off-bridge spectrum _____ a reliable tool to distinguish between car-related and bridge-related peaks.

9. More _____ are provided by comparing the passes over pin-pin and fixed-fixed bridges.

10. Because operating cash flow changes are not fully persistent, this leaves _____ for dividend changes to provide some incremental information about the permanence of post-dividend cash flow changes.

Ⅶ Rearrange the words and phrases in each group into clear and coherent sentences.

1. faster, in reality, the earthquake, when, we have a denser phone network, we would, expect, the application to, detect.

2. undergoes, as a nonequilibrium complex system, in megacities critical transitions, almost every day, urban traffic.

3. it has also been suggested that, can determine the overall flow conductance of the network, indeed, long-range connections.

4. that the system experiences strong persistence, in the metastable regime, precisely, we observe.

5. based on, several future implications, our current results, there are.

Ⅷ Below are the sentences from a Discussion section. Put the sentences into a proper order to work out the Discussion section. The Discussion section falls into four paragraphs. The first sentence is given for the first paragraph. But the rest sentences of each paragraph are not yet in order. Rearrange the sentences in the order that you think the author originally wrote them.

Paragraph 1

__1__ A. The main contribution of this study is that it represents the first attempt to empirically examine how corporate diversification-performance relationships of BG-affiliated firms differ across manufacturing and service sectors.

_____ B. Given the inherent differences in these two sectors (Brouthers & Brouthers, 2003; Capar & Kotabe, 2003) and given the growing literature devoted to business groups in emerging economies (Carney et al., 2011; Kedia et al., 2006; Zhao, 2010), this study has addressed two important and timely research questions.

_____ C. Prior BG research has overlooked such distinctions.

_____ D. The results of this study have important implications for research and practice.

Paragraph 2

__1__ A. First and foremost, our findings suggest that the diversification-performance relationship of affiliated firms indeed varies across sectors and the relationship is stronger for service firms than manufacturing firms.

_____ B. But, the influence of BG size and diversity is greater for service firms than manufacturing firms.

_____ C. Second, findings reveal that various measures of group size and group diversity impact corporate diversification-firm performance relationships differently for manufacturing and services sectors.

_____ D. The results also suggest that the influence of domestic ownership on corporate diversification-firm performance relationship is practically nonexistent for both manufacturing and service firms.

_____ E. Finally, the results suggest that the influence of foreign ownership on corporate diversification-performance relationship does not significantly differ across the two sectors. All the above findings are new and contribute to corporate diversification literature in general and BG scholarship in particular. Our findings add to the existing knowledge base relating to Indian BGs and affiliated firms (George, 2007; George & Kabir, 2012).

Paragraph 3

__1__ A. Practicing managers of affiliated firms will find the study findings useful.

_____ B. While diversification can lead to enhanced or decreased performance, the impact of diversification, in general, will be more for service firms than manufacturing firms.

_____ C. They need to understand that although service and manufacturing firms may belong to the same BG, corporate behavior and subsequent performance of these firms can be very different when it comes to corporate diversification.

_____ D. Thus, managers need to prepare themselves differently for the after-effects of diversification depending on the industrial sector to which they belong. In addition, managers of affiliated service firms whose group market capitalization is high must prepare for greater benefits (firm performance) from diversification compared to their counterparts in manufacturing.

_____ E. Moreover, managers of BG-affiliated firms need to understand that their firms' domestic and foreign nonfinancial corporate ownership does not exert a meaningful impact on the performance that they expect from pursuing diversification.

_____ F. However, managers of manufacturing firms whose group total assets are high should prepare for decreased benefits from diversification compared to the benefits that managers in service firms would experience.

_____ G. Therefore, managers need not deploy excessive resources to align their interests with those of their corporate owners.

_____ H. In other words, monitoring and guidance from nonfinancial corporations will neither add to nor diminish the benefits that they can generate for their firms by pursuing diversification on their own.

Paragraph 4

_____ A. First, the study relies on a five-year timeframe (2004–2008).

_____ B. Although this lends greater validity than relying on single year data, running similar analysis for different or longer timeframes may generate more fine-grained results. Future research therefore needs to execute similar studies utilizing time spans that are different from this study's time period.

__1__ C. Despite the study's new findings, it is not without limitations.

_____ D. Second, the study utilizes data of firms from only one country—India. This limits the generalizability of findings.

_____ E. Future research should conduct similar analysis for firms from other nations such as China, Russia, Japan, South Korea, and so forth (Carney et al., 2011), or engage in comparative studies across nations.

_____ F. Third, the study focuses on three heterogeneous features of business groups: group size, group diversity, and share ownership.

_____ G. Future scholarship needs to examine other BG features such as interfirm relationships, power dependence, and social ties among others (George & Kabir, 2012) in investigating how such attributes influence diversification and performance in BGs.

_____ H. Finally, future research can compare and contrast the above results across group-affiliated and nongroup or independent firms (Carney et al., 2011).

_____ I. Fourth, future research needs to theorize and investigate in detail how sector influences the impact of related and unrelated diversification on firm performance.

_____ J. We sincerely hope this study inspires scholars to undertake similar research in the future that examines the influence of sector on other BG dynamics.

IX Translate the following sentences into English.

1. 我们之前认为，多维方法对于了解这件事情非常重要，即电子政务的进展是否代表了管理城市所必需的一系列技术和人为因素。
2. 反之，当满足3D重建条件时，通过立体视觉重建的点云（point cloud）信息与通过激光雷达获取的点云信息会进行融合，从而得到目标点云数据。
3. 确定这样的机制是否在那些重点国家发挥作用超出了我们的研究范围，不过未来可以进行研究。
4. 从政策的角度来看，这表明更好的法治和司法的执行是减少非正规性的一个重要渠道，通过提高市场互动的效率，使正规信贷市场的参与更具吸引力。
5. 互联网技术或许能够通过将一家公司的活动与其在一个更独特的系统结合来加强这些优势，但不太可能完全取代这些优势。

X Translate the following paragraphs into Chinese.

　　The major conclusion from this work is the general finding that positive emotions account for more variance than negative or anxiety-related emotions in willingness to interact with robots. This suggests that person-to-person variation in the extent of positive responses such as excitement is a more important factor than variation in negative feelings such as anxiety. Our Bayesian multilevel analysis shows that these effects hold across variation between studies and conditions in participant populations, types of robots used, live or video interaction, and many other factors. This pattern suggests that there may be some robustness and generality to these effects.

　　At the broadest level, this work demonstrates benefits of conceptualizing HRI as an instance of intergroup interaction. This not only allows the application of well-developed social psychological theories to help understand HRI but also challenges and strengthens intergroup theories by stretching them to different contexts from those for which they were developed. In future research, studies should be conducted on effects of positive and negative emotions on willingness to engage in human intergroup interaction, for which similar patterns of findings might be expected. Surprisingly, as far as we are aware, no such studies have been conducted [although Barlow et al. (2019) examined a related issue, effects of past contact on one positive and one negative emotion].

Unit 6
Conclusion

📝 Warm-up Questions

1. What is the purpose of the Conclusion section?

2. What information elements are included in the Conclusion section?

3. What are the salient linguistic features of the Conclusion section?

6.1 Overview

6.1.1 Purpose of the Conclusion Section

The purpose of the Conclusion section is to tie up the whole article by drawing conclusions in accordance with the questions raised in the Introduction section. Following the preceding logic development of research questions, research procedure, and research results and discussion in the article, the final Conclusion section serves to tease out the important findings in the article, support the end-results of the present research by deduction and induction, and direct for the succeeding research.

It is not easy to work out a qualified Conclusion section since it tests the writer's abilities of abstract thinking, analytical generalization, and value judgement. In this section, the writer needs to refine the research contents for the purpose of establishing the reliability and validity of the research results. The writer should also pinpoint the significance of the present study by illuminating its research value. Apart from this, the writer should shed light on the broader implications and applications for future work.

Perspicuous and perspicacious, the Conclusion section may enlighten readers for further research. Inspired by a good conclusion, readers could probe into new areas in which they will harvest new fruits. To a large extent, a reader is more interested in the Conclusion section for its easy and rapid access to relevant information which will continuously bring a new breakthrough to humanity. Even the smallest breakthrough can mean a great deal.

If a research article is compared to a pearl necklace, the Conclusion section should be the brightest pearl in this necklace. Coherent, rigorous and rational, the Conclusion section fits together well with other pearls in a research article. The Conclusion section should be a climatic part in an article, which will leave readers a deep impression. Sometimes, the Conclusion section mingles with the Results and Discussion sections as an integrated part. However, it still plays a crucial part in these cases.

6.1.2 Information Elements of the Conclusion Section

Contrary to the writing of the Introduction section in a research article, the composition of the Conclusion section bears resemblance to a pyramid in which writers begin with more specific information and end with more general ideas. In other words, the Conclusion section usually goes from narrow to broad.

The Conclusion section may start with a very brief summary of the Results and Discussion sections and then come to the conclusion statements, followed by the contribution to the research fields and suggestions for the future work. Sometimes, the summary is inclined to be integrated into the concluding remarks while some statements in this section may function as suggestions as well. Some research articles could add other necessary information elements or exclude a certain element as per the content. Nevertheless, the composition of the Conclusion section should follow a clear logical line, putting the essential information into a proper order. Figure 6.1 exhibits the order of typical information elements in the Conclusion section.

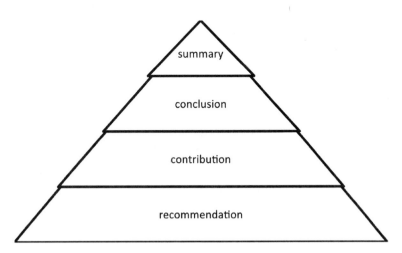

Figure 6.1   The Order of Typical Information Elements in the Conclusion Section

As indicated generally in the pyramid above, the Conclusion section should, with a focus on one aspect or several ones, include such information elements as:

- a brief summary of the main points/results;
- the conclusion from the end-results;
- the reliability of the conclusion;
- the points different from the conventional ones;
- the comparative advantages of the research;
- the significance and implication of the research;
- the limitations of the research;
- the prediction for follow-up work;
- the questions for further research;
- the well-supported proposals on succeeding research.

Different research articles may highlight different aspects in the Conclusion section. However, it may go through the following basic stages as indicated in Table 6.1:

Table 6.1 Basic Stages of Writing the Conclusion Section

Basic Stages	Information Elements	Questions to Be Answered
Stage 1	Brief summary	What is the gist of the main findings?
Stage 2	Conclusion	What are the conclusions from the main findings?
Stage 3	Contribution	What is the contribution of this work to the research field?
Stage 4	Recommendation	What would be done in the future?

6.1.3 Principles of Writing the Conclusion Section

Built on solid data and discussion, an article should reach the research conclusion in a matter-of-fact way. Make clear the application range of a conclusion. On the other hand, avoid jumping at a hasty conclusion, an over-simplified one or an over-generalized one. The Conclusion section should also leave readers a sense of completeness of the present research and may suggest the follow-up work.

To write a good Conclusion section, writers should stick to the following principles:

- echo the Introduction section;
- answer the question(s) in the Introduction section;
- generalize the present important findings without adding unnecessary details;
- exclude the citations of others' studies;
- evaluate the relevant points;
- come to a clear and concise conclusion;
- highlight the originality or novelty of the present research;
- strive for a sense of completeness of the present work;
- direct for future research;
- end with a memorable statement.

6.1.4 Common Problems of Writing a Conclusion Section

When writing a Conclusion section, a writer should also avoid some common problems as follows:

- re-elaborate the research background;
- present a verbose summary;

- draw a vague or ambiguous conclusion;
- copy some sentences from the Results and Discussion sections without further refinement;
- include too many details when coming to a conclusion;
- introduce ideas irrelevant to the research question, procedure, or results and discussion;
- provide an over-simplified or an over-generalized conclusion;
- lack the essential coherence and cohesion devices;
- end the whole article abruptly.

6.2 Sample Analysis

Now let's try to analyze the following samples from these aspects: Identify the information elements of the following Conclusion samples and trace the logic underlying the text; highlight the coherence and cohesive devices deployed in the text, as well as the tentative language used; change the information in each of the Conclusions into a mind-map, as Sample 1 and Sample 2 do respectively in Figure 6.2 and Figure 6.3; comment on the writing strategies in these samples.

Sample 1 (From the Field of Biomechanics)

Sentence 1: Conclusion **Sentence 2:** Significance **Sentence 3:** Application	1) The similarity of stability characteristics between lipid bilayer vesicles and carbon nano tubes does exist. 2) This quantified similarity enables us to understand better the stability characteristics of vesicles in micro or nano scales, and provides beneficial enlightenments in curing cancer cells. 3) Besides, the simple, precise and quantified method to measure vesicle's curvature rigidity may be used for discriminating the mechanical property of carbon nano tubes, and may be broadly applied to various fields such as biophysics, biology and biomedicine as well. **Source:** Yin, Y. J., Yeh, H. Y.& Yin, Y. 2006. Stability similarities between shells, cells and nano carbon tubes. *IEE Proceedings: Nanotechnology, 153*(1): 7–10.

Figure 6.2　The Mind-Map of Sample 1

Sample 2 (From the Field of Language Education)

Sentences 1–3: Summary of the end results	1) We have looked at ways of conceptualizing second language learning and understanding its nature and causes. 2) First, we dealt with creative construction and skill learning as alternative models of second language learning. 3) Then, we discussed how these two models might be integrated, either by viewing one from the perspective of the other, or by placing them both within a broader framework based on social learning theory.
Sentence 4: Conclusion	4) To conclude, we should stress that to view the problem in terms of two different kinds of learning is a simplification which, however useful, may also be misleading. 5) Between the most subconscious process of "acquisition" at one extreme and the most conscious forms of "learning" at the other, it would probably be more realistic to think in terms of a continuum, in which subconscious and conscious processes are mingled to varying degrees. 6) As research continues, we may hope to gain more detailed and reliable knowledge about how these and other processes interact with each other in the development and use of second language ability. **Source:** Littlewood, W. 1994. *Foreign and Second Language Learning*. Cambridge: Cambridge University Press.
Sentence 5: Further explanation of conclusion	
Sentence 6: Suggestion for future work	

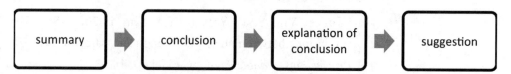

Figure 6.3　The Mind-Map of Sample 2

Unit 6 Conclusion

Sample 3 (From the Field of Law)

Sentences 1–3: Necessity and feasibility of the research work	1) The growing threat of cyber crime is real and serious. 2) The new breed of criminal activities and offenders in cyber space also present law enforcement officials and prosecutors with issues and challenges in the investigating of cyber crime and prosecuting of cyber criminals. 3) While there exists a sizable and growing body of literature on cyber crime, there are also research gaps that need to be addressed. 4) In this article, we outline and propose five salient and pertinent areas of inquiry that we feel constitutes a sufficient basis to advance our knowledge and the scholarship on cyber crime. 5) We hope our proposed agenda will serve as a helpful guide for researchers, scholars, and practitioners interested in understanding, combating, and preventing cyber crime. **Source:** Ngo, F. & Jaishankar, K. 2017. Commemorating a decade in existence of the *International Journal of Cyber Criminology*: A research agenda to advance the scholarship on cyber crime. *International Journal of Cyber Criminology*, *11*(1): 1–9.
Sentence 4: Summary and conclusion	
Sentence 5: Significance of the research work	

Sample 4 (From the Field of Journalism)

In this sample, the discussion and the conclusion are an integrated part. This is the extract of the last two paragraphs. **Sentences 1–4:** Concluding remarks from one perspective	1) In concluding the study, an important note must be made regarding the digital architectures framework: Digital architectures are subject to rapid and transformative change. 2) Even though Snapchat's architecture, for example, offered only rudimentary analytics to campaigns during the primaries, the platform was updated by the general election to provide campaigns with a sophisticated means of acquiring users' emails. 3) The Trump campaign, says Oczkowski, gathered "hundreds of thousands of emails off the Snapchat platform" by presenting users with advertisements encouraging them to "swipe up" and enter their

Sentence 5: Restatement of study purpose	email addresses. **4)** Even in the interim between the 2016 primaries and the writing of this article, all of the platforms included here have undergone significant transformations in their digital architectures. **5)** Nevertheless, the study purpose has been to elucidate how the digital architectures of social media platforms can be compared, systematically, at a particular point in time.
Sentences 6–7: Recommendation to future work	**6)** Future scholars may wish to engage with the question of how changes in a platform's digital architecture influences campaign practices longitudinally, as well as how the digital architectures of platforms not analyzed here (e.g., YouTube or WhatsApp) influence campaigns' communication strategies. **7)** Moreover, data from other sources such as voter turnout, donation, or polling figures should be incorporated in future research designs, to corroborate how digital communication is affected by offline dynamics critical for campaigns and their strategies. **Source:** Bossetta, M. 2018. The digital architectures of social media: Comparing political campaigning on Facebook, Twitter, Instagram, and Snapchat in the 2016 U.S. election. *Journalism & Mass Communication Quarterly,* *95*(2): 471–496.

Sample 5 (From the Field of Computer Science)

Paragraph 1: Summary of the research work	**Para. 1)** In this paper, a brief history of industrial robotics in the 20th century was presented. The evolution of the industrial robots was conventionally categorized into four generations, of which the first three cover the timespan from the 1950s to the end of the century.

Paragraph 2: Comparative advantage of the research work	**Para. 2)** In this historical sketch, not only the scientific and technical evolution was taken into account, but some considerations about the economic and geopolitical issues that determined the diffusion of industrial robots, were also done.
Paragraph 3: Conclusion and implication for follow-up work	**Para. 3)** The evolution of industrial robotics is not over, but is still developing in the current days. Innovative ideas and novel hardware devices, together with some new programming techniques connected with Artificial Intelligence, are revolutionizing the concept of industrial automation and giving a new youth to the factory environment. **Source:** Gasparetto, A. & Scalera, L. 2019. A brief history of industrial robotics in the 20th century. *Advances in Historical Studies, 8*: 24–35.

6.3 Linguistic Features of the Conclusion Section

6.3.1 Lexical Features

1. ABC principle

Similar to other section compositions, the Conclusion section should stick to the ABC principle in which A means accuracy, B stands for brevity and C represents clarity (Zheng & Xu, 2008). Based on the research results and discussion, many writers prefer an accurate, clear and concise conclusion to an inaccurate, unclear and verbose one. Appropriate wording, from the linguistic point of view, plays a crucial part in working out not only an impressive conclusion but a superior abstract, introduction, method, and results and discussion as well.

1) Accuracy

With respect to the selection of words, two aspects deserve special attention: connotation and collocation. Writers should understand the accurate meaning of a word. At the same time, they must have a good command of the word collocations. Compare the words in the following examples. The sentence with a "★" is more acceptable.

✓ ①Hitler was **famous** for his cruelty.

②Hitler was **notorious** for his cruelty. ★

✓ ①We **have met a consensus** on the reciprocal trade.

②We **have reached a consensus** on the reciprocal trade. ★

2) **Brevity**

As the last section in the textual development, a conclusion should be explicit and concise. Below are some lexical methods to serve the purpose of brevity. Compare the two sentences in each method. The sentence with a "★" is more acceptable.

(1) Conversion

✓ ①In this article, we **make an outline** and propose five salient and pertinent areas of inquiry that we feel constitutes a sufficient basis to advance our knowledge and the scholarship on cyber crime.

②In this article, we **outline** and propose five salient and pertinent areas of inquiry that we feel constitutes a sufficient basis to advance our knowledge and the scholarship on cyber crime. ★

(2) Compound

✓ ①The traditional method **may waste a lot of time**.

②The traditional method **may be time-consuming**. ★

(3) Nominalization

✓ ①In this small town, if the house price **is increased**, it will **make the purchasing power decreased**.

②In this small town, **the increase** in house price will **lead to the decrease in purchasing power**. ★

(4) Noun clusters

✓ ①**The limitations of our research** should be noted as well to provide insight on **additional measures for controlling depression**.

②**Our research limitations** should be noted as well to provide insight on **additional depression-controlling measures**. ★

(5) Affixation

✓ ①In these 60 students' articles, **there are twice as many lexical errors as grammatical ones**.

②In these 60 students' articles, **lexical errors outnumber grammatical ones by 2:1**. ★

3) Clarity

Writers should avoid any ambiguous and vague expressions in their conclusions. They should select the specific words when writing. Support the idea with convincing data, if necessary. Compare the words in the following examples. The sentence with a "★" is more acceptable.

- ✓ ①Trash recycling is becoming an increasingly **good** option for waste disposal.

    ②Trash recycling is becoming an increasingly **green/feasible/sensible/practical** option for waste disposal. ★

- ✓ ①Sales were down **quite a bit** last year because of the pandemic.

    ②Sales were down **by 40% / sharply** last year because of the pandemic. ★

2. Tentative language

Different from ambiguous and vague expressions, tentative or hedging language is a kind of cautious and scrupulous language, which is used especially in the Literature Review, Discussion, and Conclusion sections. Writers use this kind of language to show their prudent and precise attitude towards their research work since a claim sometimes may be not very definite. The tentative expressions may include some nouns, verbs, modal verbs, adjectives, determiners, adverbs of uncertainty, adverbs of frequency, adverbs of degree and phrases. For the sake of unity, tentative sentence patterns are also placed in this part.

Table 6.2 lists some tentative words, expressions and sentence patterns often used in the Conclusion section. The tentative language may also emerge in other sections such as the Literature Review and the Results and Discussion.

Table 6.2 Tentative Words, Expressions and Sentence Patterns

Nouns	assumption, hypothesis, possibility, postulation, probability, speculation, etc.
Verbs	allow, appear, argue, assume, believe, consider, doubt, hypothesize, indicate, postulate, propose, seem, speculate, suggest, suppose, tend, think, etc.
Modal verbs	could, may, might, should, will, would, etc.
Adjectives	conceivable, possible, probable, etc.
Determiners	many, some, one of, etc.
Adverbs of uncertainty	conceivably, likely, perhaps, possibly, probably, seemingly, etc.
Adverbs of frequency	frequently, often, sometimes, usually, etc.
Adverbs of degree	broadly, considerably, clearly, closely, extensively, generally, largely, markedly, etc.

(Continued)

Phrases	generally speaking, broadly speaking, to some extent/degree, to our knowledge, according to, as far as we know, in broad outline, etc.
Sentence patterns	The results suggest/indicate that… This appears to be… We believe/think/speculate/argue that… It is likely that… It would probably be more realistic… It seems that… It might be suggested that… It is possible that…

Read the following examples and pay special attention to the words and expressions in bold:

- ✓ As research continues, we **may hope** to gain more detailed and reliable knowledge about how these and other processes interact with each other in the development and use of second language ability.

- ✓ Like first language learners, second language learners **tend to follow** natural sequences in internalizing the system.

- ✓ In many respects, these sequences **seem to be** independent of the learners' mother tongue.

- ✓ They **suggest** that learners use "intralingual" strategies which are also found in first language learning, such as generalizing rules and reducing redundancy.

- ✓ **It seems**, therefore, **that** habit-formation principles **should not be** discarded but integrated into a broader framework.

- ✓ **Perhaps**, these discrepancies are due to the lack of purity in the substance.

- ✓ The overall prevalence of CUD **appears to be** considerably higher in our sample than in the general population of young adults.

- ✓ The younger age of our sample and the certain cultural aspects of college life **may account for some of** these differences.

- ✓ The findings clearly **indicate** that the amount of exposure to a foreign language **could have** a marked effect on student performance.

6.3.2 Syntactical Features

1. Tense and mood

Generally, the present simple tense, the past simple tense, the present perfect tense and the future simple tense are often used in writing the Conclusion section. Some modal verbs often emerge in the section as well. Below are examples at different stages when writing a Conclusion section.

A brief summary in a Conclusion section usually uses the present simple tense, the past simple tense and the present perfect tense. Fox example:

- ✓ These data **confirm** the positive transfer between the two languages.
- ✓ We **dealt with** creative construction and skill learning as alternative models of second language learning.
- ✓ We **have looked at** ways of conceptualizing second language learning and understanding its nature and causes.

It is more liable to employ the present simple tense and modal verbs when drawing conclusions. For example:

- ✓ The various studies **seem to allow** a number of general conclusions.
- ✓ To conclude, we **should stress** that to view the problem in terms of two different kinds of learning is a simplification which, however useful, may also be misleading.
- ✓ Between the most subconscious process of "acquisition" at one extreme and the most conscious forms of "learning" at the other, it **would be** probably more realistic to think in terms of a continuum, in which subconscious and conscious processes are mingled to varying degrees.

When writing the statements of the research significance and contribution, the writer tends to use the present simple tense, the present perfect tense and the future simple tense, apart from modal verbs. For example:

- ✓ This study **lends** further support for our theory.
- ✓ Our work **has shown** promising potential for commercial applications.
- ✓ We hope our study **will serve as** a helpful guide for other researchers' work.
- ✓ The simple, precise and quantified method to measure vesicle's curvature rigidity **may be broadly applied** to various fields such as biophysics, biology and biomedicine.
- ✓ These preliminary results **would also highlight** the value of online education in remote areas.

The present simple tense and the future simple tense, as well as modal verbs frequently appear when a conclusion predicts the research tendency or puts forward some suggestions for the succeeding work. For example:

- ✓ Future studies **will help** to address that question by observing whether cannabis-related problems with concentration and class attendance predict long-term problems with grades and occupational attainment.

- ✓ The studies **draw attention** not to ignore the role of processes associated with behaviorism, such as imitation and memorization.

2. Recapitulative and objective language

Contrary to an Introduction section which attempts to attract readers' attention to the research work by stating the research purpose, research question, and research value, the Conclusion section, while echoing the Introduction section, should tie up the whole article in conclusive and objective language. Therefore, the sentences in the Conclusion section should deliver a sense of abstracting, reasoning, generality, and objectivity in accordance with logical development of the Results and Discussion sections. The sentences will also direct for follow-up research. Here are some sample sentences. Pay attention to the recapitulative and objective language in bold.

- ✓ **This article has studied some of the sequences** which learners have been observed to follow in mastering various aspects of a second language.
- ✓ **From the forgoing, it follows that** different constituents of sunlight are treated in different ways as they struggle through the earth's atmosphere.
- ✓ **To conclude, we should stress that** to view the problem in terms of two different kinds of learning is a simplification which, however useful, may also be misleading.
- ✓ However, **the various studies seem to allow a number of general conclusions**.
- ✓ **The main conclusions** reached in this work **can be summarized as follows**: …
- ✓ Besides, **the simple, precise and quantified method** to measure vesicle's curvature rigidity **may be used for discriminating the mechanical property** of carbon nano tubes, **and may be broadly applied to various fields** such as biophysics, biology and biomedicine as well.
- ✓ **We hope our proposed agenda will serve as a helpful guide** for researchers, scholars, and practitioners interested in understanding, combating, and preventing cyber crime.
- ✓ **These preliminary results would also highlight the value** of online education in remote areas.
- ✓ **How to manipulate this approach** in the writing class of large size **remains further research**.
- ✓ **The studies draw attention not to ignore the role of processes** associated with behaviorism, such as imitation and memorization.

3. Non-complicated sentences

Since the Conclusion section should enable readers to catch the gist without miscomprehension, writing an explicit and concise conclusion is a must. A writer will certainly use simple sentences, compound sentences, complex sentences, and even compound-complex sentences. However, a writer should avoid any redundant coordination and subordination in the Conclusion section. Try to avoid long-winded and over-complicated sentences which are very liable to some misunderstandings. Split a lengthy sentence into two or three concise sentences. On the other hand, a writer will certainly not overuse simple sentences either, which may destroy the unity and coherence of the Conclusion section. The sentences in the following sample are acceptable.

- ✓ From the forgoing, it follows that different constituents of sunlight are treated in different ways as they struggle through the earth's atmosphere. A wave of blue light may be scattered by a dust particle, and, therefore, turned out of its course. At last, it enters our eyes by a path as zigzag as that of a flash of lightening. Consequently, the blue waves of the sunlight enter our eyes from all directions. That is why the sky looks blue.

However, one of the sentences in Version 1 below is too long, in which the underlying logic is not rigorous enough. It is suggested to split this long sentence up into several concise ones. Compare Version 1 with Version 2 and comment on the writing strategies.

Version 1:
- ✓ Advances in computers, software and sensors have brought the dream of self-driving cars to reality, and already, many luxury models can largely drive themselves on highways and in stop-and-go traffic, but the real challenge is driving on city streets and in suburbs where scatter complex intersections and pedestrians, so companies from both inside and outside the auto industry are working on these problems. Several automakers have promised to put self-driving cars on the road in just a few years…

Version 2:
- ✓ Advances in computers, software and sensors have brought the dream of self-driving cars to reality. Already, many luxury models can largely drive themselves on highways and in stop-and-go traffic. However, the real challenge is driving on city streets and in suburbs where scatter complex intersections and pedestrians. Companies from both inside and outside the auto industry are working on these problems. Several automakers have promised to put self-driving cars on the road in just a few years…

6.4 Useful Expressions for the Conclusion Section

Below are some sentence patterns describing information elements at different stages of the Conclusion section.

1. Summarizing the end results

- ✓ To sum up, we have discovered…
- ✓ We provide new insights into the dynamic process of…
- ✓ These results confirm the presence of…
- ✓ This review paper reveals the overall scenario of… under different aspects.
- ✓ In summary, the effective mitigation of such a global crisis is possible…
- ✓ This work reports for the first time that…
- ✓ The current paper shows relations between… and…
- ✓ Our results support the idea that…
- ✓ In this research, a sustainability framework was proposed by considering economic and environmental aspects.
- ✓ The present research demonstrated the viability of the working hypothesis and the proposed models.
- ✓ These data provide compelling evidence that…
- ✓ In this paper, we have discussed/found that…
- ✓ This paper discusses how AI provides safe, accurate and efficient imaging solutions to…
- ✓ In our opinion, the current recommendation to… does not appear to be justified.

2. Drawing conclusions

- ✓ Through the analysis of…, we may state the following: …
- ✓ Based on the discussion above, we may conclude as follows: …
- ✓ The result(s) obtained in this work lead(s) us to the following conclusions.
- ✓ The analysis of… allows the conclusion that…
- ✓ From the forgoing, it follows that…
- ✓ On the basis of…, the following conclusion can be drawn.
- ✓ Concluding the above discussion, we may state the following: …
- ✓ In conclusion, the research indicates…
- ✓ In conclusion, taking into account… we can infer that…
- ✓ Statistically significant differences were found regarding…
- ✓ It was evident from the experimental data that…
- ✓ It is clear that…
- ✓ The results clearly demonstrate that…

- ✓ This evidences the existence of…
- ✓ There is no evidence that…

3. Stating the significance

- ✓ The detection of… is of great clinical significance in tumor diagnosis.
- ✓ The results of these studies may change the ways in which… are managed in the future.
- ✓ The data presented here may provide the framework for future studies to…
- ✓ These preliminary results will provide new insights into the role and importance of…
- ✓ Our/This study lends further support for…
- ✓ This approach indicates that…
- ✓ These findings would also highlight the value of…
- ✓ This study could have potential in areas such as…
- ✓ Our work has shown promising potential for…
- ✓ The research work has brought about a discovery of…
- ✓ The present results illustrate that…
- ✓ This could eventually lead to the identification of novel biomarkers.
- ✓ This work could prove to be a promising surgical technique.
- ✓ This work showed that… have high potential for application in…
- ✓ Though this study obviously has its limits, it nevertheless provides specific evidence that can…
- ✓ Maintaining the efficacy of… will be of utmost importance in…

4. Putting forward recommendations

- ✓ Future work should focus on the efficacy of…
- ✓ An important question for future studies is to determine the antidepressant effects of…
- ✓ In addition, more pilot or full-scale investigations of… should be performed.
- ✓ More research on other approaches for using rather than losing this valuable resource is also needed.
- ✓ Clearly, the study also raises further questions for future investigation on this topic.
- ✓ It is nevertheless certain that… must be urgently addressed.
- ✓ More attention should be paid to… in the future.
- ✓ There are growing incentives for the finance and governance models to be explored…
- ✓ These will be the hotspots for…
- ✓ We must continue to pursue a goal that is within our grasp and facilitated through…

- ✓ Hence, further work is still needed to address global plastic waste challenges.
- ✓ Future research is needed to apply and further develop the approach with respect to its conceptual robustness and its applicability in…

6.5 Reflections and Practice

❶ Answer the following questions.

1. What are the functions of the Conclusion section?
2. What are the basic information elements in the Conclusion section?
3. What are the differences between the Conclusion section and the Introduction section?

❷ Analyze the information elements of the two Conclusion sections. Text 1 is in the field of language education and Text 2 in the field of environment engineering.

› Text 1

1) In light of the problems occurring in students' writing, the paper analyzed the process of EFL learning and the effectiveness of two different approaches to the teaching of writing: the product-oriented approach and the process-oriented one. 2) The paper postulated four points in the teaching of writing and put forward the assumptions on the nature of writing process and the features of the product approach and the process approach.

3) The data were collected in the form of questionnaires and error records. 4) The questionnaire results support writing methodologists' view that the act of composition goes through different phases of planning, writing and revising. 5) The result of the error records reveals that the problems of both HOCs and LOCs in the students' compositions occur less frequently in the process-oriented class than in the product-oriented one.

6) Teaching practice in different writing classes showed that the process-oriented approach to writing seems to be more effective than the product-oriented one since the former places more stress on writers' thinking and writing process, whereby the nature of writing is probed into. 7) In the process of generating ideas, selecting appropriate words and sentences for the intended meaning and organizing compositions, the process approach provides writers with the opportunities of discovering the strong and weak points of their own and obtaining the valuable and thought-provoking feedback from peers and the teacher. 8) Thus they not only activate their inner thinking but also get in touch with the real audience.

9) The interaction and cooperation between the teacher and students and among the peers, as well as the input from reading materials facilitate writers in developing ideas, organizing the ideas and struggling for the exact expressions of these ideas, by drawing on mutual writing experiences and language resources.

10) Like the product-oriented approach to writing, the process approach also has its own limitations. **11)** The implementation prefers the writing class of small size where students could get more individual attention from the teacher, which seems to be unrealistic in the present situation of English teaching for non-English majors. **12)** How to manipulate this approach in the writing class of large size remains further research.

Sentence Number	Information Element
1)	
2)	
3)	
4)	
5)	
6)	
7)	
8)	
9)	
10)	
11)	
12)	

〉Text 2

1) The aim of this study was to investigate organic-inorganic combined fouling in a spiral-wound reverse osmosis membrane. **2)** The main conclusions reached in this work can be summarized as follows:

3) The experiments showed that membrane fouling is governed by individual foulant concentrations where there is an increasing fluxdecline rate with increasing foulant concentration in the system.

4) Our findings demonstrate a synergistic effect in the combined fouling experiment where combined foulants caused a more rapid flux decline than with individual foulants. **5)** An exacerbated synergistic effect on membrane fouling was observed when the concentration of sodium alginate was equal to or higher than the concentration of silica. **6)** In these cases of combined fouling, a more severe flux decline was observed compared to the additive sum of the flux decline of the individual foulants.

7) The fouling potential (kf) parameter was used to characterize and quantify the fouling potential of the feed water and was applied to a commercial spiral-wound RO membrane.

8) Fouling caused by silica colloids, sodium alginate and combinations thereof was mostly reversible since significant membrane restoration was achieved after appropriate chemical cleaning.

Sentence Number	Information Element
1)	
2)	
3)	
4)	
5)	
6)	
7)	
8)	

III Select two or three Conclusion sections in your research field and complete the following tasks.

1. Identify the information elements in these Conclusion sections.

2. Analyze the logic underlying the text in these Conclusion sections.

3. Comment on the strong points and weak points of these Conclusion sections.

IV Following are the sentences in a Conclusion. Match the information elements in Column A with the sentences in Column B.

Column A	Column B
Research conclusion	1) This surgical approach is gaining acceptance in many centers worldwide of late.
Research significance 1	2) However, well-designed multicenter clinical studies are necessary to provide a validation of this surgical strategy in the treatment of refractory traumatic intracranial hypertension.

Research significance 2	3) The positive effect on brain oxygenation and metabolism obtained after cisternostomy suggests that it addresses the pathophysiologic processes underlying elevated ICP.
Succeeding work	4) It could prove to be a promising surgical technique by itself or as a complement to DC.

Ⅴ Fill in each blank with the appropriate form of the verb given in the brackets, adding modal verbs where necessary.

This article 1) _____ (study) some of the sequences which learners have been observed to follow in mastering various aspects of a second language. It also 2) _____ (look) at ways in which learners use imitation and memorization, in addition to creative process of rule-formation.

We 3) _____ (be) wary of generalizing too widely from the available evidence, since this is still very limited in scope. Many aspects of language development 4) _____ (not study) at all; most of the studies are concerned only with the learning of English and the results need to be 5) _____ (confirm) with larger groups of learners. However, the various studies seem to 6) _____ (allow) a number of general conclusions:

First, like first language learners, second language learners 7) _____ (tend) to follow natural sequences in internalizing the system. In the main outline, these sequences 8) _____ (be) similar for different learners, but there 9) _____ (be) some individual variation in the details of the development.

Second, in many respects, these sequences seem to be independent of the learners' mother tongue. They 10) _____ (suggest) that learners use "intralingual" strategies which are also found in first language learning, such as generalizing rules and reducing redundancy.

Third, there is also evidence that the learner's mother-tongue knowledge 11) _____ (influence) the sequences. From the learners' viewpoint, this strategy 12) _____ (be) another way of generalizing rules acquired by previous learning.

Last, as well as forming rules on the basis of the data they are exposed to, learners also 13) _____ (imitate) and 14) _____ (memorize) specific utterances, without analyzing their internal structure. It seems, therefore, that habit-formation principles 15) _____ (not discard) but integrated into a broader framework.

In general, then, the studies 16) _____ (tend) to confirm that learners construct their knowledge of the second language through active learning processes and that they

17) _____ (incline) to do this according to a natural "inbuilt syllabus". The studies 18) _____ (draw) attention not to ignore the role of processes associated with behaviorism, such as imitation and memorization.

Ⅵ Select the appropriate word or phrase in the box to complete each sentence. Change the form where necessary.

| conclusion | lead... to | preliminary | in the course of | evident |
| state | provide | draw | reveal | investigation |

1. From this work, we can _____ the following conclusions.
2. Though this study obviously has its limits, it nevertheless _____ specific evidence that certain physical activity has benefits for human brain.
3. Clearly, the study also raises further questions for future _____ on this topic.
4. The analysis of the four research results _____ us _____ the following conclusions.
5. Concluding the above discussion, we may _____ the following.
6. _____ results indicate that brick and mortar sales are still popular.
7. The results obtained _____ this investigation clearly demonstrate a boom in automobile industry.
8. It was _____ from the experimental data that our research result agrees with the previous study.
9. These research results have led the author to the _____ that light music could help health.
10. To sum up, we _____ that staying up late is closely linked to liver diseases.

Ⅶ Rearrange the words and phrases in each group into clear and coherent sentences.

1. the lack of, the brain drain, of the company, cohesion, accounted for.
2. listening to, a psychologist, in the ear, speculates, that, self-stimulation, extremely loud music, at, is, a form of, the University of Manchester.
3. consumers, may, an effect, environmental concerns, bottled water sales, on, among, have had.
4. children's development, the social structure, research results, of peer interactions, that, influenced, is, most, by, show.
5. communication, the gender differences, women and men, such different expectations,

clarify, in marriage, why, have, about.

Ⅷ Rearrange the following sentences into a coherent paragraph.

1. This paper has discussed Marx's unfinished, compelling and, at times, prophetic views on the role of credit in the development of advanced capitalism, particularly its part in expediting the realization of surplus-value as well as its changing and ultimately destabilizing effect on the industrial cycle.

2. Moreover, Marx's analysis was not just confined to any one nation.

3. Max also tried to identify both supply-side and demand-side factors that set up real barriers and limits to the further expansion and reproduction of industrial capital in the course of the business cycle.

4. Max's analysis further showed that he did not remain content to just describe the pernicious effects of excessive credit, debt and speculation in an advanced capitalist economy such as England.

5. The discussion also highlighted Marx's relatively neglected but highly important analysis of the separation of ownership from management in the advanced capitalism of his day, England, and its modern-day implications for excessive risk-taking and debt-fueled speculation up until the eve of the crash.

6. Far ahead of his contemporaries, Max viewed the business cycle and the recurring crises as a world-market phenomenon and outlined how contagion took place in the commercially advanced nations of his day, viz., England and France.

Ⅸ Rewrite the following sentences to make them more tentative.

1. There are five social causes that lead to the use of alcohol by teenagers.
2. Water price is an important factor that affects the water consumption in these countries.
3. The results confirm the view that many L2 learners employed more certainty markers than their L1 counterparts did.
4. Positive attitudes towards children and childrearing account for earlier child-bearing and higher marital fertility.
5. Further follow-up of the on-line education study supplies more data testifying its extensive feasibility.

Ⅹ Translate the following sentences into English.

1. 从以上讨论我们可以得出结论：自行车的优点远大于缺点，在现代社会中自行车仍将发挥重要作用。

2. 随着研究继续，骨髓干细胞（stem cells）的潜在特质将有助于治疗多种类型的严重疾病。
3. 在过去的几年里，这个地区的犯罪率急剧下降，这说明其治安管理是成功的。
4. 有助于加快全球化进程的其他因素还包括新型通信技术和日趋完善的运输系统。
5. Drake 博士创造了著名的 Drake 方程，用于估算发现外星生命存在的概率。这个方程表明，我们的银河系里可能存在一万种可探测到的文明。

XI Translate the following paragraphs into Chinese.

Over very many years there has been an increase in the population of towns in many countries. This development has led to huge expansions of towns both upwards into the sky and outwards into the surrounding countryside. In spite of all the efforts of governments and business, many areas still suffer from a serious shortage of housing.

The new idea put forward here is to utilize areas which have no other obvious commercial potential. These are the ponds, small lakes, disused docks and other areas of water, many of which can be found near, or even in the suburbs of big towns.

The new style of construction which has been designed will provide a house for less than half the cost of the conventional building. The main saving is the land because the new houses will float on water. There will be no need for foundations; instead the house will be built on a frame made of steel. Above this the builders will make a house with two, three or four bedrooms and all the usual modern conveniences, as well as a roof garden. Each house will be joined to the main services supplying water, gas and electricity and each will have a vacuum sewage disposal system. All the service links will have enough flexibility to allow for small differences in the water level caused by wet and dry periods of weather. It is clear that there will be a very good potential market for the new system. As the cost is comparatively low, young people and common citizens would like to purchase.

Unit 7
Title and Abstract

Warm-up Questions

1. What are the purposes of the Title and Abstract sections?

2. What information elements are included in the Title and Abstract sections?

3. What are the salient linguistic features of the Title and Abstract sections?

7.1 Overview

7.1.1 Purposes of the Title

The title of a research article plays a very important role since it provides the key words of the article, indicates the content, and helps readers retrieve relevant information. A good title can usually fulfill the purposes of:

- drawing readers' attention;
- serving information retrieval;
- informing research orientation;
- clarifying research paradigm;
- generalizing the central theme of the article;
- presenting research clue;
- indicating research area;
- stimulating readers' research inspiration.

In the information era, readers usually decide on whether they would read an article just by browsing the title of the article. Therefore, the diction of title deserves much attention. A good title should pinpoint the gist of a research article in clear and concise wording to attract readers' attention.

7.1.2 Principles of Writing a Title

A good title should abide by the following principles:

- Be consistent with the document. Like a clean French window, a title should accurately exhibit the research article.
- Try to be objective. Avoid any subjective and groundless ideas.
- Select appropriate key words to generalize the research article. Include the most important key words in the Abstract section.
- Be informative to readers. Short as a title may be, it should not be too general or even ambiguous. Instead, it should cover the most relevant ground.
- Report specific research which may include new discoveries, new problems, new contradictions, new phenomenon, new methods, new causes and effects, new solutions, etc.
- Weigh words to catch readers' attention to the research article.
- Be clear in wording. Try to avoid any miscomprehension and make clear the

correlation between the different parts in a title.

- Be concise in wording. Avoid any redundant expressions and highlight straightforwardly the most important information in a title. Keep a title concise but explicit.

7.1.3 Types of Titles

Generally speaking, there are three types of titles. The most common ones are noun-phrase, gerund-phrase, and preposition-noun-phrase titles which frequently serve research articles. Apart from those, statement titles or question titles are also applicable, though not as common as those titles. Statement titles are more useful for research articles that "address a specific question and present a non-complex answer" (Cargill & O' Connor, 2013: 66). They are also suitable when writers are eager to clarify their attitudes in a straightforward way. If the research issues may arouse arguments with no simple and definite answers, it is more appropriate to use question titles. A statement title has no period at the end of the sentence while a question title should have a question mark at the end.

Sometimes a subtitle steps after the major title for the purpose of supplementing or highlighting something, attracting readers' attention, or further explaining something. In this case, a colon or a dash mark may lie in between the two titles. Subtitles often emerge in some research fields, such as medical research articles.

Below are some examples of different types of titles.

1. Noun-phrase titles / gerund-phrase titles / preposition-noun-phrase titles

✓ The Application of the Models of Nonlinear Regression

✓ Neighborhood Environment and Positive Mental Health in Older People: The Hertfordshire Cohort Study

✓ Cross-Lingual Countability Classification: English Meets Dutch

✓ An Analysis of the Product Approach and the Process Approach to the Teaching of EFL Writing at Tertiary Level

✓ Using Laser Technology on the Glaucoma Surgery in Modern Medicine

✓ On the Fatigue Life Prediction of Spot Welded Components

2. Statement titles

✓ Capital Punishment Should Be Lawful

✓ Academic English Is No One's Mother Tongue

✓ The Conformational Dynamics of SARS-CoV-2 N Protein Packaging Virus RNA Are Revealed by Single-Molecule FRET

✓ The Coordinate Transformation Coefficient Is Indeed a Tensor

- ✓ Near-Real-Time Monitoring of Global CO_2 Emissions Reveals the Effects of the COVID-19 Pandemic

3. Question titles

- ✓ Euthanasia, for or Against?
- ✓ What Are the Costs of Environmental Degradation? The Case of Morocco
- ✓ How to Treat Polycystic Ovary Syndrome?
- ✓ Does Electromagnetic Field Affect the Way Plants Grow?
- ✓ Which Firms Get Punished for Unethical Behavior? Explaining Variation in Stock Market Reactions to Corporate Misconduct

7.1.4 Capitalization of the Title

A writer should observe the writing formats of a title and appropriately capitalize the letter of a word. Then how to capitalize the letter? Below are three cases of which a writer should be aware. Upon submission of an article to a journal, the writer needs to check the title format.

The first one is to capitalize all the letters in a title. This case is not very common. For example:

- ✓ SIMULATION OF THE NATURAL SMOKE FILLING IN SUBWAY TUNNEL FIRE
- ✓ NEAR-REAL-TIME MONITORING OF GLOBAL CO_2 EMISSIONS REVEALS THE EFFECTS OF THE COVID-19 PANDEMIC

The second one is to capitalize the initial letter of the first word in a title, except for the proper nouns. For example:

- ✓ Simulation of the natural smoke filling in subway tunnel fire
- ✓ Near-real-time monitoring of global CO_2 emissions reveals the effects of the COVID-19 pandemic

The third one is to capitalize the letter in the following contexts:

- the initial letter of the first word in a title;
- the initial letter of the last word in a title;
- the initial letter of nouns, verbs, adjectives, adverbs, and pronouns;
- the initial letter of proper nouns;
- the initial letter of auxiliary verbs;
- the initial letter of the word after a hyphen in a compound when it is a noun or adjective;

- the prepositions with more than four or five letters.

This case is very common. For example:

✓ Simulation of the Natural Smoke Filling in Subway Tunnel Fire

✓ Near-Real-Time Monitoring of Global CO_2 Emissions Reveals the Effects of the COVID-19 Pandemic

7.1.5 Purposes of the Abstract

The purpose of an abstract is to tell readers the important information of a research article. As an overview of an article, an abstract helps readers to catch the central theme in the article in a very limited time and space. Usually readers preview the abstract of an article before reading through it. Therefore, an abstract plays a crucial part in introducing writers' research work to readers and a writer pours considerable time and effort into its composing. Involving more detailed information than a title, an abstract may further fulfill the purposes of:

- drawing readers' more attention;
- indicating the previous mistakes and research gaps;
- summarizing the present research work;
- helping readers catch the gist of the research work;
- clarifying research field;
- introducing the research method and technique;
- putting forward new concepts and discoveries;
- pointing out the research significance;
- reminding the difficulties and challenges in the research;
- highlighting the comparative advantages of the research work.

7.1.6 Information Elements of the Abstract

An abstract summarizes the important information in a journal article. It is more appropriate to compose an abstract for a journal article in about 200 words since the information beyond this word limit may not be included in a database. However, some journals may allow for 250 words or even 350 words, so a writer should verify the word limit before submission. Completed in full sentences, an abstract usually consists of the information elements as follows:

- background information of the research;
- purpose of the research work;

- research question or hypothesis put forward in the article;
- method(s) used to conduct the research work;
- research results or the tendency of the results;
- conclusion(s) of the research work;
- significance of the research work;
- recommendations for the future work.

An abstract should usually contain less background information and may include the basic stages as indicated in Table 7.1.

Table 7.1　Basic Stages of Writing an Abstract

Basic Stages	Information Elements	Questions to Be Answered
Stage 1	Research purpose and/or question	What do the researchers want to do?
Stage 2	Research method and technique	How did the researchers do the work?
Stage 3	Research results	What results did the researchers get?
Stage 4	Research conclusions	What conclusions could the researchers draw?
Stage 5	Research contribution	What are the researchers' comparative advantages in the work?

Generally, the idea in an abstract is highlighted with its key words. Below the abstract, the key words listed are separated by space, comma or semi-colon. Usually, the number of key words ranges from three to eight. Look at the formats shown in Table 7.2.

Table 7.2　Key Words Formats

Format 1	**Key words:** traditional teaching method modern teaching method class structure
Format 2	**Key words:** traditional teaching method, modern teaching method, class structure
Format 3	**Key words:** traditional teaching method; modern teaching method; class structure

7.1.7 Types of Abstracts

Basically, there are two types of abstracts: descriptive abstract and informative abstract. A descriptive abstract outlines the article, sometimes without reporting the specific information about the article. It indicates the scope of an article, so a descriptive abstract is also called a table-of-contents abstract.

Different from a descriptive abstract, an informative abstract tells such specific information of an article as the research question, the method used, exact research results and clear research conclusions.

However, a third type of abstracts integrates both a descriptive abstract and an informative one. It is thus entitled a descriptive-informative abstract which is a combined form that bears specific information about the research question, methods used, main findings and conclusions, and general information about the rest of the article. Many abstracts may fall into the category of descriptive-informative ones.

A structural abstract comes to the fourth type of abstract which follows a fixed format when listing the important information in a research article. This type of abstracts could be identified in disciplines like medicine.

7.1.8 Common Problems of Writing the Abstract

While writing an abstract, writers should avoid some common problems, which are listed and illustrated as follows.

1. Inconsistency with the paper

A good abstract should exclude all the information irrelevant to the original paper. Do not make any modification in meaning.

2. Over-simplified statements

Short as an abstract may be, it should not over-simplify the gist of the research work in the paper. Below is an example of over-simplified statements, which is too short to reflect all of the main ideas in the article.

> ✓ The paper compares the similarities and differences of the cognitive behavior between the writers of native language and of target language.

3. Over-elaborated background information

The purpose of an abstract is to summarize the important research work in an article. Therefore, an abstract should lay more stress on the research information in a paper. Do not over-elaborate the background knowledge.

4. Unnecessary details

Do not include examples, details or elaborate explanations. It is better to avoid such phrases or clauses as "for example", "such as", "as indicated in Figure 1" or "…which was shown in Table 1" in an abstract.

5. Overuse of the passive voice

Overuse of the passive voice in an abstract may lead to monotony. Short as an abstract may be, the sentence patterns should be varied. Therefore, avoid working out an abstract in the following example.

> ✓ This study is intended to answer an essential question, i.e. what determines the order of the fractional operator in fractal space? To answer this question, the concept of fractal cell defined in the previous paper is generalized, and the tree-like and net-like fractal spaces with higher-order topology are abstracted. The algebraic equations satisfied by the fractal operators are derived. It is proved that the solutions of the lower-order algebraic equations for fractal operators are deterministically related to the fractional temporal operators that are usually of fractional orders. By the Vieta theorem, the relation between the solutions of algebraic equations for fractal operators and the physical component operators is clarified, and the duality constraints between them are revealed…

7.2 Sample Analysis

7.2.1 Title Analysis

Samples

Numbers 1–2: Clear and informative; Number 1 is relatively longer	1) Simulation of a Two-Turn Railgun and Comparison Between a Conventional Railgun and a Two-Turn Railgun by 3D FEM
Numbers 3–4: Concise but not relevant and informative; too general as a title of journal article	2) Stationary Resistive Field Distribution Along Epoxy Resin Insulators in Air Under DC Voltage
	3) Innovation and the Materials Revolution
	4) The Study of an Efficient Simulation Method
Number 5: Grammatically redundant, though specific and informative	5) A Cultural Communication Learning-Teaching Model (CCLT) Which Is Established Based on Practical Experience

Number 6: A subtitle after the major title for supplement and explanation	6) Problems with Scientific Research: How Science Goes Wrong
Number 7: A question title with no simple and definite answers	7) Why Is It So Hard for Men and Women to Talk to Each Other?
Number 8: A question title followed by a subtitle for supplement and explanation	8) Which Firms Get Punished for Unethical Behavior? Explaining Variation in Stock Market Reactions to Corporate Misconduct
Number 9: A statement title addressing a specific question	9) Bottled Water Sales Dry Up; Industry Asks "Why?"
Number 10: A statement title to clarify the author's attitude straightforwardly	10) Capital Punishment Should Be Lawful

7.2.2 Different Types of Abstracts

Read the following samples and analyze the types of the abstracts.

Sample 1 (From the Field of Language Education)

This is a descriptive abstract. It outlines the article without reporting the specific information about the article.	In accordance with Cognitive Psychology and System Science, this article studies the class structure in conventional English class, multimedia English class and online English class. By comparing the different kinds of class structure, the article analyzes the similarities and the differences of the information storage and information transfer, and discusses the strengths and weaknesses of the three different classes. In addition, the paper presents the most recent long-distance class, online live-broadcasting class. This study may help English instructors to better manipulate different classes. **Source:** Zhang, Y. 2020. An analysis of the class structure of traditional and modern English teaching. In Wu Jiangmei, Peng Gong & Ju Fang'An (Eds.), *Modern Language Teaching and Research*. Beijing: China Renming University Press, 111–115.

Sample 2 (From the Field of Architecture Design)

This is an informative abstract. It tells the specific information of the article.	In the contemporary human community relations, great attention is paid to social sustainability due to its ties with the local identity and social culture. The common spaces are considered as the social arena that creates an opportunity for people to bond and interact. In light of this, this study aims at highlighting the importance of such spaces through a case study of the apartment building in Amman, and its impact on social sustainability. A mixed-method approach was adopted in this research that entailed spatial analysis of layouts of 65 apartments, building, an on-line survey of 197 residents of apartments, buildings, and face-to-face interviews with 30 architects and developers. The results of this study bring to notice that apartment building in Amman is deficient in indoor common spaces in terms of functionality and that a few indoor common spaces are mainly limited to circulation paths with no hierarchical system. This finding underlines a crucial need for formulation of design guidelines for multi-family housing with the consideration of social sustainability as an integral part in the infrastructure. These design guidelines, once formulated and enacted, will guarantee provision of indoor common space qualitatively as a hub for a wide range of activities. **Source:** Abed, A. & Al-Jokhadar, A. 2021. Common space as a tool for social sustainability. *Journal of Housing and the Built Environment, 37*: 399–421.

Sample 3 (From the Field of Environment Science)

This is a descriptive-informative abstract. It bears specific information about the research question, methods used, main findings and conclusions, and general information about the rest of the document.	To address current challenges regarding sustainable development of wastewater treatment and provide scientific support in decision procedures towards sustainable solutions, new approaches, frameworks and methodologies about different possible solutions and their potential sustainability implications are

needed. One way to facilitate sustainability assessment of wastewater is Life Cycle Assessment (LCA) methodology; however, it fails to map the full scope of wastewater impacts. This paper presents a framework to evaluate the performance of Wastewater Treatment Facilities (WWTF) taking into consideration various factors for insuring environmental sustainability. A total of nine indicators, seven environmental and two economic related to four wastewater treatment facilities, were assessed. Apart from evaluating the sustainability, this study also discussed the link of life cycle approach and social aspects of wastewater. The results show that for the environmental dimension using LCA provides information on different types of environmental activities and different impact categories. LCA can thus be used to quantify and compare the multiple types of impacts caused by one type of use or emission, as well as the various resource uses or emissions that contribute to one type of impacts. For the economic dimension, there is still a need for consistent and robust indicators and methods. The empirical results suggest that the environmental sustainability framework can be used in the first phase of the decision procedure that leads to a strategic choice for sustainable resource recovery from wastewater in developing countries. This motives researchers and decision-makers to consider the whole picture, and not just individual aspects, when considering different futures scenarios.

Source: Padilla-Rivera, A., Morgan-Sagastume, J. M. & Guereca-Hernandez, L. P. 2019. Sustainability assessment of wastewater systems: An environmental and economic approach. *Journal of Environmental Protection*, *10*: 241–259.

Sample 4 (From the Field of Medicine)

This is a structural abstract. It follows a fixed format.	**BACKGROUND:** The current surgical treatment of choice for refractory intracranial hypertension after traumatic brain injury (TBI) is decompressive craniotomy. Despite efficacy in control of intracranial pressure (ICP), its contribution to an improved outcome is debatable. **CASE DESCRIPTION:** We describe a case of refractory intracranial hypertension successfully managed with cisternostomy. The rationale for this surgical technique is discussed, with a focus on the pathophysiologic processes underlying elevated ICP and its improvement after surgery. **CONCLUSION:** Cisternostomy proved to have an immediate effect in controlling ICP and improving brain oxygenation and metabolism. **Source:** Giammatte, L., Messerer, M., Oddo, M., Borsotti, F., Levivier, M. & Daniel, R. T. 2018. Cisternostomy for refractory posttraumatic intracranial hypertension. *World Neurosurgery*, *109*: 460–463.

7.2.3 Textual Analysis of the Abstract

Read the following samples and identify the information elements in the abstracts. Pay attention to the logic underlying the text. Put the information in each of the abstracts into a mind-map, as Sample 1 does in Figure 7.1.

Sample 1 (From the Field of Natural Science)

Sentence 1: Research background **Sentence 2:** Research background	1) For centuries, flow visualization has been the art of making fluid motion visible in physical and biological systems. 2) Although such flow patterns can be, in principle, described by the Navier-Stokes equations, extracting the velocity and pressure fields directly from

Sentence 3: Research problem and method	the images is challenging. **3)** We address this problem by developing hidden fluid mechanics (HFM), a physics-informed deep-learning framework capable of encoding the Navier-Stokes equations into the neural networks while being agnostic to the geometry or the initial and boundary conditions. **4)** We demonstrate HFM for several physical and biomedical problems by extracting quantitative information for which direct measurements may not be possible. **5)** HFM is robust to low resolution and substantial noise in the observation data, which is important for potential applications.
Sentence 4: Research result	
Sentence 5: Research conclusion and recommendation	
	Source: Raissi, M., Yazdan, A. & Kamiadakis, G. E. 2020. Hidden fluid mechanics: Learning velocity and pressure fields from flow visualizations. *Science* (New York, NY), *367*(6481): 1026–1030.

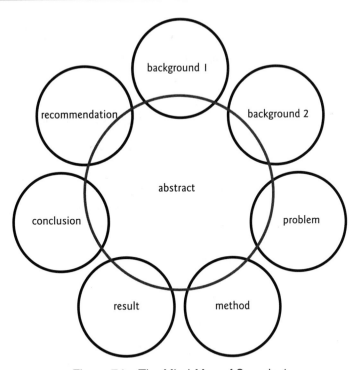

Figure 7.1 The Mind-Map of Sample 1

Sample 2 (From the Field of Law)

Sentences 1 and 2: Research background	1) Corporations are primary actors in transitioning to a climate neutral society. 2) This is also reflected in the green policy agenda of the European Union, including the latest "Green Deal", which is seeking to improve and introduce legislation that will control and provide more insight into the impact of corporations on the environment. 3) The focus of some of this legislation, and of this article, is on the reporting by larger corporations on their non-financial impact. 4) In particular, the revision of the Non-Financial Reporting Directive, the new Taxonomy Regulation and the new Sustainable Finance Disclosure Regulation are examined. 5) These will trigger newly available non-financial information which can be used by investors. 6) As this article sets out, the European policy agenda is based on the notion that providing the markets with such information will unlock private investments, ensuring a shift towards a climate neutral economy. 7) This does, however, require some form of "enlightened" share holdership. **Source:** Hartman-Ohnesorge, L. & Ebbe, R. 2021. Europe's green policy: Towards a climate neutral economy by way of investors' choice. *European Company Law*, *18*(1): 34–39.
Sentence 3: Research purpose	
Sentence 4: Research problem	
Sentence 5: Research significance	
Sentences 6 and 7: Research result	

Sample 3 (From the Field of Language Education)

Sentence 1: Research purpose	1) Based on Cognitive Psychology and System Science, this article is mainly devoted to the information feedback in conventional English class, multimedia English class and online English class. 2) By comparing the different information feedback, the article studies the impact of these differences on the cognitive characteristics of both teachers and
Sentence 2: Research method and several aspects of the problem	

Sentence 3: Research suggestions **Sentence 4:** Another research aspect	students, and discusses the strengths and weaknesses of the three different classes. 3) In addition, the article proposes some suggestions on the better manipulation of class. 4) Finally, the paper briefs the information feedback of the most recent long-distance class, online live-broadcasting class. **Source:** Zhang, Y. 2020. An analysis of the information feedback of traditional and modern English teaching. *New Silk Road*, *186*(4): 244–245.

7.3 Linguistic Features of the Title and the Abstract

7.3.1 Lexical Features

1. Using common wording

Since one of the purposes of a title or an abstract is to help readers catch the gist of the research work before reaching for the textual development, the diction in a title or an abstract should be simple and straightforward. Avoid the "big" words or unfamiliar words which may prevent the readers from catching the exact information. Try to use common words to get the idea across. Compare the two sentences below. Readers are more familiar with "elaborate" than "expatiate on". The sentence with a "★" is more acceptable.

✓ ①This article **expatiates on** the design of system architecture and business logic layer.

②This article **elaborates** the design of system architecture and business logic layer. ★

2. Using concise wording

For the reason of limited words in a title or an abstract, it should summarize the main idea without any redundancy. Therefore, eliminate any unnecessary words and highlight the most important information in a title; replace a phrase with a word or a sentence with a phrase in an abstract, whenever necessary. Compare the titles and the sentences in the following examples.

✓ ①**A Comprehensive Survey on the Prerequisite** for Rural Online Education in America

②**On Prerequisite** for Rural Online Education in America

③**Prerequisite** for Rural Online Education in America

✓ ①**There are four factors which determine** the success of business.

②**Four factors determine** the business success. ★

✓ ①This problem **is so urgent that it needs to be solved immediately**.

②This problem **presses for urgent solution**. ★

✓ ①We have devised **an engine which is able to save a lot of fuel**.

②We have devised **a fuel-efficient engine**. ★

3. Using prepositions in titles frequently

Prepositions are frequently used in titles, as indicated in the following examples:

✓ Experimental Study **of** High-Velocity Impact and Fracture **of** Ice

✓ The Statistical Analysis **of** Peak Ice Loads **in** a Simulated Ice-Structure Interaction Process

✓ A Review **of** Concrete Properties at Cryogenic Temperatures: **Towards** Direct LNG Containment

✓ Simultaneous Heterotrophic Nitrification and Aerobic Denitrification **by** a Novel Isolated Pseudomonas Mendocina X49

✓ Tai Chi and Postural Stability **in** Patients **with** Parkinson's Disease

4. Adjacent verbs and subjects in abstracts

It is more appropriate to place the verb in a sentence as close as possible to its subject. This could prevent readers from any misunderstanding, especially in a complex sentence. Do not insert a long parenthesis between the subject and its verb. The subject and its verb are close to each other in the following examples:

✓ **The aim of this study is to explore** the annual growth rings in the main tree species in Mount Gutian subtropical forest of China.

✓ **The results showed** that four out of eight species in the samples collected had visible and cross-datable rings.

✓ **The results obtained from this study may help** to understand growth dynamics in other subtropical forests with these tree species.

In the following two sentences, the subject is not close enough to its verb in the first example, so it is more appropriate to split it into two sentences. The sentence with a "★" is more acceptable.

✓ ①**A spring-dashpot fractal network with the self-similar topology**, which is further constructed into the II-type fractal ladder hyper-cell (FLHC), **is** abstracted from the micro-nano structure of ligaments and tendons (LTs).

②A spring-dashpot fractal network with the self-similar topology is abstracted from the micro-nano structure of ligaments and tendons (LTs). This fractal network is further constructed into the II-type fractal ladder hyper-cell (FLHC). ★

5) Hyphenated or unhyphenated compounding words

Sometimes more than one noun or adjective will be used to modify the key noun in a sentence. Replace the group of nouns or adjectives with hyphenated or unhyphenated compounding words where necessary. For example:

- ✓ However, existing viscoelastic models neglect the internal correlation between the fractal structure of biomaterials and their **fractional-order** temporal responses.
- ✓ To demonstrate the utility of an FHC, **tree-like**, **ladder-like** and **triangle-like** FHCs were abstracted from human cartilage, tendons and muscle **cross-sections**, respectively.
- ✓ This article proposes a **self-similar resistor-capacitor** network to relate the spiny dendritic structure with fractional spiking properties.

6) Verbs and phrases commonly used in abstracts

Short as the abstract may be, it will outline the article with the aid of different verbs and phrases. Below is a list of verbs and phrases commonly used in abstract composition.

account for	admit	adopt	address	agree
aim at	analyze	apply	argue	arrive at
assess	attempt to	characterize	comment	compare
compose of	concern	conclude	concur	conduct
consider	consist of	construct	contend	contribute
deal with	defend	define	demonstrate	describe
design	devise	devote to	discuss	draw
elaborate	emphasize	establish	examine	exhibit
explain	explore	expound	evaluate	focus on
formulate	give	hold	illustrate	indicate
intend	interpret	introduce	investigate	lie in
make	maintain	measure	observe	outline
perform	point out	predict	present	press for
proceed	propose	prove	provide	recommend

(Continued)

relate	report	result in	reveal	review
seek	select	show	speculate	study
suggest	suppose	test	verify	work out

7.3.2 Syntactical Features

1. Tense usage

Generally speaking, the present simple tense, the past simple tense and the present perfect tense are often used in writing an abstract. Below are the tenses of different stages in an abstract.

1) Research background

The past simple tense and the present perfect tense are often used in the introduction to the research background of an article. Sometimes the present simple tense is also used if the background information is a fact. For example:

- ✓ Researchers **demonstrated** that people could restructure their emotional relationships with others.
- ✓ Researchers **have demonstrated** that people could restructure their emotional relationships with others.

2) Research purpose or the problem to be solved

When stating the research purpose or the problem to be solved, a writer usually uses the present simple tense. For example:

- ✓ This paper **discusses** the bio-fuel process technologies over the past decade.
- ✓ The purpose of this study **is** to explore new models which could predict inflation.

3) Research methods

In different cases, a writer may use the present simple tense, the past simple tense or the present perfect tense in the description of research methods. For example:

- ✓ The method used in this study **is** known as radiocarbon dating.
- ✓ We **sampled** the blood and urine of 200 patients who had been infected with flu virus.
- ✓ Thirty tests **have been conducted** to judge how these babies react to the changes.

4) Research results

When presenting research results, a writer may use the past simple tense in the case of an action or the present simple tense in the case of a truth. For example:

- ✓ The results of calculation **show** that inflation runs at 8 percent.

✓ Our research results **provided** support for this reading strategy.

5) Research conclusion and recommendation

The writing of a conclusion and recommendation embraces varied tenses based on different situations. For example:

✓ On the basis of the research results, the following conclusions **can be** drawn.

✓ The research **has led** to the discovery of unusual objects.

✓ We **concluded** by experiment that this remedy could perform the traditional ones.

✓ It **is suggested** that the experimental data should be rechecked.

✓ This **will pave the way for** the further development of this theory.

2. Point of view in person

The third person or the first person should be used in writing an abstract. The second person is not usually used in an abstract. For example:

✓ **This paper** attempts to deal with the issue in a new way—by using the grey system theory.

✓ **We** found that Internet addiction was closely related to students' poor academic performance.

3. Voice usage

The composition of an abstract should appropriately employ sentences both in the active voice and the passive voice. Do not overuse the passive voice in an abstract, which would lead to monotony. Below are two good examples that use different kinds of voice:

✓ Torsades de Pointes (TdP) **is** a type of ventricular arrhythmia which **could be observed** as an unwanted drug-induced cardiac side effect, and it **is associated with** repolarization abnormalities in single cells. The pharmacological evaluations of TdP risk in previous years mainly **focused on** the hERG channel due to its vital role in the repolarization of cardiomyocytes. However, only considering drug effects on hERG **led to** false positive predictions since the drug action on other ion channels can also **have** crucial regulatory effects on repolarization. To address the limitation of only evaluating hERG, the Comprehensive in Vitro Proarrhythmia Assay initiative **has proposed** to systematically integrate drug effects on multiple ion channels into in silico drug trial to improve TdP risk assessment. It is not clear how many ion channels are sufficient for reliable TdP risk predictions, and whether differences in IC_{50} and Hill coefficient values from independent sources can **lead to** divergent in silico prediction outcomes. The rationale of this work **is to investigate** the above two questions using a computationally efficient population of human ventricular cells optimized to favor repolarization abnormality. Our blinded results based on two independent data sources

confirm that simulations with the optimized population of human ventricular cell models **enable** efficiency in silico drug screening, and also **provide** direct observation and mechanistic analysis of repolarization abnormality. Our results **show** that 1) the minimum set of ion channels required for reliable TdP risk predictions are Nav1.5 (peak), Cav1.2, and hERG; 2) for drugs with multiple ion channel blockage effects, moderate IC_{50} variations combined with variable Hill coefficients can **affect** the accuracy of in silico predictions.

- ✓ Toxic organic solvents **are widely used** in fabricating perovskite solar cells, which **pose a** potential threat to human health and the environment. Here, we **attempt to** prepare high-quality all-inorganic perovskite films from all aqueous solutions using a traditional two-step method. A continuous $PbBr_2$ precursor film **is first prepared** from a HBr/H_2O solution added with a certain amount of poly (ethylene glycol) (PEG). The PEG **plays** important roles in adjusting the viscosity of the aqueous solution and affecting the growth of the $PbBr_2$ precursor crystals. A high concentration of the $CsBr/H_2O$ solution **is then spin-coated** on the $PbBr_2$ precursor film followed by annealing to form a high-quality $CsPbBr_3$ film. The $CsPbBr_3$ perovskite solar cells prepared from the aqueous solutions **show** an efficiency of 7.19%, which **is higher** than those prepared from the organic solvents in the same conditions. It **is** a facile and green method to eliminate the solvent toxicity derived from organic solvents in fabricating perovskite solar cells.

4. Non-complicated sentences

An abstract will certainly deploy a variety of sentence patterns such as simple sentences, compound sentences, and complex sentences. However, a good abstract will not use lengthy and over-complicated sentences which could impede readers' comprehension. Writers should avoid ineffective coordination and excessive subordination when composing an abstract. They also usually split a lengthy sentence into two or three concise sentences. On the other hand, they will certainly not overuse simple sentences either in an abstract. For example:

- ✓ The Australian red meat industry is an important contributor to the national economy and international markets. A focus on reducing greenhouse gas (GHG) emissions from this sector presents an important opportunity for the sustainability of the industry, enabling Australia to achieve its commitments set under the Paris Climate Agreement. Here we show that through changes in land management and application of technologies to reduce enteric methane emissions from grazing livestock, it is possible for the Australian red meat industry to substantially reduce GHG emissions, and even become carbon neutral. We calculated baseline (2005) and current (2015) GHG emissions for the red meat sector, and examined the mitigation potential and costs of potential pathways to reduce and offset emissions. Emissions from the Australian red meat industry have decreased from 124.1 Mt CO_2e in 2005 to 68.6 Mt CO_2e in 2015, primarily through reductions in land clearing. Achieving carbon neutrality is possible with continued improvements in vegetation management combined with methods to reduce livestock emissions, sequester carbon, and maintain animal numbers. While possible, this ambitious target will require timely and substantial investment and policy support from private and government bodies.

7.4 Useful Expressions for the Abstract

Below are some sentence patterns for abstracts describing different information elements.

1. Introducing the research purpose or the problem to be solved

- ✓ The purpose of this paper is to discuss…
- ✓ The aim of this paper is to survey…
- ✓ The goal/rationale of this study is to investigate/reveal…
- ✓ This article aims at…
- ✓ The article discusses the reasons of…
- ✓ This study offers an insight into…
- ✓ This paper presents a framework to evaluate the performance of…
- ✓ The article reports / examines / focuses on / addresses / deals with…
- ✓ This article analyzes the relationship between… and…
- ✓ This paper explores the political and social forces that…
- ✓ This paper surveys the design system of…
- ✓ This study aims to clarify…
- ✓ This article is intended/designed to…
- ✓ This article is devoted to raising awareness on…
- ✓ This article is concerned with the analysis of…
- ✓ In this paper, we attempt to define… in terms of…
- ✓ In this review paper, we focused on highlighting different aspects related to…
- ✓ The authors intend to…

2. Describing the methods used

- ✓ The approach adopted is…
- ✓ The method used in this study is referred to…

- ✓ This formula is used to calculate…
- ✓ The formula is verified by…
- ✓ The tests were carried out on…
- ✓ Approximately thirty tests were conducted to…
- ✓ Experiments were performed to check…
- ✓ Using patch-clamp experiments, we confirm that…
- ✓ To obtain empirical data, a face-to-face survey was conducted in…
- ✓ We apply a cascading failure model to quantify…
- ✓ Our experiment consists of two steps: …
- ✓ The experiment is composed of three tasks: …

3. Presenting results

- ✓ The results of the experiments suggest/show/support that…
- ✓ Our analysis suggests that…
- ✓ The findings indicate/reveal that…
- ✓ It is/was found/observed that…
- ✓ Our results based on two independent data sources confirm that…
- ✓ Our results demonstrate/show that…
- ✓ Our research results provide support for… that…
- ✓ The results are consistent with…
- ✓ The study found/showed that…
- ✓ We found that…

4. Drawing conclusions or stating significance

- ✓ In conclusion, the report states…
- ✓ In conclusion, our computational modeling experiments provide novel mechanistic explanations for…
- ✓ On the basis of…, the following conclusions can be drawn: …
- ✓ From the experiment, we concluded that…
- ✓ We concluded by experiment that…
- ✓ The paper concludes/suggests that…
- ✓ All our preliminary results throw light on the nature of…
- ✓ The research work leads to…
- ✓ Based on these findings, the paper provides guidance for an improved management of…

✓ The study represents an element of novelty by proposing an effective and widely applicable solution to…

✓ It is suggested/concluded/recommended that…

✓ This review could help clarify… from the perspective of…

7.5 Reflections and Practice

I Answer the following questions.

1. What are the functions of a title?
2. How can you work out an appropriate title?
3. What are the functions of an abstract?
4. What is an abstract usually composed of?
5. What kind of titles and abstracts do you often read in your research field?
6. What are the linguistic features of a title and an abstract?

II Complete the following titles with the prepositions in the box. Some of the prepositions may be used more than once.

towards	of	for	on	under	into
between	to	in	by	with	among

1. Regulation of Cyber Space: An Analysis of Chinese Law _____ Cyber Crime
2. The Multiple Middle-Grounds _____ Civil and Criminal Law
3. Responding _____ Rural Social Care Needs: Older People Empowering Themselves, Others and Their Community
4. What Is the Best Biological Process _____ Nitrogen Removal: When and Why?
5. _____ Maximal Service Profit in Geo-Distributed Clouds
6. Protecting One's Own Privacy _____ a Big Data Economy
7. A Study _____ How Experts and Non-Experts Make Decisions on Releasing Genetically Modified Plants
8. _____ Teacher Appraisal

9. Comparing Subjective and Objective Neighborhood Deprivation and Their Association _____ Health over Time _____ Older Adults in England

10. Preliminary Evaluation _____ Super GTOS in Pulse Application

11. Experimental Validation of a Model _____ Prediction of Dynamic Ice-Structure Interaction

12. Near-Real-Time Monitoring of Global CO_2 Emissions Reveals the Effects _____ the COVID-19 Pandemic

13. Investigating the Complex Arrhythmic Phenotype Caused _____ the Gain-of-Function Mutation KCNQ1-G229D

14. Heterotrophic Nitrifying / Aerobic Denitrifying Bacteria: Ammonium Removal _____ Different Physical-Chemical Conditions and Molecular Characterization

15. A Critical Review of Aerobic Denitrification: Insights _____ the Intracellular Electron Transfer

(II) Analyze the types and information elements of the three abstracts. Then comment on the strong points and weak points of these abstracts.

Text 1

1) In recent years, it is commonly believed that different disciplines should integrate with each other. 2) However, how to integrate the different disciplines seems to have no acknowledged answers yet. 3) This paper speculates that aesthetics may converge many different disciplines by elaborating the case of a beautiful fractal snowflake. 4) It could be confirmed that many disciplines are correlated with the fractal snowflake. 5) Reversely, the fractal snowflake may, beyond all expectations, bridge the interrelationships of many different disciplines.

Key words: fractal snowflake; discipline integration; correlation

Sentence Number	Information Element
1)	
2)	
3)	
4)	
5)	

Unit **7** Title and Abstract

> **Text 2**

1) This paper elaborates that highly curved matter spaces, at micro/nano scales, may induce abnormal driving forces. **2)** Such abnormal driving forces are controlled by two fundamental factors: One is the bending extent of surfaces (curvature) and the other is the non-uniform extent of bending surfaces (the gradients of curvatures).

Key words: abnormal driving forces; curvatures; gradients of curvatures; micro/nano curved surfaces

Sentence Number	Information Element
1)	
2)	

> **Text 3**

1) Environmental degradation is costly—to individuals, to societies and to the environment. **2)** This paper makes these costs clear in the context of Morocco, a country marked by rapid economic development and urbanization. **3)** Although Morocco has made impressive efforts to strengthen its policies and strategies to protect its environment and natural resources, environmental degradation is still an issue. **4)** Using the most updated methodology and data sources, the paper estimates that environmental degradation imposed costs on Moroccan society of about US$3.9 billion, or 3.5 percent of the country's GDP in 2014. **5)** Water-related problems and air pollution are the most pressing challenges, followed by agricultural land degradation. **6)** Based on these findings, the paper provides guidance for an improved management of the country's environmental priority areas.

Key words: Cost of Environmental Degradation (COED), Valuation

Sentence Number	Information Element
1)	
2)	
3)	
4)	
5)	
6)	

Ⅳ Select two or three abstracts in your research field and analyze the strong points and weak points of them.

Ⅴ Match the information elements in Column A with the sentences in Column B to arrange the abstract in order.

Column A	Column B
Research background	1) It is concluded that project success is the outcome of the interaction between a variety of techniques, and that partnering, associated with incentives, is a basic management method through which risk management and TQM can be strongly improved.
Research question	2) However, little research outlines the mechanism behind its application.
Research method	3) This paper presents the findings of a study that was conducted to develop and test a partnering model that reveals the relationships between the critical success factors (CSFs) of partnering and demonstrates their importance to construction.
Research result	4) Partnering and its principles have increasingly been introduced to the construction industry to improve the efficiency of project delivery.
Research conclusion	5) With support of data collected from the Chinese construction industry, this study has revealed strong correlations among partnering CSFs, risk management, total quality management (TQM), use of incentives, and project performance.

Ⅵ Select the appropriate verb in the box to complete each sentence. Change the form where necessary. There may be more than one choice.

| draw | confirm | examine | devote | play | indicate |

1. As in every aspect of human life, Information and Communication Technologies (ICT) _____ an important role in education.

2. Results _____ that all participants used their L1 while writing in their L2 to some extent.

3. On the basis of our research results, the following conclusions can be _____.

4. The multiphase intergrowth in the system _____ by the present research.
5. This paper is mainly _____ to the principle and methodology of language teaching.
6. This article _____ the changes in attitudes towards marriage and children in Great Britain.

| throw | deepen | discuss | provide | conclude | conduct |

7. The paper _____ the correlation between the frequency of Internet surfing and personality characteristics.
8. Approximately thirty tests _____ to check the possibility of cross-compatibility in distant hybridizations.
9. Our research results _____ support for our theory.
10. From the experiment, we _____ that there are no negative side effects with this therapy.
11. This statistical analysis will _____ the understanding of how the human brain works.
12. All the preliminary results _____ light on the nature of language learning.

| investigate | prove | present | carry | contribute | survey |

13. Our laboratory studies _____ to be encouraging.
14. Vulnerable analysis _____ out to evaluate the air pollution stress at different locations.
15. This study _____ the language learning strategy use of 85 ESL students enrolled in a college English program.
16. The author's pioneer work _____ to our present understanding of depression controlling.
17. The purpose of this paper is to _____ the cause of falling fertility rate in the past ten years.
18. This paper _____ the mathematical model and its algorithm used for predicting the wave propagation.

Ⅶ Fill in each blank with the appropriate form of each verb given in the brackets.

The dynamic development of biotechnology in recent years 1) _____ (raise) serious public concerns about the possible risks 2) _____ (arise) from genetically

183

modified organisms (GMOs). The aim of this study 3) _____ (be) to investigate consumer opinions regarding genetically modified (GM) foods. The research also 4) _____ (aim) at verifying the differences in the attitudes of respondents from two relatively culturally diverse research sites. To obtain empirical data, a face-to-face survey 5) _____ (conduct) in 2015. It 6) _____ (cover) a total of 976 randomly selected individuals. The study 7) _____ (perform) in London and Warsaw. The results of the study 8) _____ (show) that almost half of the respondents 9) _____ (be) familiar with the GMO concept. According to the respondents, the greatest benefits arising from the genetic modification 10) _____ (be): enhanced shelf-life of food and crops' resistance to extreme climatic conditions. The main disadvantages 11) _____ (be): unpredictable consequences of deoxyribonucleic acid (DNA) modification, production of species-specific toxins and food allergenicity. Over two thirds of people surveyed 12) _____ (support) the idea of the obligatory labeling of GM foods. An almost equal number of respondents 13) _____ (show) an intention for purchasing GM food products, an intention to act otherwise, or undecided intention. As many as 27.7% of survey participants 14) _____ (show) negative attitudes towards GM foods, whereas only 19.8% predominantly positive. It 15) _____ (be) worth noticing that no statistically significant differences 16) _____ (observe) between the opinions of Polish and British respondents.

Ⅷ Following is the notes of the abstract of a paper in the field of bio-engineering. Write the complete abstract based on the notes given.

Research purpose	to apply biomimetic designed composites to artificial structures
Research question	the solid-fluid composite structure of the cancellous bone, from the viewpoint of the bio-joint mechanism, play an important role in the load transmission
Research methods	(1) establish: the solid-fluid composite model equal to the cancellous bone, use honeycomb structure (2) carry out: static indentation testing (3) measure quantitatively: in-plane deformation conditions of the solid-fluid composite specimens
Results	the hydrostatic pressure of the fluid phase, great influence on the in-plane deformation condition of the solid phase
Conclusion	the compressive load dispersion by the solid-fluid phase interaction, expect, under the framework of the solid-fluid composite models

IX Rearrange the following sentences into a coherent paragraph.

1. This article discusses a basic question.
2. To reveal the essence of the coordinate transformation coefficient, the basic concept of the tensor is revisited and extended.
3. The conventional viewpoint is that the coordinate transformation coefficient is not the component of a tensor.
4. Is the coordinate transformation coefficient the component of a tensor?
5. Thus, the concept of tensors is extended.
6. That is to say, the coordinate transformation coefficient is the hybrid component of a metric tensor.
7. On the basis of the new concept, the conventional viewpoint is negated: The coordinate transformation coefficient is indeed the component of a tensor.
8. A new concept, i.e., the hybrid tensor, is therefore defined.

X Translate the following sentences into English.

1. 在过去的几十年里，医疗技术的进步已经使人们寿命比过去更长成为可能。
2. 东亚的经济灾难很大程度上归因于银行业和投资业出现危机，进而导致投资者信心崩溃。
3. 早在儿童能够听懂和说出某种语言之前，他们就会通过面部表情和发出声音来与人交流。
4. 骑自行车既对人体健康有益，又能缓解交通堵塞。
5. 自从骨髓干细胞20世纪60年代被发现以来，对于它的研究已经引起了许多科学家的兴趣。

XI Translate the following paragraph into Chinese.

The paper carefully analyzes the connotation and denotation of the feedback in the process approach to the teaching of writing and subtly delineates its forms and functions at different stages of writing. The paper also discusses the effect of feedback on the subject's cognition and indicates its limitations in the process approach to writing. In general, the introduction of the feedback to the process approach blazes new and significant trails, since it facilitates not only the establishment of interactive writing environment but the development of the effective error-correction mechanism as well. Without feedback, the process approach will not be a successful teaching method.

Unit 8
Referencing

📝 Warm-up Questions

1. Why do we need to cite others' work?

2. What citation style(s) is (are) commonly used in your research field?

3. What reporting verbs can be used to introduce the source in the text?

8.1 Overview

8.1.1 Purpose of Referencing

Most academic writing projects require you to gather, evaluate, and use others' work. When you draw upon others' work, you must give proper credit. Referencing is the practice of acknowledging in your own writing the intellectual work of others that has been presented in some way into the public domain. Failure to do so constitutes plagiarism. Several reasons have been proposed for referencing, including six knowledge-related and three student-related reasons (Neville, 2010: 7–13), as listed below:

Six knowledge-related reasons:

- facilitate the tracing of the origin of ideas;
- help you to build a web of ideas;
- support your own voice in academic writing;
- validate arguments;
- help to spread knowledge;
- acknowledge the work of others.

Three student-related reasons:

- illustrate the range of your reading;
- serve as marking criteria;
- avoid plagiarism.

It is important to fully understand the documentation style to be used in your paper and to apply it consistently.

8.1.2 Information Elements of Referencing

All referencing styles require every source you use to be documented twice: first in an in-text citation in the main body of your work, and then an entry in the end-text reference. While the in-text citation specifies the source of literature, the end-text reference list presents the complete publication details. Table 8.1 shows examples of in-text citation and end-text reference in two referencing styles, respectively, i.e., name-referencing style and numerical-referencing style (Neville, 2010).

Table 8.1 Examples of In-Text Citation and End-Text Reference

Referencing Style	Example	Information Element
name-referencing style	Due to the fact that developing as an EAP practitioner is reported as being a potentially limitless process, and because of the wide range of backgrounds and levels of experience new EAP teachers bring with them from other contexts, it seems unhelpful and arbitrary to continue to artificially categorize "novices" and "experienced teachers", as much of the professional literature tends to do. There does not appear to be a magic moment where the "novice", who is capable of very little, becomes an "expert", with all the implied competencies and authority, and indeed there are no particular observations to be made from the present study about differences in responses between the more and the less experienced teachers involved in this study, suggesting that differences in beliefs between more and less experienced EAP teachers may not be as marked as **Alexander (2007)** suggests. **Reference** Alexander, O. (2007). Groping in the dark or turning on the light: Routes into teaching English for academic purposes. In T. Lynch (Ed.), *Teaching Languages for Academic Purposes*. Edinburgh: IALS, Edinburgh University.	in-text citation end-text reference

(Continued)

Referencing Style	Example	Information Element
numerical-referencing style	**6 Related Work** Babcock & Olston [1] and Olston et al. [18] show how to trade precision for performance using approximations in a distributed system. A central station coordinates a number of distributed sites and installs individual constraints in each site. These constraints specify the amount of deviation that a site value can have from its last reported value to the station without violating the query invariants. As long as the invariants hold at each site, no message communication is necessary. This work is complementary to our work, where we need to identify the top-k least frequent event set continuously. Chu et al. [4] extend the above work to a sensor network setting and exploit the spatial correlations among the attributes to further reduce communication costs. This work can be considered to be an optimization over strategies, which employ only the push mechanism. **Reference** [1] B. Babcock & C. Olston. "Distributed Top-K Monitoring," *Proc. ACM SIGMOD*, 2003: 22–39	in-text citation end-text reference

8.1.3 Referencing Styles

A search at your university's library website will show you a list of commonly used referencing styles. Figure 8.1 is an example from Tsinghua University Library.

We can tell from Figure 8.1 that choosing the appropriate referencing style depends on disciplinary variations. For instance, AMA (American Medical Association) style is used throughout disciplines in biomedical sciences, while APA (American Psychological Association) style is commonly used in psychology, education and other fields in social sciences.

Unit 8　Referencing

英文文章写作:

1 **Citation Style for Research Papers** 由美国长岛大学（Long Island University）整理的各种参考文献格式，包括：MLA、APA、CMS、AMA 等。
2 **Citation Guide** 由 SourceAid, LLC 公司整理的各种参考文献格式，包括：MLA、APA、CMS、CSE。

MLA 格式 (Modern Language Association, 现代语言协会)
主要用于人文科学领域
http://www2.liu.edu/cwis/cwp/library/workshop/citchi.htm
美国长岛（Long Island）大学整理
另外，MLA格式可参考图书：

作者名	吉巴尔迪, J. (Gibaldi, Joseph), 1942- 著
题名	MLA文体手册和学术出版指南 mla wen ti shou ce he xue shu chu ban zhi nan 第二版 (美) 约瑟夫·吉巴尔迪著 沈弘, 何姝译
出版发行	北京 中国标准出版社 2003

收藏于逸夫馆一层中文社科区和三层的工具书阅览室，索书号为H315 J062

ACS 格式 (American Chemical Society 美国化学学会)
主要用于化学领域
ACS Style Guidelines Quick Guide
另外，可参考本馆图书：

题名	The ACS style guide : effective communication of scientific information.
出版发行	Washington , DC : American Chemical Society ; Oxford ; New York : Oxford University Press, 2006
版本	3rd ed. / Anne M. Coghill, Lorrin R. Garson, editors.

收藏于逸夫馆三层工具书阅览室，索书号为 06-62 FA511

题名	The ACS style guide : a manual for authors and editors / Janet S. Dodd, editor ; Marianne C. Brogan, advisory editor.
出版发行	Washington, DC : American Chemical Society, 1986.

收藏于逸夫馆二层大厅出纳台，索书号为O6 FA51

AMA 格式（American Medical Association 美国医学协会)
主要用于生物医学领域
http://www2.liu.edu/cwis/cwp/library/workshop/citama.htm
美国长岛 (Long Island) 大学整理
APA 格式 (American Psychological Association 美国心理学会)
主要用于心理、教育等社会科学领域
APA Citation Style
美国长岛（Long Island）大学整理
Chicago Manual of Style (简称 CMS，芝加哥格式，又称 Turabian Style 或 Humanities Style)
广泛应用于图书、杂志、报纸以及人文科学领域
http://www2.liu.edu/cwis/cwp/library/workshop/citchi.htm
美国长岛（Long Island）大学整理
Vancouver Style　(温哥华格式)
主要用于生物医学期刊
Harvard Style　(哈佛格式，也叫Author-date system, 作者-日期体系)
广泛应用于各学科，南澳大利亚大学整理

Figure 8.1　Screenshot of the Website of Tsinghua University Library

In addition, you also need to take the requirements of the particular course or those of your target journal or conference guidelines into consideration when choosing the appropriate referencing style. Figure 8.2 is a screenshot of the website of the journal *Scientific Study of Literature*, showing guidelines for authors, with the section on specific requirement for referencing styles highlighted.

Figure 8.2　Screenshot of the Website of the Journal *Scientific Study of Literature*

Figure 8.3 is taken from the website of a conference (The 18th USENIX Symposium on Networked Systems Design and Implementation) held by the Advanced Computing Systems Association. As part of authors' resources, the LaTeX template and sample PDF files are provided by the organizing committee of the conference.

Unit **8** Referencing

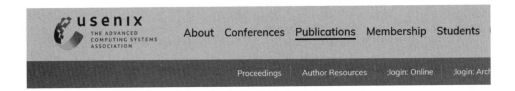

Figure 8.3 Screenshot of a Conference Website

All citation practices can be attributed to the understanding of academic writing as social practices (Lea & Street, 1998). From this social constructivism perspective, academic writing is perceived as collective literacy practices situated in a specific disciplinary culture. Discipline is defined as a human institution where actions and understandings are influenced by personal, interpersonal, institutional, and sociocultural factors (Hyland, 2004).

Referencing styles can be generally divided into two types: name-referencing style and numerical-referencing style (see Table 8.1), each including several variations. In the following section, APA style and IEEE (Institute of Electrical and Electronic Engineers) style will be briefly illustrated with examples. For full information on each style, please visit their offical websites.

Table 8.2 Commonly-Used Referencing Styles

Name-Referencing Style	Numerical-Referencing Style
American Psychological Association (APA). https://www.apa.org/	Institute of Electrical and Electronic Engineers (IEEE). https://www.ieee.org

(Continued)

Name-Referencing Style	Numerical-Referencing Style
Modern Language Association of America (MLA). https://www.mla.org/	Vancouver Style (The complete guide to the Vancouver Style referencing is *Citing Medicine* by the National Library of Medicine (NLM). https://www.ncbi.nlm.nih.gov/books/NBK7256/pdf/Bookshelf_NBK7256.pdf)
Chicago/Turabian. https://www.chicago-manualofstyle.org/turabian/citation-guide.html	Council of Science Editors. https://www.councilscienceeditors.org/
American Medical Association (AMA). https://www.amamanualofstyle.com/	

Following is an example of end-text referencing for one journal article using different referencing styles:

Table 8.3　An Example of End-Text Referencing

	Name-Referencing Style
APA	Salovey, P. & Mayer, J. D. 1990. Emotional intelligence. *Imagination, Cognition and Personality,* 9(3): 185–211. https://doi.org/10.2190/DUGG-P24E-52WK-6CDG
MLA	Salovey, Peter & Mayer, J. D. "Emotional Intelligence." *Imagination, Cognition and Personality,* 9(3): 185–211. 3, Mar. 1990 doi:10.2190/DUGG-P24E-52WK-6CDG.
Chicago	Salovey, P. & John D. Mayer. "Emotional Intelligence." *Imagination, Cognition and Personality* 9, no. 3 (March 1990): 185–211. https://doi.org/10.2190/DUGG-P24E-52WK-6CDG.
	Numerical-Referencing Style
Vancouver	1. Salovey, P., Mayer J.D. Emotional Intelligence. *Imagination, Cognition and Personality.* 1990; 9(3): 185–211. doi:10.2190/DUGG-P24E-52WK-6CDG

Unit 8 Referencing

1. APA style

APA style is primarily used in social sciences, so if you're taking a psychology or sociology course or writing a journal article in this field, you may be expected to write papers in APA style.

The APA style calls for three kinds of information to be included in in-text citations:

- the author's last name (obligatory);
- the work's date of publication (obligatory);
- the page number (optional; appears only in a direct quotation).

Listed below are examples of three different types of in-text citations.

✓ ① Shrinking markets are also evident in other areas. As **Smith (2000)** pointed out, the wool industry is experiencing difficulties related to falling demand worldwide since the development of high-quality synthetic fibers.

✓ ② Shrinking markets are also evident in other areas. The wool industry is experiencing difficulties related to falling demand worldwide since the development of high-quality synthetic fibers **(Smith, 2000)**.

✓ ③ Shrinking markets are also evident in other areas. **Several authors** have reported that the wool industry is experiencing difficulties related to falling demand since the development of high-quality synthetic fibers **(Smith, 2000; Wilson, 2003; Nguyen, 2005)**.

The first type of in-text citation, as exemplified in ①, is named author-prominent citation (Cargill & O'Connor, 2013), or integral citation (Swales, 1990), or narrative citation (American Psychological Association [APA], 2020), in which the name of the author is foregrounded in a prominent position to highlight the scholar who proposed the idea. By contrast, in example ② above, the idea/information per se is emphasized rather than the exact person who proposed the idea. Thus, this type of in-text citation is called information-prominent citation (Cargill & O'Connor, 2013), or non-integral citation (Swales, 1990), or parenthetical citation (APA, 2020). Example ③ shows another type of in-text citation, namely weak author-prominent citation (Cargill & O'Connor, 2013), in which the writer provides a summary of previous research and list several authors' last names and their works' dates of publication in the parentheses. The format of the author element of the in-text citation changes depending on the number of authors and is abbreviated in some cases. See Table 8.4 for examples of the basic in-text citation styles (APA, 2020: 266; The Writing Center—University of Wisconsin-Madison, 2022).

Table 8.4   Basic In-Text Citation Styles (APA)

Author Type		Author-Prominet Citation	Information-Prominent Citation
One work	one author	Luna (2020)	(Luna, 2020)
	two authors	Salas and D'Agostino (2020)	(Salas & D'Agostino, 2020)
	three or more authors	Martin et al. (2020)	(Martin et al., 2020)
	group author with abbreviation first citation	National Institute of Mental Health (NIMH, 2020)	(National Institute of Mental Health [NIMH], 2020)
	subsequent citations	NIMH (2020)	(NIMH, 2020)
	group author without abbreviation	Stanford University (2020)	(Stanford University, 2020)
Two or more works	several researchers (arrange by order of the reference list; use a semicolon between works)		(Alibali, Phillips & Fischer, 2009; Siegler, 1976)
	same researcher(s) (don't repeat name[s]; earliest year first)		(Hyland, 2004, 2008, 2013)
Secondary reference	only the secondary reference goes in the reference list		According to Coie et al. (as cited in Greenbert, Domitrovich & Bumbarger, 2000), …

With regard to end-text referencing, please ensure that all authors cited in the text must appear in the reference list, and all authors listed must have been cited in the text. Table 8.5 shows a correspondence between the end-text referencing and in-text citations (APA style) in one journal article.

Table 8.5 Correspondence Between End-Text Referencing and In-Text Citation (APA)

End-text referencing	Salovey, P. & Mayer, J. D. (1990). Emotional intelligence. *Imagination, Cognition and Personality, 9*(3), 185–211. https://doi.org/10.2190/DUGG-P24E-52WK-6CDG
In-text citation	Narrative citation (integral citation): Salovey and Mayer (1990) Parenthetical citation (non-integral citation): (Salovey & Mayer, 1990)

Please notice that "APA publications and other publishers and institutions using APA style generally require reference lists, not bibliographies. A reference list cites works that specifically support the ideas, claims, and concepts in a paper; in contrast, a bibliography cites works for background or further reading and may include descriptive notes" (APA, 2020: 281).

A reference generally has four elements: author, date, title, and source. Figure 8.4 shows an example of a journal article title page highlighting the locations of the reference elements and showing their placement in a reference list entry (APA, 2020: 283).

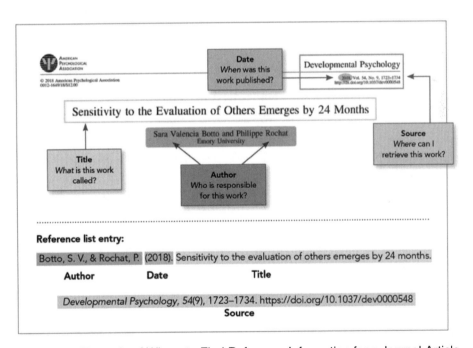

Figure 8.4　Example of Where to Find Reference Information for a Journal Article

Please see Table 8.6 for basic end-text referencing styles (APA).

Table 8.6 Basic End-Text Referencing Styles (APA)

Reference Category		Basic Rule/Template	Example
Book	first edition, single author	Author's last name, First initial. Middle name initial. (Year of publication). *Book title*. City of publication, State's 2-letter abbreviation: Publisher.	Baxter, C. (1997). *Race equality in health care and education*. Philadelphia, PA: Ballière Tindall.
	later edition, two authors	First author's last name, First initial. Middle initial. & Second author's last name, First initial. (Year of publication). *Book title* (Edition number). City of publication, State's 2-letter abbreviation: Publisher.	Hyde, J. S. & Delamater, J. (2008). *Human sexuality* (10th ed.). New York, NY: McGraw-Hill.
	editors in place of authors	First editor's last name, First initial. Middle initial., Second editor's last name, First initial. Middle initial. & Third editor's last name, First initial. (Eds.). (Year of publication). *Title*. City of publication, State's 2-letter abbreviation: Publisher.	Castellanos, J., Gloria, A. M. & Kamimura, M. (Eds.). (2006). *The Latina/o pathway to the Ph.D.: Abriendocaminos*. Sterling, VA: Stylus.
	Chapter in edited work	Author's last name, First initial. Middle initial. (Year of publication). Chapter title. In Editor's first initial. Middle initial. Last name (Ed.), *Edited work title* (pp. Pages). City of publication, State's 2-letter abbreviation: Publisher.	Alibali, M. W. (2005). Mechanisms of change in the development of mathematical reasoning. In R. V. Kail (Ed.), *Advances in child development and behavior* (pp. 79–123). New York, NY: Academic Press.

(Continued)

Reference Category		Basic Rule/Template	Example
Scholarly journal article	single author, print	Author's Last name, First initial. Middle initial. (Year of publication). Article title. *Journal name, Volume number,* Pages.	Alibali, M. W. (1999). How children change their minds: Strategy change can be gradual or abrupt. *Developmental Psychology, 35,* 127–145.
	two authors, read online, with digital object identifier (doi)	First author's last name, First initial. Middle initial. & Second author's last name, First initial. Middle initial. (Year of publication). Article title. *Journal name, Volume number,* Pages. doi: number	Gaudio, J. L. & Snowdon, C. T. (2008). Spatial cues more salient than color cues in cotton-top tamarins (*Saguinusoedipus*) reversal learning. *Journal of Comparative Psychology, 122,* 441–444. doi: 10.1037/0735-7036.122.4.441
Dissertation	unpublished dissertation, obtained from database	Author's last name, First initial. Middle initial. (Year of publication). *Title of dissertation* (Type of dissertation, Name of Academic institution). Available from Database name. (Accession or Order number)	Hostetter, A. B. (2008). *Mind in motion: The gesture as simulated action framework* (Doctoral dissertation, University of Wisconsin-Madison). Available from ProQuest Dissertations and Thesis database. (UMI No. 3327832).
Conference paper or poster session	Paper or poster presented at a meeting	First author's last name, First initial. Middle initial. & Second author's last name, First initial. Middle initial. (Year, Month of publication). *Title of poster/paper.* Poster presented at Conference name, City, State.	Lindberg, S. M. & Hyde, J. S. (2007, March). *Mother-child interactions during mathematics homework: Socialization of gender differentiation?* Poster presented at the biennial meeting of the Society for Research on Adolescence, Chicago, IL.

(Continued)

Reference Category	Basic Rule/Template	Example
Internet source	Author's last name, First initial. Middle initial. (Year of publication) Website Name. http://web address	Driscoll, D. & Brizee, A. (2016). Commas: Quick rules. https://owl.english.purdue.edu/owl/owlprint/607/

2. IEEE style

IEEE style, the official style of the Institute of Electrical and Electronics Engineers, is standard for all IEEE journals and magazines and is frequently used for papers and articles in the fields of engineering and computer science. IEEE style requires endnotes and that references be cited numerically in the text.

Citing references in a paper using IEEE style is fairly straightforward. References are cited using the reference number enclosed in square brackets: [1], [2], etc. The organization of the references section depends upon the order in which you refer to sources in the body of your paper. If you cite a single publication more than once, use the original citation number instead of creating a new reference. For example:

✓ …Booske et al. [6]; however, as mentioned earlier [1]–[3], [5]…

In the IEEE style, in-text citations are treated like either footnotes (though they are never placed in superscript; similar to information-prominent citation in APA style) or nouns (similar to author-prominent citation in APA style) in your sentences. In the example above, the citations are treated like footnotes. You might also cite the same sources treating the references as nouns, as exemplified in the following:

✓ …was proven incorrect, as demonstrated in [1]–[3], [5].

Note that reference citations are placed inside the punctuation.

With regard to end-text referencing, IEEE reference section lists only those sources cited in the paper, and they are organized according to the order in which sources are cited. The author's first initial appears first (B. Smith) in each entry. The first line of each reference entry should be numbered in square brackets and be flush left. Please see Table 8.7 for examples of basic IEEE end-text referencing styles.

Table 8.7 Basic End-Text Referencing Styles (IEEE)

Reference Category	Example
Book, one author, first edition	[1] R. S. Lakes, Viscoelastic Materials. Cambridge, UK: Cambridge Univ. Press, 2010.
Book, one author, later edition	[2] M. W. Carbon, Nuclear Power: Villain or Victim? 2nd ed. Madison, WI: Pebble Beach Publishers, 2006.
Book, two authors	[3] J. J. Duderstadt and G. A. Moses, Intertial Confinement Fusion. New York, NY: Wiley, 1982.
Book, more than two authors	[4] V. Bier et al., Effects of Deregulation on Safety: Implications Drawn from the Aviation, Rail, and United Kingdom Nuclear Power Industries. New York, NY: Kluwer Academic Publishers, 2003.
Edited collection	[5] Applications of Cell Immobilization Biotechnology, V. Nedovic and R. Willaert, Eds. New York, NY: Kluwer Academic Publishers, 2005.
Chapter in an edited collection	[6] J. H. Booske et al., "Plasma Implantation," in Wiley Encyclopedia of Electrical and Electronics Engineering, vol. 16, J. G. Webster, Ed. New York, NY: John Wiley and Sons, 1999, 520–527. [7] R. S. Lakes, "Composit Biomaterials," in The Biomedical Engineering Handbook, 2nd ed., J. D. Bronzino, Ed. Boca Raton, FL: CRC Press, 2000, 40.1–40.7.
Journal article	[8] M. Morse, J. M. Patel, and W. I. Grosky, "Efficient evaluation of bioinformatics research and applications," International J. of Bioinformatics Research and Applications, vol. 3, no. 1, pp. 24–41, 2007. [9] E. L. Haseltine, V. Lam, J. Yin, and J. B. Rawlings. "Image-guided modeling of virus growth and spread," Bulletin of Math. Biology, vol. 70, no. 6, 2008. doi: 173048
Conference article	[10] C. Prakash et al., "PGA: using graphs to express and automatically reconcile network policies," in SIGCOMM'15, 2015 © ACM. doi: 10.1145/2785956.2787506

(Continued)

Reference Category	Example
Online source	[11] B. Curtin. (1999, July). Internationalization of the File Transfer Protocol, RFC 2640 [Online]. Available: http://tools.ietf.org/html/rfc2640
Patent	[12] N. Hershkowitz et al., "Non-ambipolar radio-frequency plasma electron source and systems and methods for generating electron beams," U.S. Patent 7 875 867, Dec. 3, 2008.
Standard	[13] IEEE Standard Critera for Digital Computers in Safety Systems of Nuclear Power Generating Stations, IEEE Standard 7-4.3.2-2010.
Thesis or dissertation	[14] Z. Li, "Signature-Driven Fault Management Metholdologies for Complex Engineering Systems," Ph.D. Dissertation, Indust. Eng., UW-Madison, Madison, WI, 2007.

8.2 Sample Analysis

Sample 1 (Name-Referencing Style)

information-prominent citation	**Approaching doctoral supervision and its differentiation** The quality of academic supervision is of major importance for increasing completion rates and quality of dissertations (Holdaway et al., 1995; Hockey, 1991; Lipschutz 1993; Mainhard et al., 2009; Zhao et al., 2007), as well as for maintaining high rates of students' satisfaction (Harman 2003; Zhao et al., 2007) and decreasing TTD (De Valero, 2001; Jiranek, 2010; Seagram et al., 1998; Wao & Onwuegbuzie, 2011). Three aspects are discussed in literature in this relation. The first is concerned with the professional and personal qualities a supervisor should possess to promote Ph.D. students' development in the best way. For instance,

	particularly important are accessibility for students and willingness to support (Johnson & Huwe, 2003; Taylor et al., 2018), as well as knowledge of the research field (Donald et al., 1995). The second aspect is related to supervisors' behavior, i.e., the functions they perform and the manner (or style) in which they do them (Zhao et al., 2007). The third aspect emphasizes that successful supervision is also a result of establishing a good student-supervisor relationship (Ali et al., 2016; Fillery-Travis & Robinson, 2018; Golde, 2000; Grant et al., 2014; Linden et al., 2016; Mainhard et al., 2009; Pyhältö et al., 2015; Taylor et al., 2018). We argue that supervisors' behavior is the least studied among these three aspects. Although, as pointed out by Lee (2008), many works concentrate on listing functions of doctoral supervision, most of them analyze what supervisors should do (e.g., Taylor et al., 2017) instead of what they actually do. In this regard, Halse and **Malfroy (2010)** give a comprehensive description of supervisors' functions, experiences, and professional expertise. Based on the data from 26 semi-structured interviews, they describe doctoral supervision through 5 categories: the learning alliance, which is about establishing relations with the student and organizing the work around a common goal, habits of mind that allow supervisors to show empathy and curiosity towards student's experience, scholarly expertise that accounts for participating in the production of knowledge, and techne that deals with the educational function of supervision and contextual expertise about institutional and disciplinary context of a student's research. However, their work is qualitative by method and aims to separate doctoral supervision as a whole by approaching it as professional work. It does not account for differences within supervisors' work and their relation to outcomes of supervisor-student interaction.
author-prominent citation	

	Source: Gruzdev, I., Terentev, E. & Dzhafarova, Z. 2020. Superhero or hands-off supervisor? An empirical categorization of Ph.D. supervision styles and student satisfaction in Russian universities. *Higher Education*, *79*(5), 773–789.

Sample 2 (Numerical-Referencing Style)

In-text citations are treated like footnotes (similar to information-prominent citation in APA style)	**2 Related Work** Several algorithms [18], [19], [20], [21] have been proposed for finding MFIs in a finite data set. These algorithms are not suitable for an online data stream since they require multiple scans on an input data set. Pincer-Search [20] constructs the candidate sets of MFIs in a bottom-up manner like a priori [12] along with top-down searching. If an infrequent item set is found in the bottom-up direction, it can be used to prune its supersets in the top-down direction of the next pass. The algorithm reduces the required number of scans on a data set by eliminating those frequent item sets that are not maximal as early as possible. Since the set of candidate MFIs is usually much larger than that of actual MFIs, the overhead of maintaining the set of candidate MFIs can be very costly in general. MaxMiner [21] performs a breadth-first search on an item set tree by employing a look-ahead pruning technique to reduce the number of scans on a data set. MAFIA [18] traverses an item set tree in a depth-first manner to prune any nonmaximal item set. It stores the transactions of a data set as a series of vertical bitmaps. For each distinct item, a bitmap represents whether the transaction that corresponds to a particular bit position has the corresponding item or not. Candidate item sets generation and support counting are efficiently processed by a series of bitwise operations. The algorithm may extract a superset of MFIs so that it requires a postpruning step to eliminate any nonmaximal item set obtained in the previous step. GenMax [19] employs a progressive focusing operation for maximality

	testing and a diffset propagation operation for frequency checking. A progressive focusing is a superset checking technique to narrow down the group of possible supersets, i.e., the set of MFIs. As a result, a considerable number of superset/subset checking operations can be reduced. Furthermore, between an item set and its superset, a diffset is defined to be a set of transaction identifiers, which contain the superset only. While traversing an item set tree, a diffset between a node and its child node is propagated for fast frequency testing. Consequently, the supports of each item set can be computed efficiently. These algorithms are not suitable for finding MFIs over a data stream since they require to scan a data set multiple times. **Source:** H. J. Woo & W. S. Lee, "estMax: Tracing Maximal Frequent Item Sets Instantly over Online Transactional Data Streams," in IEEE Transactions on Knowledge and Data Engineering, *vol. 21, no.* 10, pp. 1418–1431, Oct. 2009, doi: 10.1109/TKDE.2008.233.

8.3 Reflections and Practice

❶ Answer the following questions.

1. Why do we need to cite others' work?
2. How do you use references when you read articles in your research field?
3. What is the danger attached to the author-prominent citation style?

❷ Select four research articles in your research field (one classic; one latest [published within three years]; one from authoritative scholars; one from your target journal). Then analyze the referencing style used in each article and fill in the following table.

	Information of the Article (include all four elements that a	Referencing Style (name-referencing or numerical-refe	Specific Referencing Style (APA, MLA, AMA, IEEE, Chicago, etc.)

	reference requires: author, date, title, and source)	rencing)	
Classic article			
Latest article			
Article from authoritative scholars			
Article from your target journals			

Ⅲ **Match the reference categories in Column A with the corresponding end-text references (APA style) in Column B.**

Column A	Column B
Book, later edition, two authors	1) Castellanos, J., Gloria, A. M. & Kamimura, M. (Eds.). (2006). *The Latina/o pathway to the Ph.D.: Abriendocaminos*. Sterling, VA: Stylus.
Book, editors in place of authors	2) Hostetter, Autumn B. (2008). *Mind in motion: The gesture as simulated action framework* (Doctoral dissertation, University of Wisconsin-Madison). Available from ProQuest Dissertations and Thesis database. (UMI No. 3327832).
Chapter in edited work	3) Lindberg, S. M. & Hyde, J. S. (2007, March). *Mother-child interactions during mathematics homework: Socialization of gender differentiation?* Poster presented at the biennial meeting of the Society for Research on Adolescence, Chicago, IL.
Scholarly journal article, two authors, read online, with digital object identifier (doi)	4) Hyde, J. S. & Delamater, J. (2008). *Human sexuality* (10th ed.). New York, NY: McGraw-Hill.

Unpublished dissertation, obtained from database	5) Driscoll, D. & Brizee, A. (2016). Commas: Quick rules. https://owl.english.purdue.edu/owl/owlprint/607/
Paper or poster presented at a conference	6) Gaudio, J. L. & Snowdon, C. T. (2008). Spatial cues more salient than color cues in cotton-top tamarins (*Saguinusoedipus*) reversal learning. *Journal of Comparative Psychology, 122*, 441–444. doi: 10.1037/0735-7036.122.4.441
Internet source	7) Alibali, M. W. (2005). Mechanisms of change in the development of mathematical reasoning. In R. V. Kail (Ed.), *Advances in child development and behavior* (pp. 79–123). New York, NY: Academic Press.

IV Rearrange the words and phrases in each group into clear and coherent sentences.

1) define, as, meetings and conventions, Kozlowski and Farr [17], professional activities.

2) several reasons, outline, Bliese and Hanges (2004), it is, to, important, why, model.

3) Agichtein et al. (2006), these techniques, as mentioned in, well, on average, perform.

4) academic supervision, of, and, quality of dissertations, (Holdaway et al., 1995), the quality, is, for, of major importance, increasing, completion rates.

5) describes, as, Petress (2003: 624), "plague on our profession", plagiarism, a.

V Rearrange the following sentences into a coherent paragraph.

1	A.	Thomas Eakins (1844–916) is now recognized as one of the greatest American painters, alongside Winslow Homer, Edward Hopper, and Jackson Pollock.
___	B.	In many ways, Eakins was a modern late nineteenth century figure since he was interested in science, anatomy, and the fast-growing "manly sports" of rowing and boxing.
___	C.	Over the last thirty years, there have been many studies of his life and work, and in 2002 there was a major exhibition devoted entirely to his art in his home city of Philadelphia.
___	D.	The non-portraits are distinguished by compositional brilliance and attention to detail, while the portraits—most of which come from his later period—are thought to show deep insight into character or "psychological realism".
___	E.	His best-known pictures include a number of rowing and sailing scenes, several domestic interiors, the two large canvasses showing the surgeons Gross and Agnew at work in the operating theater, and a long series of portraits, including several of his wife, Susan McDowell.

_____ F. These included his wish to get inside the marsh landscape, to stress the hand-eye coordination between the shooter and "the pusher", and to capture the moment of concentration before any action takes place.

_____ G. Apart from a chapter in Foster (1997), this series has been little discussed by critics or art historians. For example, these pictures were ignored by Johns in her pioneering 1983 monograph, perhaps because their overall smallness (physically, socially and psychologically) did not fit well with her book's title, *Thomas Eakins: The Heroism of Modern Life*.

_____ H. In his best work, he painted what he knew and whom he knew, rather than being an artist-outsider to the scene in front of him.

_____ I. However, in this paper I will argue that Eakins focused his attention on these featureless landscapes for a much more complex set of motives.

_____ J. Among Eakins' pictures, there is a small series of scenes painted between 1873 and 1876 showing hunters preparing to shoot at the secretive marsh birds in the coastal marshes near Philadelphia.

_____ K. These pictures are usually thought to have come about simply because Thomas Eakins used to accompany his father on these hunting/shooting trips to the marshes.

Ⅵ Translate the following references into English.

1. 蔡基刚，廖雷朝. 2010. 学术英语还是专业英语——我国大学 ESP 教学重新定位思考. 外语教学（6）：47–50；73.
2. 蔡基刚，武世兴. 2003. 引进多媒体网络技术，改革传统的教学模式. 外语界（6）：2–7.
3. 严明. 2009. 大学专门用途英语（ESP）教学理论与实践研究. 哈尔滨：黑龙江大学出版社.
4. 李稻葵，刘霖林，王红领. 2009. GDP 中劳动份额演变的 U 型规律. 经济研究（1）：70–82.
5. 陈元芳. 1994. 非负自回归模型的提出及估计回归系数的新方法. 水利水运科学研究（Z1）：141–146.

Ⅶ Translate the following paragraph into Chinese.

Excellence in writing is critical for success in many academic and professional pursuits. APA style is a set of guidelines for clear and precise scholarly communication that helps authors, both new and experienced, achieve excellence in writing. It is used by millions of people around the world in psychology and also in fields ranging from nursing to social work, communications to education, business to engineering, and other disciplines for the preparation of manuscripts for publication as well as for writing student papers, dissertations, and theses. APA style provides a foundation for effective scholarly communication because it helps authors present their ideas in a clear, concise, and organized manner. Uniformity and consistency enable readers to (a) focus on the ideas being presented rather than formatting and (b) scan works quickly for key points, findings, and sources. Style guidelines encourage authors to fully disclose essential information and allow readers to dispense with minor distractions, such as inconsistencies or omissions in punctuation, capitalization, reference citations, and presentation of statistics. When style works best, ideas flow logically, sources are credited appropriately, and papers are organized predictably and consistently.

Unit 9
Common Mistakes in Students' Writings

Warm-up Questions

Can you spot the errors in the following three sentences?

1) The present paper provides a reliable criteria for choosing proper penalty function.

2) Compared with numerical models, statistical models like deep neural networks has exhibited similar performance.

3) There are two ways to learn a language: take private lessons or learn it in the country where the language is spoken, but this entails spending a lot of money.

9.1 Common Mistakes

This chapter focuses on common mistakes in students' academic writings and modifications that increase linguistic accuracy, readability, and empathy for the reader. Precise expression and appropriate phrasing are required in terms of academic English expectations to be highly articulate and well proofread (Kumar & Stracke, 2007; Baskurkmen et al., 2014; Morton et al., 2014). Apart from being precise, being considerate to increase empathy for the reader is another requirement. Being considerate means considering the broad readership of the target journal and describing the problem configuration adequately and clearly to set the context for the reader. As argued by Wallwork and Southern (2020: 49), the aim of academic writing is "not to force your reader to decide what certain phrases mean, but instead to make those phrases so clear that reading your paper is effortless".

The problems outlined in the following section are the most common and severe faults in scientific writing and should be avoided at all costs. It will be presented from the following four aspects: the lexical level, the syntactical level, the textual level, and academic conventions (the appropriate use of citations and references).

9.1.1 Lexical Level

1. Confusion of similar words

There are many groups of words that students tend to confuse when using. Table 9.1 lists some examples from students' writings. The original version with "*" is illogical.

Table 9.1   Examples of Confusion of Similar Words

Original Version	Revised Version	Reason for Modification
1. *... compare the data with observational data using **statistic** analysis.	... compare the data with observational data using **statistical** analysis.	**statistic**: *n.* (usually plural) **statistical**: *adj.*
2. *the relatively unequal **economical** and educational status…	the relatively unequal **economic** and educational status…	**economical**: *adj.* not requiring a lot of money to operate something **economic**: *adj.* concerned with the organization of the money, industry, and trade of a country, region, or society

(Continued)

	Original Version	Revised Version	Reason for Modification
3.	*The present paper provides a reliable **criteria** for choosing proper penalty function…	The present paper provides a reliable **criterion** for choosing proper penalty function…	**criterion**: *n.* (singular) **criteria**: *n.* (plural)
4.	*It is a multisystem disease that **has affected on** many organs and regulatory pathways (Byrne & Targher, 2015).	It is a multisystem disease that **has affected** many organs and regulatory pathways (Byrne & Targher, 2015). It is a multisystem disease that **has effect on** many organs and regulatory pathways (Byrne & Targher, 2015).	**affect**: *v.* **effect**: *n.*
5.	*In this article, Higgs' method is used to *analysis* systems of spin-1/2 particles.	In this article, Higgs' method is used to **analyze** systems of spin-1/2 particles.	**analysis**: *n.* **analyze/analyse**: *v.*
6.	*Then we applied eye drop of the rosmarinic acid **everyday** and photographed every week by slit lamp.	Then we applied eye drop of the rosmarinic acid **every day** and photographed every week by slit lamp.	**everyday**: *adj.*, meaning happening every day **every day**: adverbial phrase, meaning each day or daily
7.	*Next, **a serious of** tribology experiments had been done to indicate how microcapsules affected the wear and friction of a fabric liner.	Next, **a series of** tribology experiments had been done to indicate how microcapsules affected the wear and friction of a fabric liner.	**serious**: *adj.* severe in effect; bad **series**: *n.* a number of similar or related events or things, one following another
8.	*factors affecting community governance during the period of **emergence**	factors affecting community governance during the period of **emergency**	**emergence**: (uncountable noun) The emergence of something is the process or event of its coming into existence.

(Continued)

Original Version	Revised Version	Reason for Modification
		emergency: (countable noun) An emergency is an unexpected and difficult or dangerous situation, especially an accident, which happens suddenly and which requires quick action to deal with it.

9.1.2 Syntactical Level

1. Subject-verb agreement

The most common mistake found in students' writings at the syntactical level concerns subject-verb agreement, the basic rule of which is that a singular subject should take a singular verb, whereas a plural subject should take a plural verb. It is noticed that students tend to fail in following the rule, especially when there is a long insertion between the subject and the main verb, as shown in the examples in Table 9.2.

Table 9.2 Examples of Subject-Verb Agreement Mistakes

Original Version	Revised Version
1. *This paper **focus** on the study of the composite frame structure's reaction under transverse load both in elastic and plastic conditions.	This paper **focuses** on the study of the composite frame structure's reaction under transverse load both in elastic and plastic conditions.
2. *The EBSD data **was** acquired and analyzed using Channel 5 software.	The EBSD data **were** acquired and analyzed using Channel 5 software.
3. *Compared with numerical models, statistical models like deep neural networks **has exhibited** similar performance…	Compared with numerical models, statistical models like deep neural networks **have exhibited** similar performance…
4. *The in-situ tensile tests were performed using a tensile stage (DDS-3) that could be automatically driven and **was installed** in a MIRA3 XMH field-emission scanning electron microscope with a loading maximum of 5 kN, as shown in Fig. 1(b).	The in-situ tensile tests were performed using a tensile stage (DDS-3) that could be automatically driven and **were installed** in a MIRA3 XMH field-emission scanning electron microscope with a loading maximum of 5 kN, as shown in Fig. 1(b).

2. Run-on sentences

The next group of mistakes is related to the run-on sentences, i.e., two or more independent clauses are run together without an appropriate conjunction or mark of punctuation between them, as shown in Table 9.3.

Table 9.3 Examples of Run-on Sentences

Original Version	Revised Version
1. *This design methodology must be comprehensive, **there are** three section **presents** the findings of the research, focusing on fabric design, structural design and technical design.	This design methodology must be comprehensive. **There are** three section**s** **presenting** the findings of the research, focusing on fabric design, structural design and technical design.
2. *2, 3-butanediol, a chemical product from biomass, was found in Klebsiella pneumoniae by Harden and Walpole at 1906**, several studies have also shown** that has been exploited **for** many fields.	2, 3-butanediol, a chemical product from biomass, was found in Klebsiella pneumoniae by Harden and Walpole **in** 1906. **Several studies have also shown** that **2, 3-butanediol** has been exploited **in** many fields.
3. *Photograms are also named camera-less photography that was produced without a camera or lenses, **the artist could create** images from shadows and silhouettes of objects **that were** by placing 2D or 3D objects directly **on** between the light source and light-sensitive paper or film, **and then exposing it**.	Photograms are also named cameraless photography that was produced without a camera or lenses. **The artist could create** images from shadows and silhouettes of objects ~~that were~~ by placing 2D or 3D objects directly ~~on~~ between the light source and light-sensitive paper or film **before exposing it**.

3. Attributive clauses

The problem of using "that" and "which/who" in attributive clauses is also commonly observed in students' academic writings. The first rule to remember is that "that" and "which/who" should only refer to the noun immediately preceding them. As shown in the following example in Table 9.4, the implied meaning of the original version is "Smith and Jones had died under surgery", which is ridiculous, given the context. Therefore, the attributive clause "who had died under surgery" should be moved forward and placed immediately after the noun "patients", as exemplified in the revised version.

Table 9.4　Example of Mistakes in Attributive Clause

Original Version	Revised Version
*A group of patients were compiled using this procedure, as proposed by Smith and Jones (2010), **who** had died under surgery.	A group of patients, **who** had died under surgery, were compiled using this procedure, as proposed by Smith and Jones (2010).

The second rule is concerned with the difference between "that" and "which". "That" is only used in defining clauses, whereas "which" can introduce both non-defining clauses and defining clauses. While a defining clause (also called an essential clause) gives information essential to the meaning of the sentence, non-defining clauses (also called nonessential clauses) do not limit the meaning of the sentence. You might lose interesting details if you remove them, but the meaning of the sentence wouldn't change. Sometimes, non-defining clauses are set off by commas. By identifying your clauses as defining or non-defining, you can easily remember when to use "that" and when to use "which". Here is an example. While you are reading the following two sentences, think about the question: How many sisters does the speaker have?

✓ ①My sister **that** lives in Pasadena is a researcher.

②My sister**, who** lives in Pasadena, is a researcher.

In sentence ①, you understand that the speaker has at least one other sister. Specifically, the sister he or she's talking about is distinguished from his or her other sisters by being a researcher. If you remove the clause "that lives in Pasadena", you would lose the implication that he or she has more than one sister. In sentence ②, being a researcher is simply a description of the speaker's sister. There's no implication that the speaker has more than one sister.

Here is another example commonly seen in the Results section of research articles. While you are reading, please think about the following question: Which one indicates all of the parameters are not self-explanatory?

③The table below gives details of the parameters **that** are not self-explanatory.

④The table below gives details of the parameters**, which** are not self-explanatory.

In sentence ③, you understand that the parameters can be divided into two categories: self-explanatory and non-self-explanatory. Specifically, the parameters the writer is talking about (included in the table) are distinguished from other parameters by being not self-explanatory. If you remove the clause "that are not self-explanatory", you would lose the implication that the parameters can be divided into self-explanatory and non-self-explanatory. In sentence ④, being not self-explanatory is simply a description of the parameters the writer is talking about (included in the table). There's no implication that there are other self-explanatory parameters, which are not included in the table.

9.1.3 Textual Level

1. Pronouns

Pronouns are the greatest source of ambiguity in academic writing. To write an ambiguity-free sentence, you need to remember the following rules:

- Do not use a pronoun before the noun it refers to has been mentioned (as exemplified in the first sentence in Table 9.5).
- Do not use a pronoun when there is more than one noun that the pronoun could refer to (as exemplified in the second sentence in Table 9.5).
- Ensure it is clear what "this" refers to in phrases such as "this study" (as exemplified in the third sentence in Table 9.5).
- Avoid "the former" and "the latter" (as exemplified in the fourth sentence in Table 9.5).

Table 9.5 Examples of Ambiguity Caused by Pronouns

Original Version	Revised Version	Reason for Modification
1. *Although **it** is a very stable and chemically inert material, focused studies have verified that the composition of **beeswax** found in…	Although **beeswax** is a very stable and chemically inert material, focused studies have verified that the composition of **beeswax** found in…	The pronoun "**it**" is used in the original version before the noun it refers to (beeswax) has been mentioned.
2. *There are two ways to learn a language: take private lessons or learn it in the country where the language is spoken, **but this** entails spending a lot of money.	There are two ways to learn a language: take private lessons or learn it in the country where the language is spoken. **However, living in a foreign country** entails spending a lot of money.	There is more than one noun that the pronoun "**this**" could refer to: • take private lessons • learn it in the country where the language is spoken
3. *Smith el al. (2018) explored the influence of institutional pressures from different stakeholders. **In this study** it was highlighted how institutional pressures generally strengthen the internalization of proactive environmental practices.	Smith el al. (2018) explored the influence of institutional pressures from different stakeholders. **Their study** highlighted how institutional pressures generally strengthen the internalization of proactive environmental practices.	It is not clear what "**this**" refers to in "this study" in the original version. "**This study**" may refer to Smith et al.'s study or the current study the author is writing about.

(Continued)

Original Version	Revised Version	Reason for Modification
4. *Weed control in maize can be both direct (e.g., mechanical tools or flaming) and indirect methods (Sartorius, 2020)… **The latter** include any practices that prevent…	Weed control in maize can be **extremely challenging and relies on an integrated strategy through the application of both direct** (e.g., mechanical tools or flaming) and indirect methods (Sartorius, 2020)… **Indirect methods** include any practices that prevent…	When using words such as "**the latter**", you are assuming that the reader has actually read the previous sentence. Readers may simply be browsing the text, and if they see "**the latter**", they won't know what it refers to.

A commonly used strategy to avoid ambiguity is to replace pronouns with the nouns that they refer to. Repeating the nouns is not considered a bad style in academic English.

2. Dangling modifiers

A dangling modifier refers to the subordinate phrase that does not appear to be modifying the subject. As shown in the following examples in Table 9.6, the subordinate phrases in bold seem not to be modifying the subjects respectively.

Table 9.6   Examples of Dangling Modifiers

Original Version	Revised Version	Reason for Modification
1. ***Using commercial software,** the electric-thermal-mechanical coupling of the 3D bonding wires under normal operation and under the effect of rectangular voltage pulses is calculated.	Using commercial software, **we calculated** the electricthermal-mechanical coupling of the 3D bonding wires under both the normal operation and the effect of rectangular voltage pulses.	The subordinate phrase "**Using commercial software**" seems not to be modifying the subject "**the electric-thermal-mechanical coupling of the 3D bonding wires under normal operation and under the effect of rectangular voltage pulses**".

(Continued)

Original Version	Revised Version	Reasons for Modification
2. ***Considering the complexity of analyzing the corresponding continuum dynamics,** the finite element method [22-25] (FEM) was applied to develop the strategies to modulate bandgaps.	Considering the complexity of analyzing the corresponding continuum dynamics, **we applied** the finite element method [22-25] (FEM) to develop the strategies to modulate bandgaps.	The subordinate phrase "**Considering the complexity of analyzing the corresponding continuum dynamics**" seems not to be modifying the subject "**the finite element method [22-25] (FEM)**".
3. ***To record images of pathological slices (several cm² in size) with a Gaussian beam,** there would be two problems: (1) it is susceptible to move out of focus… (2) a single 2D imaging cannot completely capture all axial information of the samples.	**Recording** images of pathological slices (several cm² in size) with a Gaussian beam **would induce two problems**: (1) it is susceptible to move out of focus… (2) a single 2D imaging cannot completely capture all axial information of the samples.	The subordinate phrase "**To record images of pathological slices (several cm² in size) with a Gaussian beam**" seems not to be modifying the subject "**there would be**".

3. Misplaced modifiers

A misplaced modifier is a word, phrase, or clause that is improperly separated from the word it modifies or describes. Because of the separation, sentences with this error often sound awkward, ridiculous, or confusing. Furthermore, they can be illogical. This kind of mistakes can usually be corrected by moving the modifier to a more sensible place in the sentence, generally next to the word it modifies. There are several kinds of misplaced modifiers, as shown in the following examples in Table 9.7.

Table 9.7 Examples of Misplaced Modifiers

Types of Misplaced Modifiers	Original Version	Revised Version
Misplaced adjectives	When **gasoline ample** supplies returned, consumers again bought **American large** cars.	When **ample gasoline** supplies returned, consumers again bought **large American** cars.
Misplaced adverbs (Watch out for adverbs such as "only", "just", "nearly", "merely", and "almost". They are often misplaced and cause an unintended meaning.)	I **only** contributed $10 to the fund for orphaned children. (Implied meaning: I only contributed the money.)	I contributed **only** $10 to the fund for orphaned children. (Implied meaning: I contributed only $10.)
Misplaced phrases	People have different attitudes towards GM foods **in Western Europe and Central and Eastern Europe.**	People **in Western Europe and Central and Eastern Europe** have different attitudes towards GM foods.
Misplaced clauses	Sixteen years later Mary Lyon founded Mount Holyoke Female Seminary, the first true women's college with **directors and a campus who would sustain the college even after Lyon's death**.	Sixteen years later Mary Lyon founded Mount Holyoke Female Seminary, the first true women's college with **a campus and directors who would sustain the college even after Lyon's death**.

4. Cohesion and coherence

Cohesion and coherence are two important things considered while writing any content and are properties of written material considered in discourse analysis and text linguistics. Cohesion is how you put your ideas and views collectively together when framing your sentences, and coherence is the superset of cohesion which includes cohesive sentences and other properties like consistency and understandability of the content and how to use logically connected and related sentences while representing your ideas and transiting from one idea to another. Table 9.8 provides a list of commonly used cohesive markers.

Table 9.8 Commonly Used Cohesive Markers

Addition	Generalization
✓ New methods involving traditional farm animals are **also** being found. ✓ Being considerate means taking the broad readership of the target journal into consideration **and** describing the problem configuration adequately. ✓ These highly versatile finishing touches have many uses **besides** aesthetic appeal. ✓ **In addition**, medical examinations and records are often grossly inadequate. ✓ **Additionally**, small businesses support passing comprehensive immigration reform.	✓ **As a rule**, the simplest representation is always chosen. ✓ There are four main academic journals covering inverse problems **in general**. ✓ Modern industrial printing **mainly** uses direct printing techniques. ✓ **More often than not,** these are manifestations of ideological struggles. ✓ **On the whole**, impartiality has been well observed. ✓ Natural resource activity was very solid **overall**.
Comparison	**Illustration**
✓ **Both** X **and** Y share a number of key features. ✓ The effects of X on human health **are similar to** those of Y. ✓ Young children learning their first language need simplified input. **Likewise**, low level adult L2 learners need graded input supplied in most cases by a teacher. ✓ The mode of processing used by the right brain **is comparable to** that used by the left brain.	✓ Pavlov found that if a stimulus, **for example** the ringing of a bell, preceded the food, the… ✓ **In this case**, the scientist examined over 500 responses. ✓ **For example**, Smith and Jones (2004) conducted a series of semi-structured interviews in… ✓ The effectiveness of the X technique **has been exemplified** in a report by Smith et al. (2010). ✓ The evidence of X can be clearly seen **in the case of…**
Contrast	**Concession**
✓ It is very difficult to get away from calendar time in literate societies. **By contrast**, many people in oral communities have little idea of the calendar year of their birth.	✓ This was quite an achievement, **given that** travelling facilities were sparse. ✓ This analysis is still **admittedly** incomplete in many respects.

	(Continued)
✓ There are a number of important **differences** between X and Y. ✓ **On the other hand**, color accuracy was still pretty poor. ✓ **Whereas** oral societies tend to be more concerned with the present, literate societies have a very definite awareness of the past. ✓ All four neighboring municipalities contain extensive rural areas **despite** recent urbanization. ✓ In contrast to earlier findings, **however**, no evidence of X was detected. ✓ **However**, this system also has a number of serious drawbacks.	✓ **In spite of** abandoning precision attacks, accuracy nevertheless improved. ✓ Many online stores offer free delivery **regardless** of your local area.
Summary	
✓ **To conclude** this section, the literature identifies… ✓ **In summary**, it has been shown from this review that… ✓ **Thus** far, the thesis has argued that… ✓ **In conclusion**, considered institutional reform is necessary and urgent.	

Coherence mainly deals with logic and appropriate organization of the sentences to form meaningful and understandable content. The need for logic underlying the text is highly underscored in academic writings. It is suggested that the written texts should follow the writer's cognitive process strictly. As shown in the first example in Table 9.9, the logic shown in the original version starts with a brief introduction of the web-based speed test approach (the first sentence in the first paragraph), followed by statements on the working procedure of average speed in consecutive HTTP sessions [the italicized section in the original version (OV)], and the specific method used to research a typical example of web-based speed test approach (the underlined section in the OV). It is suggested to move the second paragraph in the original version (the underlined section in the OV; about the specific method used to research a typical example of web-based speed test approach) forward, followed by the introduction to the working procedure of average speed in consecutive HTTP sessions (the italicized section in the OV). It is only possible to get the mechanism of web-based speed test approach after you study one typical example of this approach. The thread of logic will not follow if you reverse the procedure.

A similar suggestion regarding the logic was also made in the second example in Table 9.9. The second sentence in the original version (the underlined section in the OV) is recommended to be moved to the next paragraph after the specific method of exploring the implementation of Fast.com (the italicized section in the OV) has been introduced first. Unless this statement is posted on the official website of Fast.com, it is illogical to place this piece of information before you introduce the methods, either by studying the source code or conducting black-box benchmark tests.

Table 9.9 Comparison Between the Original and the Revised Version in Terms of Coherence

Original Version	Revised Version
1. The simplest approach of web-based speed test approach is to send/receive a fixed-size file to/from a fixed server via HTTP. *During the test, the server/user sends one or more fixed-size files to the user/server via HTTP with a single thread. Each file starts to be transferred only when the previous transmission is completed. ... After the test, the user's Internet speed is measured by the average upload/download speed for all file transmission.* As a typical example of this approach, thinkbroadband.com is well-known and widely-used as an Internet speed test website. In order to uncover its workflow, we use the Chrome DevTools to monitor all the network activities during the test. By carefully filtering the network data sources, ... This specific speed test process is in consistent with the approach above.	The simplest approach of web-based speed test approach is to send/receive a fixed size file to/from a fixed-server via HTTP, which is adopted by thinkbroadband.com. As shown in Figure 1a, *there is a single HTTP session and the Internet speed is measured by the average upload/download speed for transferring a 20-MB file.* This simple approach incurs the least time and traffic costs, but bears three obvious shortcomings.

(Continued)

Original Version	Revised Version
2. Compared with SFtest, Fast.com employs a more delicate and complex approach with parallel HTTP sessions. <u>Fast.com is powered by Netflix, a famous streaming service website and the test server selection process is similar to speedof.me.</u> When exploring the inner implementation of Fast.com, *we study carefully on its source code as well as conduct comprehensive black-box benchmark tests.* Given that we conducted our research in January 2018, some slight differences may occur when we compare the latest version of Fast.com with the version we studied on. Based on the source code and test results, we figure out that Fast.com excels SFtest in two main aspects: the dynamic parallel HTTP sessions and the so-called "stable" average speed.	Compared with SFtest, Fast.com employs a more delicate and complex approach with progressive HTTP sessions. *We get the client-side JavaScript source code of Fast.com using the Chrome DevTools in January 2018, and discover that the code is not encrypted, thus greatly facilitating us to investigate the implementation of Fast.com in a white-box manner. We also conduct black-box benchmark experiments to dig deeper.* <u>According to our research, Fast.com is powered by Netflix, a major video streaming service provider in the US.</u> Before a download speed test, Fast.com conducts a pre-test to select the test server.

9.1.4 Academic Conventions

The mechanics of writing are the rules that must be followed while preparing research articles.

1. In-text citations and end-text references

Here is an example of in-text citation. How many mistakes can you spot in this example?

✓ ***Xiaoxiao Qian etc**. proposed a new and efficient method which used CsPbBr$_3$ quantum dots for the preparation of photocatalysts **(2020)** [12].

First, the writer combines the name-referencing style and the numerical-referencing style together (You may refer to Section 8.1.2 for a quick review), which is not appropriate. You can choose either name-referencing style or numerical-referencing style, but never use them together in one research article. Second, only family name of the scholar is required for in-text citation. That is to say, only "Qian" is required in the example above and the scholar's given name (Xiaoxiao) has to be deleted. Third, the writer confuses "etc." with "et al.", both of which are commonly used Latin expressions. "etc." is short for the Latin phrase "et cetera", meaning a number of unspecified additional persons or things, whereas "et al." means "and others" and is often used in bibliographical information. Therefore, "et al." should be the correct expression in this context.

2. Informal expressions

The writer should avoid informal expressions and colloquial styles in academic writings. Wallwork and Southern (2020: 47) listed three problems with informal expressions and colloquial styles as follows:

- They do not match the academic style of a research article and thus may distract the reader;
- Because they are non-academic, there is a chance that your reader may not know what they mean;
- You may mistranslate from their own language and thus make a mistake in their English writing.

Here is a list of expressions selected from students' writings that contain informal expressions and colloquial styles.

Table 9.10 Examples of Informal Expressions

Original Version	Revised Version	Reason for Modification
1. ***It's** necessary to study…	**It is** necessary to study…	Contractions, such as "**it's**" and "**can't**", are considered too informal for academic writing style. You should use the un-contracted form.
2. *LDPC codes **can't** avoid error floor…	LDPC codes **cannot** avoid error floor…	
3. *Compared with numerical models, statistical models **like** deep neural networks have exhibited…	Compared with numerical models, statistical models, **such as** deep neural networks have exhibited…	"**Like**" is a colloquial style. "**Such as**" is a better and formal alteration for "**like**".
4. ***As we all know,** the differences of the system context may lay a foundation to shape the collaborative governance regime…	**It is an established fact that** the differences of the system context may lay a foundation to shape the collaborative governance regime…	"**As we all know**" is a colloquial style. It seems to be better and more formal to start the sentence with "**It is an established fact that…**"

9.2 Reflections and Practice

I Choose the correct answer for each sentence.

1. There are no reliable _____ for the number of deaths in the battle.
   A. statistic   B. statistical   C. statistics   D. statistician

2. These financial market _____ could pose macro-economic risks.
   A. phenomenon   B. phenomena   C. criterion   D. criteria

3. According to Pew Research, most Americans believe the _____ system unfairly favors the wealthy, but 60% believe that most people can make it if they're willing to work hard.
   A. economical   B. economic   C. economics   D. economists

4. Of the 1,000 individuals polled, many expressed apprehensiveness toward Glass' high-definition camera, which can snap photos with the wink of an eye. Others feared the _____ of facial recognition applications.
   A. emergence   B. emergency   C. emergent   D. urgent

5. _____ hundreds of millions of people use their smartphones shopping, texting and searching for information.
   A. Everyday   B. Every day   C. Some time   D. Sometime

II Identify mistakes in the following sentences and correct them.

1. Ultra-low phase noise and ultra-narrow spectral linewidth laser is required to ensure the effect of each interaction is consistent.

2. Wind is one of the cheapest and easily available renewable energy source which fulfills the needs of mankind.

3. Then we applied eye drop of the rosmarinic acid everyday and photographed every week by slit lamp.

4. A number of investigations on young people tends to subjective judgments or material analyses, and little work has been done to go deep into the audience.

5. In this article, Higgs' method is used to analysis systems of spin-1/2 particles.

6. Fleischman et al. found that the in-plane elastic model produces larger frame lateral and inter-layer displacements, and the influence of the slab model is most significant when the aspect ratio is large or the number of layers is small.

7. Therefore the poor reactivity of copper (II) moieties probably due to the weak oxidation capacity of low-valent Cu (II) center.

8. The present research was devoted to find a way with good repeatability and reliability to product microcapsules effectively.

9. The UV (ultraviolet)-visible spectrum is an useful approach to study the optical properties of the cluster.

10. Moreover, it is strongly discouraged to restrain horses while monitoring their cardiac activity, because this unnatural condition leads to stressing stimuli.

11. Our method outperforms current state-of-the-art methods with a 89.66% accuracy on RAF, a 89.15% accuracy on Oulu-CASIA.

12. The fans stood in line to buy tickets to the show for twenty minutes.

13. The student pleaded with the instructor who cheated on the test.

14. We gave the old clothes to a local charity that had been piled up in the basement.

15. The job scarcely took an hour to complete.

(III) Revise the original version of an abstract and provide your corrections and feedback in the right column.

Original Version	Corrections and Feedback
computational Fluid Dynamics (CFD) is a technology used to solve the NS function with the numerical method to describe the flow in disconcrete method, so that the motion of the flow can be predicted. AS it is know, meshing is a significant preconditioner in CFD. There are two different categories of mesh in CFD: structured mesh and unstructrued mesh. In this paper, we introduce our method applied in unstructrued meshes due to its wide range of applicatiion in industry. The Finite element method and finite volume method are universally applied in unstructrued meshes. Comparing to finite element, finite volume can solve NS functions more properly Second order FV is the common choice of commercial software that cannot fit the demand for precision. Hence, an increasing number of researchers are interested in high-order accuracy FV	

(Continued)

Original Version	Corrections and Feedback
method. This study investigated the VFV method combining the volume intergration with the face intergration. We found this variational function can stay unchanged in different order accuracy. This property makes analysis of dispersion and dissipation concise. It was found that using a blend of these two different intergration would come to same accuracy with less computational cost. Meanwhile, the dissipation and dispersion of this method is also better than previous VFV method.	

IV Rearrange the following sentences into a coherent paragraph.

1. If not, then think about it and rehearse until you can.
2. For one, if you can't, it is questionable how much you "own" your project.
3. Nobody wants to hear about other people's project for the whole duration of the lunch break.
4. Can you explain the essence of your project and its implications in 60 seconds?
5. Finally, you should be confident in "pitching" to your peers, as well as to non-scientists.
6. Have you understood the key elements, is the bigger picture clear in your mind?
7. Second, treat meeting people at conferences like speed dating: you get their undivided attention for no more than a few minutes.
8. This means you have to use a different approach depending on your audience.

V Underline all the cohesive markers in the following passage.

This research has explored students' perceived benefits and challenges in an Assessment as learning (AaL)-oriented writing course. Most participants held a positive attitude towards the adoption of AaL strategies in writing. The findings imply the potential of associating criteria-referenced tasks with the process writing approach to help students develop their writing quality and enhance assessment and feedback literacy. On the other hand, the perceived challenges suggest students' need for continuing guidance in terms of emotional support, cognitive scaffolding and meta-cognitive supervision when they are involved in AaL activities.

The limitations of the study merit some attention. First, the study examined students' perceptions after the course, which cannot trace the evolving process of their affective, cognitive and behavioral changes in participating in the AaL activities over time. Second, the data collected from the six participants (all females) may not fully represent all students' perceptions and experiences in the course. Third, the teacher in the study did not fully implement the AaL strategies in the whole writing process due to the summative assessment requirement in the program.

Future research can employ multiple sources of data (e.g., observation and interviews) to track the process of students' learning engagement in a supportive learning context where teachers can fully implement the AaL-oriented approach to teaching writing. It would also be interesting to explore some extreme cases, particularly those with strong negative experiences in AaL-oriented environments.

Unit 10
Chinglish vs. English

📝 Warm-up Questions

1. What is Chinglish?

2. What are the features of Chinglish?

3. What are some of the salient differences between English and Chinese in terms of sentence structure?

10.1 Overview

10.1.1 Interlingual Errors of Chinglish

Chinglish is the interference of the mother tongue with English learning. Many learners are very liable to be influenced by Chinese when writing in English. As a result, interlingual errors occur inevitably in English writing. Below are some typical examples of Chinglish:

- ✓ * Good good study, day day up.
- ✓ * Some young people addict alcohol.
- ✓ * I'm reading my Ph.D. degree.
- ✓ * Nuclear energy makes a lot of electricity.
- ✓ * The preparation work for the experiment is complete.

10.1.2 Positive and Negative Transfer Between Two Languages

From the viewpoint of behaviorist linguistics, there exist positive transfer and negative transfer between two languages. Positive transfer is the facilitating influence of lexical and syntactical similarities between the mother tongue and the target language. However, negative transfer of the mother tongue is one of the causes for errors. It really accounts for the interlingual errors occurring in learners' writing. Learners, below the intermediate level of English, are much more liable to be influenced by the negative transfer of the mother tongue, since they have "less previous second language knowledge to draw on in making hypotheses about rules" and have to "make correspondingly more use of their first language knowledge" (Littlewood, 1994: 25). When they are incapable of thinking of any other ways to express their intended meaning, they may resort to the native language habits to collocate words and create sentences, or when they think entirely in Chinese while writing in English they are liable to write out English, sentences which are word-for-word transfer from Chinese. Thus "Chinglish" in learners' writing is not caused by translation but by the superficial negative transfer of the mother tongue.

1. Positive transfer

If the first language habits help the second language learning, that is positive transfer. Learners should make good use of positive transfer between two languages. Read the following examples of positive transfer between Chinese and English.

- ✓ 满瓶不响，半瓶晃荡。

    A full vessel sounds least; a half vessel sounds most.

- ✓ 趁热打铁。

Strike while the iron is hot.

✓ 随着研究继续，我们希望获得更多关于……的翔实可靠的信息。

As research continues, we may hope to gain more detailed and reliable information about…

2. Negative transfer

If the first language habits hinder the second language learning, negative transfer occurs. Negative transfer is also called interference. Read the following examples:

✓ 一朝被蛇咬，十年怕井绳。

Once bitten, twice shy.

✓ 江山易改，本性难移。

The leopard won't change its spots.

In the two examples above, there is no need to have a word-for-word transfer between Chinese and English. The two languages have different expressions towards the same idea.

✓ * Before I have to give a speech, I always feel nervous, **as if a little rabbit were jumping in my stomach**.

✓ * This is a **zero breakthrough** in breeding high-yielding wheat varieties.

These two examples above illustrate the negative transfer between Chinese and English. The normal English translation of the two sentences respectively should be:

✓ Before I have to give a speech / Before giving a speech, I always have a butterfly in my stomach.

✓ This is a breakthrough in breeding high-yielding wheat varieties.

10.2 Sample Analysis of Representational Chinglish Structures

Chinglish is characteristic of the interferences of Chinese culture and Chinese thinking pattern. These interferences may produce unidiomatic and inappropriate expressions of English. In broad outline, the sample analysis below categorizes Chinglish into different kinds which may, however, overlap to a certain degree.

10.2.1 Interferences of Chinese Culture

Take the idioms as examples and look at the following sentences taken from Chinese students' writings:

- ✓ * That mountain looks to be higher than this mountain.
- ✓ * She is like an ant on a hot pan.
- ✓ * Some prefer radish, but others prefer cabbage.
- ✓ * When the tiger is absent from the mountain, the monkey proclaims itself king.
- ✓ * Renting a room, you will be living under the house owner's eyes.

Influenced by different cultures and customs, people speaking different languages would deploy different metaphors to express the same ideas. Less acquainted with the culture and idioms of the target language, many Chinese learners are very inclined to have a word-for-word transfer of the native idioms. Sometimes it is, indeed, necessary to adopt literal translation of Chinese idioms. However, the acquaintance of the native culture and target culture prefers liberal translation to literal translation in many cases. These five examples above could be revised as follows:

- ✓ The grass on the other side of the valley is greener.
- ✓ She is like a cat on hot bricks.
- ✓ Tastes differ. / One man's meat is another man's poison.
- ✓ When the cat is away, mice will play.
- ✓ Renting a room, you will be living under the landlord's nose.

10.2.2 Interferences of Chinese Thinking Pattern

Lexically and syntactically, English should be concise whereas Chinglish is superfluous (Pinkham, 2000). Even if grammatically correct, Chinglish contains many redundant words and expressions, which could be attributable to Chinese thinking. Below is a brief introduction to the high-incidence cases of Chinese thinking interference from different perspectives, a few of which are selected or adapted from Pinkham's work (Pinkham, 2000) and most of which originate from students' compositions.

1. Redundant nouns

Redundant nouns may be used in Chinglish sentences. Read the following sentences and identify the redundant nouns in these sentences.

- ✓ * Playing computer games is a very popular way of lifestyle among the young people.
- ✓ * China has a long period of civilization that may be called 5,000 years old which is greatly admired by people all over the world.
- ✓ * We still need strengthen the building of national defense (Pinkham, 2000).
- ✓ * Culture shock is a common phenomenon in our life.
- ✓ * Governments in different countries are accelerating the pace of economic reform

because of the global economic crisis (Pinkham, 2000).

These five examples could be revised as follows:

✓ Playing computer games is very popular among the young people.

✓ China has a 5,000-year-old civilization which is greatly admired by people all over the world.

✓ We still need strengthen the national defense.

✓ Culture shock is common in our life.

✓ Governments in different countries are accelerating the economic reform because of the global economic crisis.

2. Redundant verbs

Redundant verbs may be used in Chinglish sentences. Read the following sentences and identify the redundant verbs in these sentences.

✓ * The birds made their nest with the mud and short sticks.

✓ * It is impossible to accomplish the transformation of the whole society overnight (Pinkham, 2000).

✓ * This can make us regain fresh spirits.

✓ * The Japanese helicopters tried to put water on the reactors at the Fukushima Daiichi Nuclear Power Plant.

These four examples could be revised as follows:

✓ The birds nest with the mud and twigs.

✓ It is impossible to transform the whole society overnight.

✓ This can refresh us.

✓ The Japanese helicopters tried to water the reactors at the Fukushima Daiichi Nuclear Power Plant.

3. Redundant modifiers

All too often, different kinds of redundant modifiers may be included in Chinglish sentences. Read the following sentences and identify the redundant modifiers in these sentences.

✓ * Staying up too late at night may injure your body.

✓ * We successfully developed the program.

✓ * We will continue to further improve bio-fuel processing technologies.

✓ * He hurriedly scribbled his witty remarks on a piece of paper.

✓ * It is reported that too many excessive X-ray can cause some serious diseases.

These five examples should be revised as follows:

✓ Staying up too late may be harmful to your health.

✓ We developed the program.

✓ We will further improve bio-fuel processing technologies.

✓ He scribbled his witty remarks on a piece of paper.

✓ It is reported that excessive X-ray can cause some serious diseases.

4. Weak verbs + redundant modifiers / inaccurate objects

In many cases, writers may fail to find a specific verb in a sentence. Likewise, they could not find an accurate verb and its appropriate object in a sentence. Read the following sentences and identify the weak verbs and the redundant modifiers or inaccurate objects in these sentences.

✓ * The municipal government will support the project with money.

✓ * The architecture in Switzerland includes both classic and novelty.

✓ * Many refugees came in great numbers to Italy.

✓ * From then on, she never dared to see my eyes straight.

These four examples should be revised as follows:

✓ The municipal government will finance the project.

✓ The architecture in Switzerland blends both antiquity and novelty.

✓ Many refugees streamed/flooded to Italy.

✓ From then on, she never dared to look me in the eyes.

5. Mistaken/unnecessary qualifiers

Some qualifiers, such as "quite" and "rather", are to weaken the force of a statement in some cases. Some other qualifiers, such as "perhaps", "possibly" and "maybe", are often unnecessary in certain contexts. Writers sometimes misuse these qualifiers. Read the following sentences and identify the mistaken/unnecessary qualifiers in these sentences.

✓ * Antibiotics are quite an important discovery in the 20th century.

✓ * We rather attached importance to this aspect when considering this problem.

✓ * Perhaps this process will take time and go through several stages.

✓ * This talk will possibly pave the way for new diplomatic relations between these two countries.

✓ * If this problem is not solved, maybe other problems will follow.

These five examples could be revised as follows:

✓ Antibiotics are an important discovery in the 20th century.

- ✓ We attached great importance to this aspect when considering this problem.
- ✓ This process may take time and go through several stages.
- ✓ This talk may pave the way for new diplomatic relations between these two countries.
- ✓ If this problem is not solved, other problems may follow.

6. Redundant sentence structures

Sometimes writers are very inclined to have a word-for-word transfer of the mother tongue and, therefore, produce redundant and unidiomatic sentences. Read the following sentences and identify the redundant sentence structures.

- ✓ * The usual methods used for… exist some disadvantages, they waste time, or they are not accurate.
- ✓ * From his accent to see, he could come from Hubei Province.
- ✓ * Some overseas students have met a problem: It is difficult for them to choose whether to return to their countries or go on receiving more education here.
- ✓ * We should not use the chopsticks which can be used only once.
- ✓ * Many undergraduates who are in the first year of their college life find the required courses they have no interest at all in.

These five examples could be revised as follows:

- ✓ The usual methods used for… has some disadvantages, either time-consuming or inaccurate.
- ✓ His accent reveals he comes from Hubei Province.
- ✓ Some overseas students are in a dilemma of whether to return home or stay for further study.
- ✓ We should not use the disposable chopsticks.
- ✓ Many freshmen find they have no interest at all in the compulsory courses.

7. Mistaken collocations

Under the influence of Chinese thinking pattern, mistaken collocations account for a large portion of Chinglish. Read the following sentences and identify the mistaken collocations in these sentences.

- ✓ * The movie has received divergent discussion after its public screening.
- ✓ * Some students indulge in the computer games, cost much money and delay many lessons.
- ✓ * The media acted a vital role in our life.
- ✓ * China got the power of being responsible for the 2008 Olympic Games.

✓ * Sophisticated experiments are fulfilled regularly in the laboratory.

These five examples should be revised as follows:

✓ The movie has aroused divergent opinions after its release.

✓ Some students indulge in the computer games, waste much money and miss many lessons.

✓ The media played a vital role in our life.

✓ China won the bid for the 2008 Olympic Games.

✓ Sophisticated experiments are performed regularly in the laboratory.

8. Unnecessary repetition of the same ideas

Some writers duplicate the same idea unnecessarily in a sentence. Read the following sentences and identify the unnecessary repetition of the same ideas in these sentences.

✓ * In my opinion, I think advertisements have both advantages and disadvantages.

✓ * One reason why these students are poor in their academic performance is because of the fact that they are addicted to computer games.

✓ * Statistics show that in the decade from 2010 to 2020 the workforce in this company doubled: In 2020 there were twice as many employees as in 2010.

✓ * We must control food waste in the canteens so as to save food.

✓ * We should pay enough attention to this problem but not neglect this problem.

These five examples could be revised as follows:

✓ In my opinion, advertisements have both advantages and disadvantages.

✓ One reason why these students are poor in their academic performance is that they are addicted to computer games.

✓ Statistics show that in the decade from 2010 to 2020 the workforce in this company doubled.

✓ We must control food waste in the canteens.

✓ We should pay enough attention to this problem.

10.2.3 Inappropriate Expressions

Inappropriate expressions may emerge due to the negative influence of Chinese culture and thinking pattern. Look at the following examples.

✓ * Our department also has other relevant courses of deeper level.

✓ * WSN is such a new and interesting area that I will keep on researching in this field deeper and deeper.

- * This will happen in the not too distant future.
- * Dalian is a city located at the end of Liaodong half island of Liaoning, a northeast province of China.
- * Our national flag flew with breeze.

These five examples could be revised as follows:

- Our department also has other relevant advanced courses.
- WSN is such a new and interesting area into which I will keep on probing.
- This will happen in the near future.
- Dalian is a city located at the end of Liaodong peninsular of Liaoning, a northeast province of China.
- Our national flag fluttered in the breeze.

10.2.4 Confusion Between Coordination and Subordination

Coordination is to link the ideas which are equal in weight while subordination is to put together ideas which are unequal in weight. A writer should distinguish the parallel ideas from the unparallel ideas and deploy the different sentence structures, and avoid both ineffective coordination and excessive subordination. Look at the following coordinate and subordinate expressions and decide on the unacceptable ones.

- ①We want to rid the world of pollution, so we must make some fundamental changes in the way many of us live.
- ②Tsinghua University is famous for her culture and history, and this is also represented by her architecture and scenery.
- ③In this study, we are not able to delineate the specific source of this anger or to determine the form in which this anger may have been expressed.
- ④Pessimism leads, by contrast, to hopelessness, sickness and failure, and is linked to depression, loneliness and painful shyness.
- ⑤In a long term study, researchers examined the health histories of a group of Harvard graduates, all of whom were in the top half of their class and in fine physical condition.
- ⑥In the front of the auditorium, it is the large grassy quadrangle, and some buildings locate along it.
- ⑦Thinking aloud test is one of the most valuable usability engineering methods and is now widely used which involves participants who speak about what they are doing and what they are thinking when they use human-computer interfaces.

- ✓ ⑧Although enlarging recruit should not deserve blame, but it is very important to carry out this plan in a suitable way so that it can avoid the relative problems, or it may bring the whole society serious after-effect which will deeply affect education in our country.
- ✓ ⑨If visitors succeed in getting some knowledge of the language and begin to get around by themselves, they are beginning to open the way into the new cultural environment.
- ✓ ⑩With the exception of the Anglo Saxons, the Germans are the largest ethnic group in the USA.

Among the ten sentences above, sentences ①, ② and ⑥ are ineffective coordination, sentence ⑦ is excessive subordination, and sentences ⑧ is both ineffective coordination and excessive subordination. The revised sentences are presented below:

- ✓ ①To rid the world of pollution, we must make some fundamental changes in the way many of us live.
- ✓ ②Tsinghua University is famous for her culture and history, which is also embodied in her architecture and scenery.
- ✓ ⑥In the front of the auditorium is the large grassy quadrangle along which locate some buildings.
- ✓ ⑦Thinking aloud test, currently in wide use, is one of the most valuable usability engineering methods. Participants involved in the test speak about what they are doing and thinking when using human-computer interfaces.
- ✓ ⑧Enlarging recruit should not deserve blame, but it should be carried out appropriately. Otherwise, its negative impact on the whole society may reach deep into the education.

10.3 Some Salient Differences Between English and Chinese

Many lexical and syntactical differences exist between English and Chinese. In terms of the differences at the syntactical level, some scholars compare English sentences to trees while Chinese sentences to bamboos (Pan, 2014; Fan, 1994; Chen, 1987). In this section, the differences mentioned are closely related to Chinglish production. In the absence of this knowledge, Chinese learners would be inclined to produce Chinglish expressions in English writing.

10.3.1 Reversed Word Order

In some cases, the word order between English and Chinese is reversed due to the different thinking patterns. Contrary to Chinese, English may express the ideas from the small-to-big point of view, near-to-far point of view, or weak-to-strong point of view. These cases may include a person's full name, forms of address, date, orientation, dish names, etc. Look at the following examples.

- ✓ Studies have shown that the right and left ear process sound differently.

  研究表明，左耳和右耳处理声音的方式是不同的。

- ✓ The movie *North and South* tells a series of stories during the Industrial Revolution in Great Britain.

  电影《南方与北方》讲述了英国工业革命时期发生的一系列故事。

- ✓ The iron and steel industry in China is in rapid development.

  中国的钢铁工业在飞速发展。

- ✓ It's my great honor to have been asked by Professor Smith to present our recent findings in sociolinguistics.

  非常荣幸，受史密斯教授邀请，我介绍一下我们近期在社会语言学领域的一些研究发现。

- ✓ This paper was published in June, 2018.

  这篇论文发表于 2018 年 6 月。

10.3.2 Postpositive Attributive in English

Many postpositive attributives in English should reverse the order when translated into Chinese. Look at the following examples.

- ✓ the matters to be discussed tomorrow

  明天要讨论的事情

- ✓ a case of theft

  盗窃案

- ✓ a country with a long history

  历史悠久的国家

- ✓ a lecture about sociolinguistics

  有关社会语言学的讲座

- ✓ the loss of many species

  诸多物种的消失

10.3.3 Static English and Dynamic Chinese

Relatively speaking, Chinese may use more dynamic words while English may use more static words (Yang & Yuan, 2007). In some cases, the actions are dominant in Chinese but covert in English. Sometimes, a Chinese sentence could have more than a verb, some of which may turn out to be a noun, a prepositional phrase or an adverbial phrase in an English sentence, or vice versa. Look at the following examples and compare the two languages.

- ✓ Failure to comply with the conditions will deteriorate the relations between the two countries.

  不遵守这些条件将会使两国之间的关系恶化。

- ✓ Enlightenment is also among the students in class discussion.

  课堂讨论中，学生之间也会互相启发。

- ✓ The ignorance of protecting the biodiversity would result in severe consequences.

  忽视保护生物的多样性将会导致严重的后果。

- ✓ This kind of butterfly is now a rare sight in this country.

  如今在这个国家，这种蝴蝶已经很罕见了。

- ✓ Poverty and ignorance are the enemies of progress.

  贫穷和愚昧阻碍进步。

- ✓ Safety measures were taken in compliance with the building regulations formulated by the country's Ministry of Construction.

  遵照国家建设部制定的建筑规程，他们采取了安全措施。

- ✓ He is a theater goer.

  他喜欢看电影。

- ✓ The pandemic is far not over yet.

  疫情远未结束。

- ✓ The union is on strike in pursuit of a 10% pay increase.

  工会在罢工，他们要求增加10%的工资。

- ✓ The sale is up by 20% this year.

  今年销售额提高了20%。

10.3.4 Multifunction of English Attributive Clauses

Apart from describing and modifying a noun, English attributive clauses may function as adverbial relations in some cases. The effective use of English attributive clauses helps to compose both idiomatic Chinese and English. Look at the following examples.

- ✓ The loss of the rainforests would mean the loss of most of the species that make their homes in the rainforests.

  热带雨林的消失意味着诸多物种的消失，因为这些物种以热带雨林为生存之地。

- ✓ Pirated software, which lowers the cost of users, cannot be installed in public computers because it is illegal.

  盗版软件尽管可以降低使用者的成本，但是不能被安装在公共电脑上，因为这样做是违法的。

- ✓ Microsoft Corporation has promoted a new Windows 11 operating system, where engineers will be able to test their programs.

  微软公司推出了全新的视窗 11 操作系统，工程师可以在该系统上测试他们的程序。

- ✓ The claim ought to succeed, in which case the damage will be substantial.

  索赔应该能成功。这样的话，索赔金额将会相当可观。

- ✓ A paragraph is composed of sentences that are composed of words and phrases.

  一个段落是由句子组成的，而句子是由单词和短语组成的。

10.3.5　Compact English and Relatively Loose Chinese

Relatively speaking, English grammar is explicit whereas Chinese grammar is, to a certain degree, implicit (Pan, 2014). In other words, English sentences, like a tree, lay much stress on the coherence and cohesion between ideas while Chinese sentences, like a bamboo, attach more importance to the idea expression. In many of the Chinese sentences, the logical connections between the ideas are underlying and unobvious. The awareness of the differences could, to some extent, prevent ineffective coordination and choppy sentences, influenced by Chinese thinking pattern, in English writing. Look at the following examples.

- ✓ 其实进来的是一个黑瘦的先生，八字须，戴着眼镜，挟着一摞大大小小的书。

  Actually, there entered a dark thin professor in glasses, with a moustache, carrying a pile of books under his arm.

- ✓ 例如，在森林中，较大的树木会掉落下残枝，在土壤中形成一个水分保护层，供其他植物利用。

  For example, within a forest the larger trees drop off little twigs and debris, making a layer that holds water in the soil for other plants to use.

- ✓ 中国北方水资源缺乏，南方水资源丰富。

  Northern China is water deficient while southern China is rich in water resources.

- ✓ 成年之后，掠水蜻蜓会飞到气候凉爽的山里度过夏季。

After emerging as an adult, a skimmer dragonfly will fly up into the mountain where the climate is cooler, staying there for the summer.

- ✓ 大熊猫咬碎并咀嚼竹子的枝叶，用牙齿把竹子的外皮剥掉，露出柔软的内部组织。

  Giant pandas crush and chew the stems and leaves of bamboos, peeling off the tough outer layers with their teeth to reveal the soft inner tissue.

10.3.6 Chinese Four-Character Sentences and English Words and Phrases

Many Chinese four-character sentences turn out to be phrases or even words. The awareness of the differences could also prevent choppy sentences and ineffective coordination in English writing. Look at the following examples.

- ✓ 中国疆域辽阔，人口众多，历史悠久，应该对人类有较大贡献。

  With a vast territory, a big population and a long history, China should make greater contribution to humanity.

- ✓ 天网恢恢，疏而不漏。

  Justice has long arms.

- ✓ 语言学习的进步是日积月累的过程，不可能一蹴而就。

  The progress in language learning is made over time, not overnight.

10.3.7 English Passive Sentences and Chinese Sentences with No Subjects

Many English passive sentences turn out to be Chinese sentences with no subjects, as indicated in the following examples.

- ✓ Approximately 50 volunteers have been recruited.

  大约招募了 50 位志愿者。

- ✓ Symptoms of depression were assessed with the Beck Depression Inventory-Ⅱ.

  采用贝克抑郁症量表Ⅱ评估了抑郁的症状。

- ✓ A mix-methods approach was used to study infant cognitive language development.

  使用混合法研究婴儿的语言认知发展过程。

- ✓ Thirty tests were conducted to evaluate the air pollution stress at different locations.

  进行了 30 项测试，以评估不同地点的空气污染程度。

- ✓ Community spirit should be strengthened.

  应该加强集体精神。

10.3.8 Inanimate Subjects in English and Chinese Sentences

Both English and Chinese sentences have inanimate subjects. However, the research of some Chinese scholars indicates that the inanimate subjects in English sentences outnumber the ones in Chinese sentences as a result of different cultures and thinking patterns (Peng, 2017). English sentences with inanimate subjects lay more stress on objectivity, logicality, and accuracy of the information. In contrast, Chinese sentences, relatively speaking, use more animate subjects. Compare the following examples.

- ✓ The country roads are taking me home. (inanimate subject)
- ✓ A detailed investigation of such disciplinary and culture variables is, however, beyond the scope of this study. (inanimate subject)
- ✓ The younger age of our sample and the certain cultural aspects of college life may account for some of these differences. (inanimate subject)
- ✓ Several important implications for research, policy, and prevention emerge from our findings. (inanimate subject)
- ✓ The frustration of not being able to relate to or communicate with other people can cause many teenagers to find refuge in alcohol. (inanimate subject)
- ✓ Many designers have also considered the issue of safety. (animate subject)
- ✓ 英语教学中，思维的碰撞和激发是思想达到新高度的助推器。(inanimate subject)
- ✓ 然而，优势和劣势是相对的，也是可以相互转化的。(inanimate subject)
- ✓ 我们常常把学员的"高自主性"视为网络课堂的重要优势。(animate subject)
- ✓ 从总体来看，英语教师已经能够借助直播课堂比较顺畅地完成英语教学。(animate subject)

On the basis of the above brief discussion, the following conclusions can be drawn:

- English focuses more on form, with more compact sentence structure, and thus more long sentences.
- Chinese focuses more on meaning, with relatively more loose sentence structure, and more short and medium sentences.
- Some verbs in a Chinese sentence appear as nouns, prepositional phrases or adverbial phrases in English, or vice versa.
- Some Chinese four-character short sentences turn out to be a word or a phrase in English.
- Sometimes, the word order and the attributive order between English and Chinese are reversed.

- English attributive clauses may function as adverbial relations in some cases.
- Many English passive sentences turn out to be Chinese sentences with no subjects.
- Inanimate subjects are more popular in English sentences.

The knowledge of these salient differences between English and Chinese would help to compose more idiomatic English sentences, reducing Chinglish expressions, to some extent.

10.4 Reflections and Practice

I Discuss the following questions.

1. What are some Chinglish expressions which are already accepted in English?
2. How can you eliminate Chinglish in your English writing?
3. How can you translate Chinese idioms into English?

II Improve the following sentences where necessary.

1. Better be the head of a cock than the tail of a dragon.
2. The same water can carry a boat and may also overturn it.
3. It seems like looking for a needle in a big sea.
4. One ant hole may cause the collapse of a thousand-li dyke.
5. Living without an aim is like sailing without a compass.
6. One cloud is enough to eclipse all the sun.
7. Without verification, the scientific research went into a blind alley.
8. Don't get upset about this result. It is never too late to mend.
9. An old frontiersman loses his horse; who knows it is a good thing or a bad thing.
10. This area's spending on education has increased, but only as a result of tearing down the east wall to mend the west wall.

III Match the phrases in Column A with the phrases in Column B to form sentences.

Column A	Column B
1. Good wine	A) but modesty takes heart.
2. Step by step	B) and frugality her left.

3. Count one's chickens　　　　　　　C) is always rugged.

4. Loquacity storms the ear,　　　　　D) does not sparkle.

5. A good medicine　　　　　　　　　E) the ladder is ascended.

6. Little chips　　　　　　　　　　　F) deserves another.

7. The path to glory　　　　　　　　　G) needs no bush.

8. An uncut germ　　　　　　　　　　H) before they are hatched.

9. One good turn　　　　　　　　　　I) light great fires.

10. Industry is fortune's right hand,　　J) tastes bitter.

IV Revise the following sentences to make them more idiomatic.

1. It makes me immediately remember my pleasant childhood memories of reading.

2. We will organize the basic essential points in three sections.

3. We must make up our minds to carry out the reform of the current system.

4. If paparazzi would keep not saying unkind things about celebrities, some of the celebrities would not be hurt.

5. In this way, clear concept can be formed and it helps the comprehending.

6. This country has placed an order of forbidding oil export since January.

7. The character of a modern society is highly changeable.

8. People's opposition to the war more and more increased day after day.

9. One should never bind himself in his own little circle; it will only make himself isolated from others.

10. Each vacuum pump has the feature of using environmentally-friendly materials and meets the requirement of Japanese design standards.

V Improve the underlined parts of the following sentences to make them more acceptable in professional papers.

1. Chongqing is in the upstream areas of the Yangtze River.

2. He is one of the cleverest people in the country.

3. This film caused heated debate among filmmakers and critics.

4. Clearly, no one wants to come near a person with a fearful face.

5. Because the traffic is crowded, people have to waste more time on their way home.

6. Severe brain damage turned him into a plant person.

7. As is well-known, who wins information wars, who wins the 21st century.

8. Seventy thousand people got cancer because of the Chernobyl.

9. They have little ability to judge whether the good or the bad.

10. To meet this challenge, we need more persons with ability.

Ⅵ **Select the appropriate word or phrase in the box to complete each sentence. Change the form where necessary. There may be more than one choice.**

attribute	contribute	the result of	impact	thanks to
effect	link	due to	as a result of	responsible for
result in	account for	cause	lead to	influence

1. Many people in the world are experiencing increasing mental stresses _____ a faster pace of life and rising competition.

2. Is it reasonable to _____ dangerous global temperature increase to the greenhouse effect?

3. The decrease in price can be _____ a rise in the number of retailers online.

4. _____ technological advances, people's life is getting more and more convenient.

5. Delay could _____ further problems.

6. Layoffs and downsizing _____ nearly half of all forced retirements.

7. This indicated that science has a very strong _____ on the everyday life.

8. The new policy _____ greatly to the commercial growth of the country.

9. There are five social causes that may _____ the use of alcohol by teenagers.

10. A mentally-ill person cannot be held _____ his actions.

Ⅶ **Rearrange the words and phrases in each group into clear and coherent sentences.**

1. themselves, refined and gentle manners, thought and action, are, an indispensable trait, of, the educated man, is, fixed habits of, which, the expression of.

2. any kind of competition, teams, from one another, to develop, need, unique approaches to, some privacy.

3. the wounds, the atmosphere, and, we, the earth's ecological system, are, healing, inflicted on.

4. there's, us, research, our habits, a lot of, the past several years, been, about, how, over, shape.

5. encounter, begin, as soon as, cultural differences, one another, communicators.

Unit **10** Chinglish vs. English

Ⅷ **Revise the following two groups of stringy sentences into coherent short paragraphs. Add or delete words where necessary.**

1. Our nation originated from the Yellow River basin, the Yellow River played a very important role through our long history, and nowadays, with the development of our economy and the increase of population, water resources become scarce, the Yellow River basin suffers great droughts, especially in the downstream, where even interruptions of channel stream flow occurred.

2. With recruiting students, the number of Ph.D students is more and more, but the number of society demand is very limited, so this is a serious problem and university administrators should pay attention.

Ⅸ **Translate the following sentences into English.**

1. 保护生物的多样性依然是一个十分棘手的问题。
2. 人们对于新型机械和驱动这些机械动力源的兴趣不断增长，这引起了18世纪和19世纪的工业革命。
3. 如果忽视这一问题，任何国家都将付出巨大的代价。
4. 在这篇论文里，我们将回顾骨髓干细胞的研究历史，总结其潜在的应用前景，并且探讨随着骨髓干细胞的研究而引起的伦理问题。
5. 作为群居动物，人类渴望与他人保持联系，也渴望被他人关爱。这种渴望与生存的愿望同样强烈。

Ⅹ **Translate the following paragraph into Chinese.**

    This paper focuses on two types of symmetry breakages in tensor analysis. One is the symmetry breakage in the concept that there is covariant differential of tensor with respect to coordinate, but there is no one with respect to time. Another is the symmetry breakage in the theory that there is covariant differential theory of tensor in space field, but there is no one in time field. This paper tries to mend the symmetry breakages on the basis of the research progresses in recent years. Firstly, the history of extending the covariance thought is reviewed. Then the process of abstracting the concept of covariant differential with respect to time is exhibited. Finally, the procedure of constructing the covariant differential theory of tensor in time field is summarized. It ultimately reveals the symmetry between the covariant differential theory in time field and the covariant differential theory in space field.

Unit 11
Posters for International Conferences and Data Presentation

Warm-up Questions

1. How can you make your research findings publicized quickly? Have you ever attended any international conferences?

2. Where can you find relevant guidelines for making posters for international conferences?

3. Have you ever made a poster for an international conference? What information elements should be included in a poster?

11.1 Overview

One way to publish your research findings is to attend an international conference and deliver a keynote speech or present a poster. An international conference is a kind of formal meeting attended by scholars from around the world. It is organized on a particular subject to bring together people who have common interests. It can also refer to a specialized professional or academic event. After the discussion with the scholars at the international level, you may further revise your paper and submit it to the proceedings which are usually published after the conference.

11.2 Pre-Conference Correspondence

Before attending an international conference or a symposium (which is usually narrower and more specific in the range of topics), you need to obtain some conference information. The available information sources include: special periodicals announcing meetings, professional journals and magazines carrying meeting announcements, conference documents, centers/departments specialized in organizing meetings or other international communication, learned societies/associations/organizations/institutions, Internet, or private channels. Some scholars or professors may also be invited to a symposium or a conference. The following are examples of invitation emails.

1. An invitation email to a symposium

From:	Gonzalo Cosa, Dr. <gonzalo.cosa@mcgill.ca>
Sent:	Tuesday, December 24, 2019 2:11 AM
To:	xuk@berkeley.edu
CC:	Peng Chen, Prof.; Tetsuro Majima (majima{a@sanken.osaka-u.ac.jp); Christy Landes (cflandes@rice.edu); wei.wang@nju.edu.cn
Subject:	Invitation to Pacifichem Symposium entitled "Single-molecule and Single-particle Fluorescence Imaging (#407)"

Dear Dr. Ke Xu,

Jointly with Christy Landes (Rice University), Peng Chen (Cornell University), Tetsuro Majima (Osaka University), and Wei Wang (Nanjing University), we are organizing a

Unit 11 Posters for International Conferences and Data Presentation

symposium on "Single-molecule and Single-particle Fluorescence Imaging (#407)" at the upcoming Pacifichem 2020, Honolulu, Hawaii (USA) from December 15–20, 2020.

This symposium will showcase the latest advances in the development and application of single-molecule fluorescence techniques. It will include both invited and contributed oral presentations, and an accompanying poster session. We were hoping that you would accept to join us at this time to give an invited talk at this symposium.

For more specific information regarding Pacifichem 2020, please visit the following url:

http://www.pacifichem.org/

Dr. Gonzalo Cosa

Chemistry Dept. of Rice University

(Tel) 941-3787

Email: Gonzalo.cosa@mcgil.ca

After getting the invitation, you can respond to it as follows.

2. A response to the invitation

From:	xuk@berkeley.edu
Sent:	Tuesday, December 24, 2019 8:28 AM
To:	Gonzalo Cosa, Dr.
Subject:	RE: Invitation to Pacifichem Symposium entitled "Single-molecule and Single-particle Fluorescence Imaging (#407)"

Dear Gonzalo,

Thank you very much for your kind invitation. Yes, I'd be happy to attend.

Happy holidays!
Ke

You may also write emails to the sponsors or organizors for some details of the conference such as the location, time of arrival, accommodations, or even information about activities before, during, and after the conference.

3. Inquiry emails about the conference

The following are some sample letters of inquiry about the themes or areas for discussion, requirements for participation, information about paper submission, details of different sessions, pre-/post-conference arrangements. Inside addresses are omitted.

253

1) An email of inquire for the deadline for the submission of the paper

Dear Professor Smith,

I am the Deputy Director of the Institute of Plasma Physics, Chinese Academy of Sciences, Beijing, China. Since we have been undertaking research on electron cyclotron emission for many years, we are very interested in attending the 16th Symposium on Electron Cyclotron Emission and Electron Cyclotron Resonance Heating, which is to be held in London, dated 5–11th December.

We should be very much obliged if you could kindly give us information on the deadline for the submission of abstracts, papers, and other written materials.

I am looking forward to hearing from you soon.

Sincerely yours,
(signature)

2) An email of inquiry for information details of the meeting

Dear Dr. Blake,

I have learned from *Progress in Physics*, No. 12, 2020 that the International Conference on Thermodynamics will be held in Sydney, Australia, from December 4 to 12, 2021. I would appreciate receiving the call for papers, circulars and other details of the conference.

I thank you in anticipation of an early reply.

Yours sincerely,
(signature)

3) An email of inquiry for current status of the submitted paper

Dear Dr. Swales,

It is more than two months since I sent to you my paper, but I have not received any information yet. As far as I know, one can be invited to the symposium only when his paper is accepted. In order to make necessary preparations for the meeting as early as possible, I would like to be informed of the present status of my submitted paper.

Yours sincerely,
(signature)

Unit 11 Posters for International Conferences and Data Presentation

11.3 Making a Research Poster

Posters are widely used in the academic community, and most conferences include poster presentations in their programs. Thus it is quite necessary for researchers to know what a poster is like and how to make an attractive poster.

11.3.1 What Is a Research Poster?

Research posters summarize information or research concisely and attractively to help it publicized and arouse discussion. It is usually a mixture of brief text mixed with tables, graphs, pictures, and other presentation formats. At a conference, the researcher stands by the poster board while other participants can come and view the presentation and interact with the author, as Figure 11.1 shows:

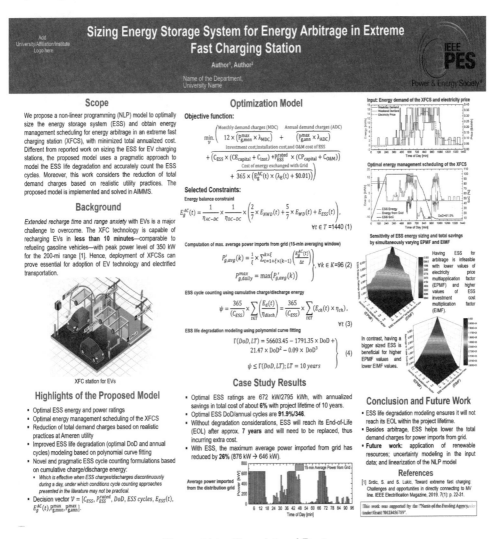

Figure 11.1　Template of Poster

From the above template, we can see the information layout: The university logo, Title, Author(s), Name of the department, Scope, Background, Highlights of the Proposed Model, Optimization Model, Case Study Results, Conclusion and Future Work, and References.

11.3.2 Instructions on Making a Poster for an International Conference

After your research has produced some results, you may want to organize them and submit the manuscript for publication. The quickest way of submitting your findings to the peers is to present your research findings at the international conference of a special field. Young researchers often have the opportunity to present a poster at the international conference or symposium instead of making a keynote speech. Different societies may have different policies for poster sessions. Figure 11.2 is American Chemistry Society's policies for poster sessions.

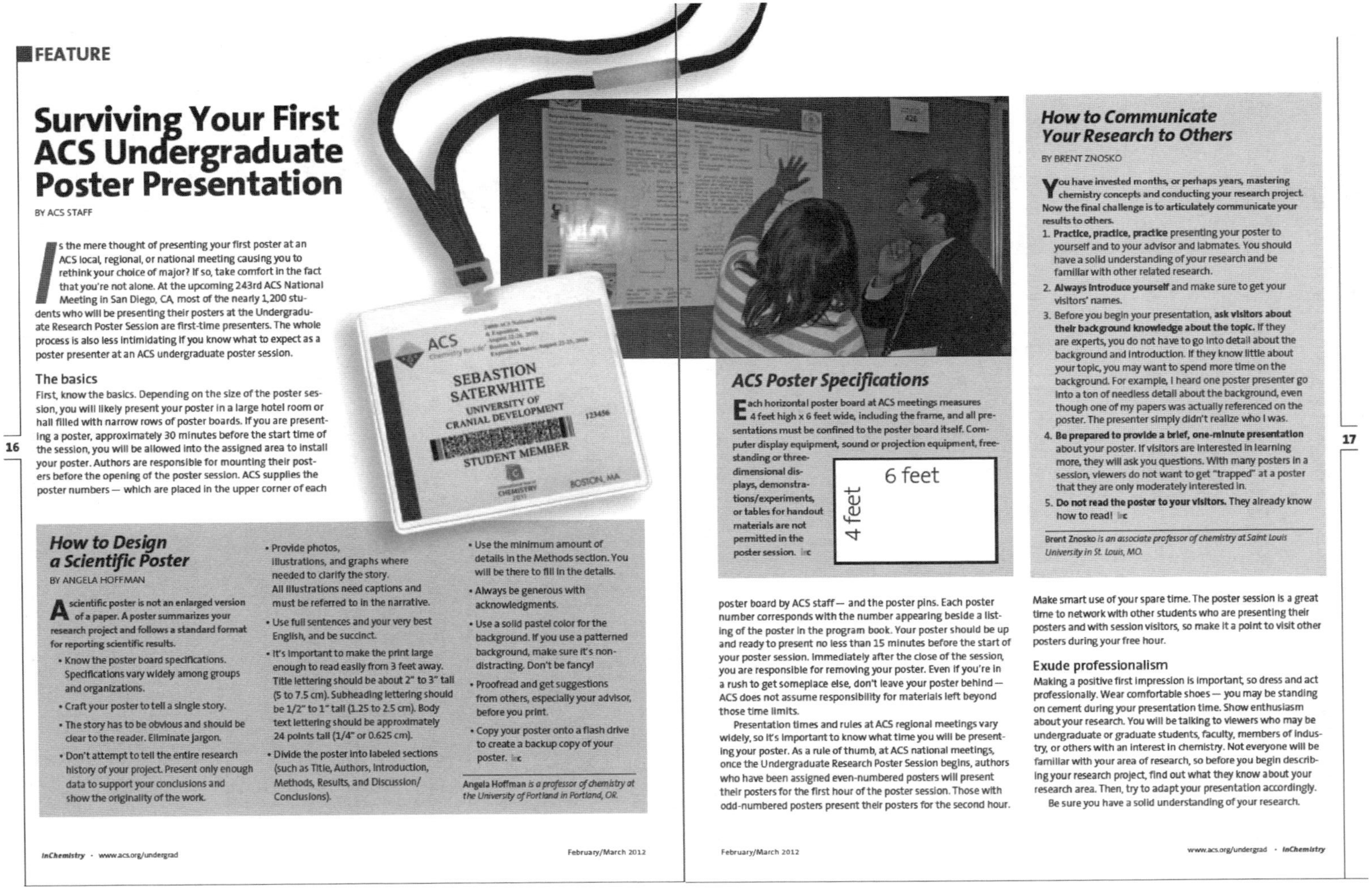

FEATURE

Surviving Your First ACS Undergraduate Poster Presentation

BY ACS STAFF

Is the mere thought of presenting your first poster at an ACS local, regional, or national meeting causing you to rethink your choice of major? If so, take comfort in the fact that you're not alone. At the upcoming 243rd ACS National Meeting in San Diego, CA, most of the nearly 1,200 students who will be presenting their posters at the Undergraduate Research Poster Session are first-time presenters. The whole process is also less intimidating if you know what to expect as a poster presenter at an ACS undergraduate poster session.

The basics

First, know the basics. Depending on the size of the poster session, you will likely present your poster in a large hotel room or hall filled with narrow rows of poster boards. If you are presenting a poster, approximately 30 minutes before the start time of the session, you will be allowed into the assigned area to install your poster. Authors are responsible for mounting their posters before the opening of the poster session. ACS supplies the poster numbers — which are placed in the upper corner of each poster board by ACS staff — and the poster pins. Each poster number corresponds with the number appearing beside a listing of the poster in the program book. Your poster should be up and ready to present no less than 15 minutes before the start of your poster session. Immediately after the close of the session, you are responsible for removing your poster. Even if you're in a rush to get someplace else, don't leave your poster behind — ACS does not assume responsibility for materials left beyond those time limits.

Presentation times and rules at ACS regional meetings vary widely, so it's important to know what time you will be presenting your poster. As a rule of thumb, at ACS national meetings, once the Undergraduate Research Poster Session begins, authors who have been assigned even-numbered posters will present their posters for the first hour of the poster session. Those with odd-numbered posters present their posters for the second hour. Make smart use of your spare time. The poster session is a great time to network with other students who are presenting their posters and with session visitors, so make it a point to visit other posters during your free hour.

Exude professionalism

Making a positive first impression is important, so dress and act professionally. Wear comfortable shoes — you may be standing on cement during your presentation time. Show enthusiasm about your research. You will be talking to viewers who may be undergraduate or graduate students, faculty, members of industry, or others with an interest in chemistry. Not everyone will be familiar with your area of research, so before you begin describing your research project, find out what they know about your research area. Then, try to adapt your presentation accordingly.

Be sure you have a solid understanding of your research.

How to Design a Scientific Poster

BY ANGELA HOFFMAN

A scientific poster is not an enlarged version of a paper. A poster summarizes your research project and follows a standard format for reporting scientific results.

- Know the poster board specifications. Specifications vary widely among groups and organizations.
- Craft your poster to tell a single story.
- The story has to be obvious and should be clear to the reader. Eliminate jargon.
- Don't attempt to tell the entire research history of your project. Present only enough data to support your conclusions and show the originality of the work.
- Provide photos, illustrations, and graphs where needed to clarify the story. All illustrations need captions and must be referred to in the narrative.
- Use full sentences and your very best English, and be succinct.
- It's important to make the print large enough to read easily from 3 feet away. Title lettering should be about 2" to 3" tall (5 to 7.5 cm). Subheading lettering should be 1/2" to 1" tall (1.25 to 2.5 cm). Body text lettering should be approximately 24 points tall (1/4" or 0.625 cm).
- Divide the poster into labeled sections (such as Title, Authors, Introduction, Methods, Results, and Discussion/Conclusions).
- Use the minimum amount of details in the Methods section. You will be there to fill in the details.
- Always be generous with acknowledgments.
- Use a solid pastel color for the background. If you use a patterned background, make sure it's non-distracting. Don't be fancy!
- Proofread and get suggestions from others, especially your advisor, before you print.
- Copy your poster onto a flash drive to create a backup copy of your poster. ic

Angela Hoffman is a professor of chemistry at the University of Portland in Portland, OR.

ACS Poster Specifications

Each horizontal poster board at ACS meetings measures 4 feet high x 6 feet wide, including the frame, and all presentations must be confined to the poster board itself. Computer display equipment, sound or projection equipment, free-standing or three-dimensional displays, demonstrations/experiments, or tables for handout materials are not permitted in the poster session. ic

How to Communicate Your Research to Others

BY BRENT ZNOSKO

You have invested months, or perhaps years, mastering chemistry concepts and conducting your research project. Now the final challenge is to articulately communicate your results to others.

1. **Practice, practice, practice** presenting your poster to yourself and to your advisor and labmates. You should have a solid understanding of your research and be familiar with other related research.
2. **Always introduce yourself** and make sure to get your visitors' names.
3. Before you begin your presentation, **ask visitors about their background knowledge about the topic.** If they are experts, you do not have to go into detail about the background and introduction. If they know little about your topic, you may want to spend more time on the background. For example, I heard one poster presenter go into a ton of needless detail about the background, even though one of my papers was actually referenced on the poster. The presenter simply didn't realize who I was.
4. **Be prepared to provide a brief, one-minute presentation** about your poster. If visitors are interested in learning more, they will ask you questions. With many posters in a session, viewers do not want to get "trapped" at a poster that they are only moderately interested in.
5. **Do not read the poster to your visitors.** They already know how to read! ic

Brent Znosko is an associate professor of chemistry at Saint Louis University in St. Louis, MO.

16 *InChemistry* · www.acs.org/undergrad February/March 2012

February/March 2012 www.acs.org/undergrad · *InChemistry* 17

Figure 11.2 CAS's Instructions on How to Design a Scientific Poster

Poster numbers supplied by ACS will be placed in the upper corner of each poster board. This number corresponds with the number assigned to each paper in the program book.

11.3.3 Design Suggestions for Scientific Posters

- Each horizontal poster board measures 4 feet high × 6 feet wide (including frame).

- Allow ample time to prepare your poster. All poster materials (illustrations, charts, and text) must be prepared in advance.

- All posters should feature a title, your name, the name of the institution where the research was performed and should credit other contributors, as appropriate.

- Use a crisp, clean design. All lettering should be legible from about 5 feet (1.5 m) away. Title lettering should be about 2 to 3 inch (about 5 to 7.5 cm). Subheading lettering should be 1/2 to 1 inch high (about 1.25 to 2.5 cm). Text lettering should be approximately 24 points tall (1/4 or 0.625 cm).

- Make illustrations simple and bold, with captions at least 3/8 inch high. Enlarge photos, tables, and charts to show pertinent details clearly.

- Do not tell the entire research history. Present only enough data to support your conclusions and show the originality of the work. The best posters display a succinct statement of major conclusions at the beginning, followed by supporting text and a summary at the end.

- Displayed materials should be self-explanatory, freeing you for discussion.

- Utilize other techniques to improve the graphic impact. Use color to add emphasis and clarity. Simplicity, ease of reading, etc., are more important than artistic design. Keep in mind that lighting may be dim inside large poster sessions, so make sure your contrasts and color combinations are easy to read.

- You may want to bring handouts of your abstract or copies of your data and conclusions to share with interested viewers. Some authors also provide sign-up sheets to record names and addresses of attendees who might wish for more information, reprints, etc.

Generally, the organizer of the conference will provide some standard templates. However, a lot of young researchers prefer to create a template of their own style. You may use PowerPoint, Adobe Illustrator, Photoshop, InDesign, etc. There are a lot of templates for making posters for reference.

Before you print, you need to double-check the spelling and grammar. You are suggested to ask a friend—a new set of eyes is more likely to catch errors!

11.4 Information Elements of Posters

The purpose of presenting a poster is to make other researchers, institutions or businessmen know what you are doing and what you have done. Thus, a poster may include the following information elements:

- the title of your presentation (obligatory);
- the introduction of the work your lab is doing (optional);
- an abstract or motivation of your research (100–150 words, obligatory);
- methods or procedures of the experiment (obligatory, often presented with figures with illustration);
- results (obligatory, often presented with figures with illustration);
- discussion (obligatory, words of simple sentences);
- references and acknowledgements (optional).

11.5 Poster Samples

Here, two samples of posters are presented. Closely read the posters and study the layout of each section.

Sample 1 (From the Field of Chemistry)

Sample 1 (see Figure 11.3) is a poster made by a professor who leads a team (Ph.D. students and postdocs) working on the intracellular physiochemical lab at Berkley. In this poster, a general introduction of the lab is given on the left top. Then what is followed is an abstract of some 150 words text. What is further followed is the limitation of previous approaches which are presented by some figures. In the middle broader column, they presented the current works they are doing, also mainly by figures and tables. On the right column, the results and discussion are presented mainly by figures and tables. At the bottom, there is a Reference and acknowledgments.

As a whole, this poster looks like a refined and colorful paper where a compete research story is told.

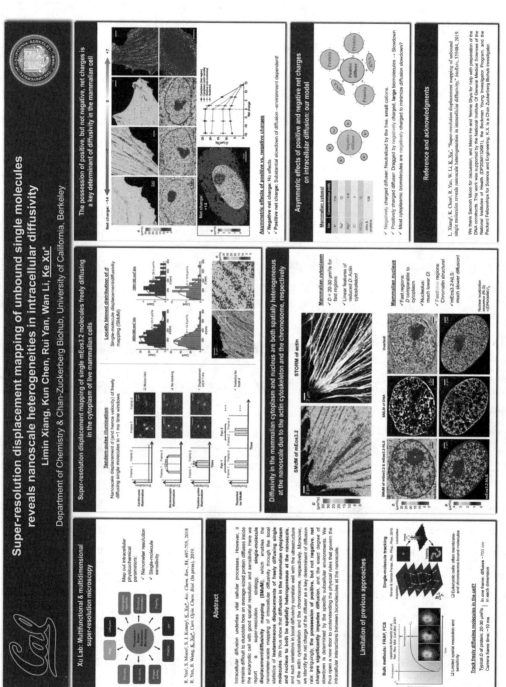

Figure 11.3　Sample Poster 1 Locally Binned Distribution of Single-Molecule Displacement

Unit 11 Posters for International Conferences and Data Presentation

Sample 2 (From the Field of Computer Science)

Sample 2 (see Figure 11.4) is a poster presented by James Jie Pan from Tsinghua University and Guoliang Li and Juntao Hu from Beijing Aeronautics and Astronautics University. Have a close look at this poster and answer the following questions:

- What is the subject title of the poster?
- Where are the two logos of the universities laid out?
- Where is the research motivation laid out?

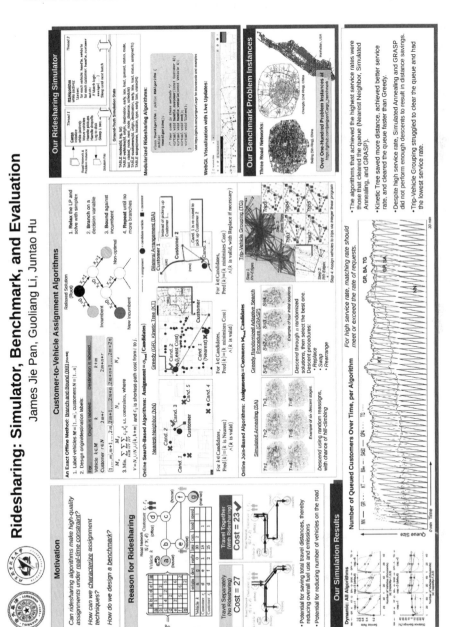

Figure 11.4 Sample Poster 2 Ridesharing: Simulator, Benchmark, and Evaluation

11.6 Linguistic Features of Posters

The poster is actually like a PPT put together. You need to prepare an outline, an abstract, some personal vocabulary, and some figures and tables. Since the specifications of a poster is only 4 feet high × 6 feet wide, each poster can only tell a single story, just like writing a light research paper. To make the viewers fully understand, you provide photos, illustrations, and graphs where needed to clarify the story. The language should be narrative and simple. Use complete sentences with simple grammar, simple words, and the active voice in the result, discussion and conclusion. To be succinct, always present your results and findings by using tables and figures with a simple illustration. The proper use of tables and figures in a poster can illustrate complicated relationships more clearly and in less space than the written words. Moreover, data, tables, and figures are very important in that they can make your research paper stand out from the crowd.

In a poster, the language expressions for referring to a graph, chart, etc. are as follows:

- ✓ **As can be seen from / It can be seen from / We can see from** / in the chart (diagram, table, graph, figures, statistics)…

The expressions for describing changes can also be omitted. For example:

- ✓ **There was a (very) barely noticeable** (slight, slow, gradual, steady, marked, dramatic, steep, sharp, rapid, sudden) rise (increase, upward trend, fluctuation, downward trend, decrease, decline, reduction, fall, drop)…

However, the above expressions may also be useful when you give an oral presentation.

Prior to the presentation, people often make preparations by writing a speech manuscript which will help overcome their tense and nervousness. Here in the following, some expressions for theme presentations are provided.

1. Initiating a new topic

- ✓ Ladies and gentlemen, **it would be very interesting to** take a look at this curve, which tells us the peak value of the signal and distribution of the light shift points…
- ✓ **The interesting thing in this experiment is** that if the amount of positive and negative charges is varied, the electron stream can be made to bend down with it, especially when…
- ✓ **It is not exaggeration to say that** professor Wu has given me many ideas for my future work, which I would not otherwise have been able to obtain, for example…
- ✓ Well, may I say boldly, **it is a common desire for everyone** that in this case the coefficient of the friction should be minimized.

In the above examples, there are clauses like "it would be very interesting to…" "The interesting thing in…" "It is not exaggeration to say that…" "it is a common desire for everyone…", which are classified as initiating phrases. The function of these clauses is to introduce a new topic or to make a contradictory comment. In a cohesive speech, there tends to be many places where topic shifting, emphasis, and attention focusing are required, as the adoption of the initiating phrases would remind the audience of the new topic or emphasis, attract their attention and achieve smooth transition to the subsequent delivery.

2. Highlighting ideas

Different parts of utterance may not be equal with one another in their importance. The most essential aspects could be highlighted in the following ways.

1) Focusing on the beginning or the ending. For example:
- ✓ Automatic driving is the very subject that we have studied for years.
- ✓ The basic idea is that, if we want to perform a real testing, then we need a driver, hopefully with great skills, a real car, drive it on a real track…

2) Using emphatic sentence structures such as "It is… that…" For example:
- ✓ It is when an object is heated that the average speed of molecules is increased.
- ✓ We can see from the equation, it is only with the reduction of the first order Doppler effect to negligible amount that a constant phase can be maintained for the…

3) Using attention-provoking words and phrases. For example:
- ✓ We must cut cost!
- ✓ We have to save!

3. Adopting direct repetition

In conference paper presentation, the repetition of key words and sentences could attract attention and highlight the main points. In fact, it is quite necessary to repeat important data, results, and conclusions so as to strengthen listeners' impression or to help them grasp the main point. For example:
- ✓ The CPU memory unit is commonly called the internal memory of the computing system. On older machines this memory usually consisted of magnetic cores… Most computing systems also incorporate components that serve as auxiliary or external memory.

4. Simplifying long/complex terms

Long technical terms that appear in the presentation of some specific subjects are often difficult to read. For example:
- ✓ …O-dichlorobenzene is employed in recording the spectrum. Our experiment shows that the testing agent has a better solubility against the sample used. But its purity

is not high enough. So it is advisable to record a spectrum of the solvent before it is employed to record the sample spectrum so as to determine the peaks of the sample.

In the above discourse, the speaker uses a very formal term "O-dichlorobenzene" when it appears for the first time. It is, then, replaced with its equivalents such as "the testing agent", "the solvent", "the sample" and so on.

5. Making some changes in the manuscript

You can compose an oral text by making some changes in the manuscript. For example:

- ✓ High operating speed shall be provided by a high-speed, motor-driven switch operator in order to assure the full inherent mechanical and electrical performance of the circuit-switcher such as power operation under 1.5-inch ice formation fault-closing capacity, close inter-phase simultaneity, long life of fault-closing arching contacts, and avoidance of excessive switching transients which can accompany prolonged or unstable pre-strike arcing.

The above paragraph has only one sentence. It would bring about a better effect in oral presentation if the following changes are made:

- ✓ A high-speed and a motor-driven switch operator shall provide high operating speed, in order to assure full inherent mechanical and electrical performance of the circuit-switcher. The performance features include power operation under 1.5-inch formation, fault-closing capability, close inter-phase simultaneity, and long life of fault-closing arcing contacts. The switch operator also assures avoidance of excessive switching transients which can accompany prolonged or unstable pre-strike acing.

Because speakers are usually tense about speaking before large audience, they often err in the direction of formality. This is especially true if the speakers have written out the whole speech, since most of them compose speeches in a written style rather than an oral one. The speeches are often stilted and stiff. For example:

- ✓ I am most pleased that you could come this morning. I would like to take this opportunity to discuss with you a subject of inestimable importance to us all—the impact of inflationary spirals on students enrolled in institutions of higher education.

Translated into the kind of oral style preferred in most speaking situations, those sentences would run like this:

- ✓ Thanks for coming. I'd like to talk today about something that everyone here has had experience with—the rising costs of going to college.

Notice the differences in the two versions. The first one is wordy, filled with prepositional phrases, larded with complex words, and formal when addressing the audience. The second one contains shorter sentences, a more direct address to the audience, and a simpler vocabulary. Comparatively, the first one is in a written style, while the second is in an oral style.

On most occasions of oral presentation, a speaker should cultivate an oral style.

11.7 Data Presentation

1. The relationship between texts and figures

From the poster samples, we may see the information presented in the poster is mainly in figures and table. Actually, all instructions on how to write a research paper diligently call for the necessity of writing a research paper in the simplest way, so that even a child can figure it out. For that purpose, you may see most of the empirical research papers present the Methods and Results sections mainly through images and figures. The texts seem to be some illustrations of the figures, in which simple grammar structures and active voice are used.

The proper use of tables and figures in a research paper can illustrate complicated relationships more clearly and in less space than the written words. To help the readers understand the data in a table or figure, a clear introduction should be provided. The introduction may be a description of the table or figure. In most cases, the writer or presenter also includes some sort of comments. The comments may be some meaningful key words or phrases as shown in Figure 11.3:

- ✓ Negatively charged diffuser: Nutralized by the free, small captions.
- ✓ Positively charged diffuser: Dragged by negatively charged large biomolecules slowdown.
- ✓ Most cytoplasmic biomolecules are negatively charged to minimize diffusion slowdown?

Other writers or presenters may also use simple sentences for some comments, as shown in Figure 11.4:

- ✓ The algorithms that achieved the highest service rates were those that cleared the queue (Nearest Neighbor, Simulated Annealing, and GRASP)
- ✓ Kinetic Tree saved more distance, achieved better service rate, and cleared the queue faster than Greedy.
- ✓ Despite high service rate, Simulated Annealing and GRASP did not perform enough descents to result in distance savings.
- ✓ Trip-vehicle Grouping struggled to clear the queue and had the lowest service rate.

2. Anatomy of tables and figures

Tables are most easily constructed using the word processor's table function or a spreadsheet like Excel. Gridlines or boxes, commonly invoked by word processors, are helpful for setting cell and column alignments but should be eliminated from the printed version.

3. How to choose graphic display tools

There are several types of graphic display tools, including (a) charts displaying frequencies (bar, pie, and Pareto charts), (b) charts displaying trends (line graphs, run and control charts), (c) charts displaying distributions (histograms), and (d) charts displaying associations (scatter diagrams).

Different types of data require different kinds of graphic display tools. There are two types of data. Attribute data are countable data or data that can be put into categories, for example, the number of people willing to pay, or the number of people who complain. Whereas variable data are remeasurement data based on some continuous scales, for example, length, time, and cost. When creating graphic displays, Table 11.1 can help you identify which tool is the most suitable one to present data in a research paper.

Table 11.1 Choosing Graphic Display Tools

To Show	Use	Data Need
Frequency of occurrence: simple percentages or comparisons of magnitude	Bar chart, pie chart, or Pareto chart	Tallies by category (attribute data or variable data divided into categories)
Trends over time	Line graph, run chart, or control chart	Measurements taken in chronological order (attribute data or variable data can be used)
Distribution: variation not related to time (distributions)	Histogram	Forty or more measurements (not necessarily in chronological order, variable data)
Association: looking for a correlation between two things	Scatter diagram	Forty or more paired measurements (measures of both things of interest, variable data)

4. Captions of figures and tables

Note that each figure and table should have a caption, legend or title that conveys concisely and clearly what the figure or table contains just like the title of a paper itself. The caption of a figure should be placed just below the figure, whereas the caption of a table

Unit 11 Posters for International Conferences and Data Presentation

should be placed above the table. Furthermore, both figures and tables should have enough information to make them understandable on their own. The proven way to achieve the result is to pace a table header that is substantial in grammar and has no relative clauses in favor of participle. A descriptive phrase is preferred as a title of a table.

5. Language focus: numbers and equations

It is common that some young writers, both Chinese and Western, do not seem to know when numbers should be written in numbers or need to be spelled out. In academic English, there are circumstances under which numerals are undesirable and full spelling of them is required.

1) Arabic numerals should never be used at the beginning of sentences. For example:

✓ ***10** parameters were selected for the experiment.

Ten parameters were selected for the experiment.

2) Larger numbers are written in numerals. Numbers that are less than ten should be spelled out rather than written in numerals. But there are three exceptions: (1) When a measurement unit is involved; (2) when numbers are shown as decimal fractions or expressed as precise mathematical relations; (3) when the number is directly linked to some category that has more than one type. For example:

✓ Distance between the two points is **8 mm**.

✓ Using the equation **S = 6A0.12**, the number of species S on an island with area A = **9 m²** would be **7.8**—or about **8** species.

✓ Only specimen **No. 13** contained trace minerals.

3) Arabic numerals should be used to give data in technical papers, however, they should not be used to provide general information.

✓ ①*The **three** authors from **three** studies grouped the **four** age classes into < 3 years, 3–6 years, 6–10 years, and >10 years.

②The **3** authors from **3** studies grouped the **4** age classes into < 3 years, 3–6 years, 6–10 years, and >10 years.

4) In academic English, dates should always have the month written in letters. For example:

✓ Aerosol samples were collected on 15 **January** 2009 in Xichuan.

5) Equations should be introduced as many as possible, not inserted in the place of words. Most journals, like the *International Journal of Production Research*, discourage the use of even short expressions within the text. For example:

✓ ①*If the power battery **SOC** > **SOCIO** and the driving torque belongs to the middle load…

267

②If the power battery **SOC is greater than SOCIO** and the driving torque belongs to the middle load...

11.8 Reflections and Practice

❶ Translate the following inquiry emails into English

Letter A: A response email for the invitation

发件人：威廉·李
发送时间：2022 年 8 月 22 日
收件人：托马斯·史密斯先生
主题：回复邀请

亲爱的托马斯先生：
　　非常感谢您的盛情邀请，我非常高兴参加此次会议并作主旨报告。
祝好！

签名：威廉·李

Letter B: An email of inquiry for current status of the submitted paper

发件人：张阳
发送时间：2022 年 8 月 10 日
收件人：斯威福特博士
主题：询问论文是否被接受

亲爱的斯威福特博士：
　　我的论文寄给您已经一个多月了，但我还没有收到任何消息。就我而言，只有在论文被接受后才能参加研讨会。为了尽早为会议做好必要的准备，我想知道我提交的论文的现状。

此致，
签名：李阳

Unit 11 Posters for International Conferences and Data Presentation

⑪ Read the following poster carefully and study both the texts and the images on it. Then make a poster of your own style to present your research work.

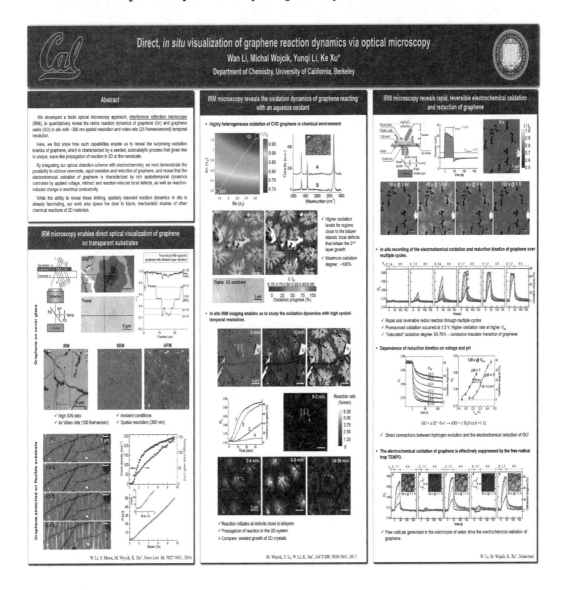

Ⅲ Translate the following sentences into English.

1. 储能系统（ESS）寿命退化建模确保它不会在项目生命周期内达到项目终止（EOL）。
2. 除了套利（arbitrage），储能系统还有助于降低从电网进口电的总需求费用。
3. 动力学树（Kineitic Tree）比格力系统（Greedy）节省了更多的距离，获得了更好的服务率，并且比格力系统更快地清除了队列（the queue）。
4. 达到最高服务率的算法是那些清除队列的算法。
5. 未来的工作是：可再生资源的应用；输入数据中的不确定性方面的建模和自然语言处理（NLP）模型的线性化。

Ⅳ Translate the following paragraph into Chinese.

A high-speed and a motor-driven switch operator shall provide high operating speed, in order to assure full inherent mechanical and electrical performance of the circuit-switcher. The performance features include power operation under 1.5-inch ice formation, fault-closing capability, close inter-phase simultaneity, and long life of fault-closing arcing contacts. The switch operator also assures avoidance of excessive switching transients which can accompany prolonged or unstable pre-strike arcing.

Unit 12
Manuscript Publication

Warm-up Questions

1. Where can you find relevant guidelines for your target journal?

2. Do you think peer review is essential for publication? Why?

3. What rules do you need to follow when you respond to editors or reviewers?

12.1 Overview

12.1.1 Aims and Scope of the Target Journal

Prior to your manuscript submission, you need to check the aims and scope of your target journal. Outright rejection or desk rejection may be the result of the manuscript being unsuitable for the target journal. The aims and scope of a journal can be easily found on its official website. For example, the aims and scope of the journal *Poetics* are shown below in Table 12.1:

Table 12.1   Aims and Scope of the Journal *Poetics*

Analysis	Aims and Scope
General introduction of the aims and scope of the journal	*Poetics* is an interdisciplinary journal of theoretical and empirical research on culture, the media and the arts. Particularly welcome are papers that make an original contribution to the major disciplines—sociology, psychology, media and communication studies, and economics—within which promising lines of research on culture, media and the arts have been developed.
Detailed descriptions of types of research suitable for the journal	*Poetics* would be pleased to consider, for example, the following types of papers: • Sociological research on participation in the arts; media use and consumption; the conditions under which makers of cultural products operate; the functioning of institutions that make, distribute and/or judge cultural products, arts and media policy; etc. • Psychological research on the cognitive processing of cultural products such as literary texts, films, theatrical performances, visual artworks, etc. • Media and communications research on the globalization of media production and consumption; the role and performance of journalism; the development of media and creative industries; the social uses of media; etc.

(Continued)

Analysis	Aims and Scope
Justification of the scope of the journal	• Economic research on the funding, costs and benefits of commercial and non-profit organizations in the fields of art and culture; choice behavior of audiences analyzed from the viewpoint of the theory of lifestyles; the impact of economic institutions on the production or consumption of cultural goods; etc. The production and consumption of media, art and culture are highly complex and interrelated phenomena. Our insight into these broad domains will be considerably enhanced by studies focusing on the interrelationships of the many factors that shape behavior towards art, culture and the media. *Poetics* publishes not only advanced research reports but also overview articles. Occasional special issues, guest-edited by specialists, present the state of the art and/or discuss new developments in a particular field. *Poetics* does not publish papers that analyze arts or literature in a more hermeneutics-oriented tradition. Thus, for papers focusing on, for example, close reading of poetry or novels, we refer to other journals.
Further instructions for potential authors	If you are in any doubt about the appropriateness of your paper for *Poetics*, please take a moment to review previous volumes of the journal. The contents of these issues will give you a good sense of the areas of research which are of interest to us. The complete back issues of the journal can be found at http://www.sciencedirect.com/science/journal/0304422X

12.1.2 Guide for Authors

Detailed guidelines for authors are available on the official website of the target journal (e.g., as shown in Figure 12.1), and the PDF version is sometimes downloadable (as shown in Figure 12.2). It is generally recommended that authors read the guidelines in full if they have not previously submitted to the target journal. It is also suggested that authors familiarize themselves with the style and content of their target journal by reading research articles recently published before their submission.

Figure 12.1   Screenshot of the Official Website of *Nature*

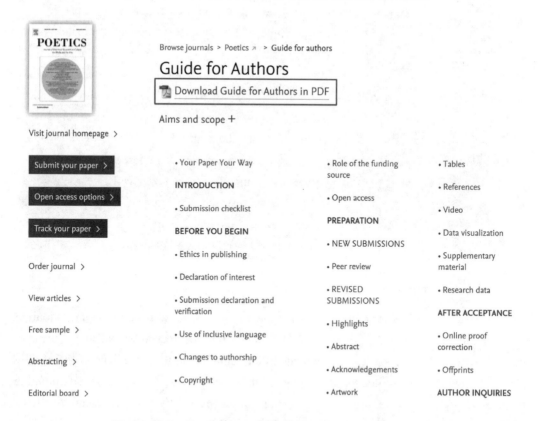

Figure 12.2   Screenshot of the Official Website of *Poetics*

12.1.3 Cover Letter

Although optional, the cover letter is an excellent opportunity to briefly discuss the context and importance of the submitted work and why it is appropriate for the journal. Please avoid repeating information that is already present in the abstract and introduction. The cover letter is not shared with the reviewers, and should be used to provide confidential information, such as conflicts of interest, and to declare any related work that is in press or submitted elsewhere. The letter must provide the corresponding author's name, postal and email addresses, and telephone and fax numbers.

A cover letter example is shown below. Please notice that you need to replace bracketed texts with your own information and writing.

[My Name

University of Research

804 Research Drive

Los Angeles, CA, USA 90210

310-555-1234

m.name@researchu.edu]

[Dr. John Editorian

Editor-in-Chief

Journal of Science]

[August 3, 2015]

Dear [Dr. Editorian]:

I am pleased to submit an original research article entitled ["Neofunctionalization of Polymerase rho in *Ustilago Maydis*" by Albert Postdoc and My Name] for consideration for publication in [the *Journal of Science*]. We previously uncovered a role for [polymerase rho in DNA repair in *U. maydis* **(citation)**], and this manuscript builds on our prior study to determine the evolution of this unique enzyme.

In this manuscript, we show that [polymerase rho… **(list a few important results)**].

We believe that this manuscript is appropriate for publication by [the *Journal of Science*] because it… **(specific link to the journal's aims and scope)**. [Our manuscript creates a paradigm for future studies of the evolution of essential enzymes in yeast.]

> This manuscript has not been published and is not under consideration for publication elsewhere. We have no conflicts of interest to disclose, but we do respectfully request that [Dr. Glen Meanie] not review our manuscript. If you feel that the manuscript is appropriate for your journal, we suggest the following reviewers:
>
> **[list reviewers and contact info, if requested by the journal]**
>
> Thank you for your consideration.
>
> Sincerely,
>
> [My Name, Ph.D.
>
> Professor, Department of Evolutionary Mycology
>
> University of Research]

12.2 Response to Editors and Reviewers

12.2.1 Peer-Review Process

A submitted manuscript is first scanned by the editor to determine whether it is suitable for the journal. If it is deemed not to be suitable, the editor will probably reject the manuscript outright before sending it for peer review. He may also reject the manuscript outright if it has a "fatal flaw." Fatal flaws could include a lack of importance of the research topic or an inappropriate study design. Other fatal flaws may include invalid data, conclusions that are not supported by the data, or material that is not original or timely. Fatal flaws cannot be corrected with additional data or clarity because they are errors in logic or approach. If it is suitable, the editor then transfers the manuscript to two or three reviewers, depending on the journal, for peer review. After the reviews are completed, dispositions may include the following:

- rejection without further submission;
- rejection with an opportunity to resubmit;
- major revision without a promise of acceptance;
- minor revision;
- acceptance subject to minor revision;
- outright acceptance.

The whole process can be shown in Figure 12.3.

12.2.2 Three Golden Rules of Responding to Reviewers' Comments

The most common form of disposition is major revision without a promise of acceptance. In such circumstances, the author will need to work hard at reading and replying to each peer

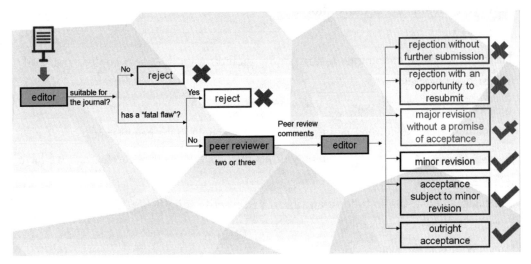

Figure 12.3 The Process of Article Submission

reviewer in turn, following three golden rules: respond completely, respond politely, and respond with evidence (Williams, 2004).

1. Respond completely

It is important that all of the reviewers' comments are responded to in sequence, however irritating or vague they may appear to you. Number them, and repeat them in your response letter using the headings such as "Reviewer 1", then "Comment 1", followed by "Response". What you are doing here is making the editor's and reviewers' jobs easy for them so they will not have to search and cross-reference a lot of scripts to discover what you have done; it will all be there in one clean document.

Typing out or paraphrasing the reviewers' comments as a means of itemizing the points also achieves two other things: (1) It forces you to listen to what the reviewers actually said, rather than what you thought they might have said when you first read their comments; and (2) it helps you to understand how many separate points are being made by the reviewers. Quite often, you will just receive a paragraph with several comments mixed together. In such a situation, you can split the paragraph into 2 or 3 separate comments (e.g., Comment 1.1, 1.2, 1.3), and then answer them in turn. Even if some of the comments are just compliments, repeat these in your response letter followed by a phrase such as "we thank the reviewer for these comments." An example of point-by-point response to reviewers' comments is shown below. Please notice that the authors even use different shades to separate and highlight their responses.

… Those changes are highlighted within the manuscript. Please see below for a point-by-point response to the reviewers' comments and concerns. All page numbers refer to the revised manuscript file with tracked changes.

Reviewers' Comments to the Authors:

Reviewer 1

There are numerous strengths to this study, including its diverse samples, and well-informed hypotheses.

Author response: Thank you!

1. Comment from Reviewer 1 noting a mistake or oversight in the manuscript.

Author response: Thank you for pointing this out. The reviewer is correct, and we have [explain the change made].

The revised text reads as follows on [insert the exact location where the change can be found in the revised manuscript]:

"[updated text in the manuscript]"

2. Comment from Reviewer 1 suggesting a specific change to the manuscript.

Author response: As suggested by the reviewer, we have [explain the specific change made, including the exact location where the change can be found in the revised manuscript].

3. Comment from Reviewer 1 suggesting a widespread change to the manuscript that would need to be updated in multiple places.

Author response: We agree with the reviewer's assessment. Accordingly, throughout the manuscript, we have revised [explain the widespread change made, for instance, switching the order in which the study variables are presented or replacing a term or acronym in the paper].

2. Respond politely

Remember that nearly all reviewers have spent at least an hour of their personal time in reviewing your manuscript without being paid for it. If you (as a lead author) receive a huge list of comments, it usually means that the reviewer is trying very hard to help you improve the manuscript to get it accepted. As illustrated below, those words highlighted in bold at the beginning of the response letter show the authors' appreciation towards reviewers.

Dear Dr. Simpson,

Thank you for giving us the opportunity to submit a revised draft of the manuscript "Poetry and the Cognitive Psychology of Metrical Constructs" for

Unit 12 Manuscript Publication

> publication in the *Journal of Poetry and Psychology*. **We appreciate the time and effort that you and the reviewers dedicated to providing feedback on our manuscript and are grateful for the insightful comments on and valuable improvements to our paper.**

It is quite all right to disagree with reviewers when replying, but do it in a way that makes your reviewers feel valued. Avoid pompous or arrogant remarks. Although it is only human nature to feel slightly offended when someone else dares to criticize your precious work, this should not come across in your reply. Your reply should be scientific and systematic. Get someone else to read your responses before sending them off. Try to avoid opening phrases such as "we totally disagree" or "the reviewer obviously does not know this field". Instead, try to identify some common ground and use phrases starting with words such as "we agree with the reviewer, however…" A list of helpful phrases is given below for guidance.

- ✓ We agree with the reviewer that…, but…
- ✓ The reviewer is right to point out…, yet…
- ✓ In accordance with the reviewers' wishes, we have now changed this sentence to….
- ✓ Although we agree with the reviewer that…
- ✓ It is true that…, but…
- ✓ We acknowledge that our manuscript might have been…, but…
- ✓ We, too, were disappointed by the low response rate.
- ✓ We agree that this is an important… that requires further research.
- ✓ We support the reviewer's assertion that…, although…
- ✓ With all due respect to the reviewer, we believe that this point is not correct.

3. Respond with evidence

If you disagree with the reviewer's comments, don't just say "we disagree", and move on. Say why you disagree with a coherent argument or, better still, back it up with some facts supported by references that you can cite in your reply. Sometimes those extra references are just to back the point you make in your cover letter, but occasionally you may add them to the revised article. Some kind reviewers go to the trouble of suggesting missed references or how you might reword important areas of your document. If providing the references or rewording makes sense to you, just go ahead and incorporate them.

Another option is to suggest that the extensive additions would be better placed in another subsequent article. Sometimes, if there are no clear published data to strongly support your methodologic approaches, you can discuss this with an expert in the field. If he or she agrees with your approach, then you can say so in your reply. For example, "although other approaches have been used in the past, we have discussed this statistical methods with Professors ×× and ×× who agree that it was the appropriate analysis."

12.3 Reflections and Practice

I Check the aims and scope, and author guidelines of your target journal.

II Which one of the following two versions of cover letter do you think is better? Why?

Version 1

Dear Dr. Carduner,

First of all, let me introduce myself to you. My name is ××, Assistant Professor of Finance, working at ×× University, a leading institution in my country. I have written several articles on microfinancing, and I would now like to contribute the enclosed paper to your distinguished journal. I hope you will be able to include it in a forthcoming issue. Please make any corrections you think necessary.

I look forward to hearing from you as soon as possible.

Sincerely,

Version 2

Dear Dr. Carduner,

I would like to submit to your journal for possible publication the enclosed paper entitled "Microfinancing in Rural Bangladesh: Causes of Microenterprise Success and Failure". The specific subject of this paper has not been submitted for publication elsewhere; it is partly based on upon research performed for the completion of my Ph.D. thesis.

I look forward to hearing from you in due course.

Sincerely,

Unit 12 Manuscript Publication

(III) Put the following reviews into the table accordingly.

Reviews Expressing Approval	Reviews Suggesting Further Improvement

A. … The introduction and literature review display a broad, sophisticated knowledge of the relevant fields and concepts. The case study itself is original and at the cutting edge in terms of the field's development. The writing is clear and concise.

B. … I do note, however, a need to clarify the key terms. I have inserted comments in the manuscript to this effect. If any trimming needs to be done, I would suggest it come from the middle section of the paper, before the case study.

C. The manuscript is well documented, well structured and relevant to genre-based ESP/EAP teaching settings. It is also extremely well written.

D. My remaining suggestions are few and editorial in nature…

E. I have two requests of the author in the interest of strengthening an already fine paper.

F. This is an outstanding piece of work, almost a model for the kinds of papers we want. As I note in my blind comments to the author, it is excellent in all respects. It certainly satisfies all five of the criteria we reviewers are asked to use in our assessment. I do note, however, …

G. There are a few minor language points to clear up…

(IV) Discuss with your partner and fill in the following table.

Disposition of Manuscript	Probability of Occurrence	Reviewer's Attitude	Probability of Acceptance	Time Wasted	Strategy
Acceptance reviews					
Minor revision reviews					
Major revision reviews					
Rewriting reviews					

(Continued)

Disposition of Manuscript	Probability of Occurrence	Reviewer's Attitude	Probability of Acceptance	Time Wasted	Strategy
Ambiguous reviews					
Rejection reviews					

Ⅴ Refer to the example cover letter in Section 12.1.3 and write a cover letter for one of your research articles following the template.

Ⅵ Read the following adapted example of a conditional acceptance letter from a journal editor and try to write a response letter based on the three golden rules you have learned in this unit.

> From: Dr AB Brown,
>
> Editor, *Journal of…*
>
> Dear Dr Zhu,
>
> I enclose the reviewers' reports on your paper entitled… The reviewers agree that the paper contains much good material. However, they have recommended that it needs considerable revision before it can be published. In particular, draw to your attention the following comments by the reviewers.
>
> **Reviewer 1:**
>
> - The Methods section does not give sufficient information, particularly about the sampling methods used.
> - The results in Tables 1 and 2 are closely related and can be combined into a single table.
> - The conclusion that there is a strong positive correlation between the number of organisms and soil salinity needs a stronger statistical basis.
> - The results in Figure 3 are very preliminary—this really requires another survey. If this is not possible, the Figure should be deleted.
>
> **Reviewer 2:**
>
> - There are inadequacies in the Methods section, as indicated on the typescript.

- The Discussion is not well focused and does not include some important relevant publications, e.g., Jones et al. (2000). "…" in the *Journal of…*
- The conclusion is interesting but can be greatly strengthened. In particular, the findings are different from those of Walter et al. (1997) in the *Journal of…*, a study done in the USA. The work in your paper is in fact the first study of its kind outside Europe and North America and this should be highlighted.

There are other comments in the enclosed reports, and some corrections have been made to the English on the typescripts. If you can revise the paper along the lines suggested and resubmit by… then I will consider its acceptability for publication in the Journal without further reference to reviewers. However, additional reviewing may be necessary.

I look forward to hearing from you.

Yours sincerely,
AB Brown

Ⅶ Translate the following sentences into English.

1. 感谢您为我们提供提交修改稿的机会，使我们的论文有机会在贵刊发表。
2. 非常感谢审稿人在百忙之中抽出时间审阅我们的论文并提出具有建设性的修改意见和反馈。
3. 本文的部分研究成果是基于本人的博士毕业论文完成的。
4. 请恕我直言，我们认为第一位审稿人提出的这一点是不正确的。
5. 本论文手稿尚未发表，也不考虑在其他地方出版发表。

Ⅷ Translate the following paragraph into Chinese.

Physicians in academic medicine have most likely submitted a scientific manuscript for publication. After all, the famous saying is "publish or perish". If all of your submitted manuscripts have been accepted straightaway without revision, you are one of the lucky few who no longer need to continue reading. The majority of authors, however, have had manuscript submissions that resulted in some form of rejection. Rejection should not be unexpected, given that only 9 percent of the 6,000 annual manuscript submissions to the *Journal of the American Medical Association* are accepted for publication. Nearly 85 percent of submissions to *Plastic and Reconstructive Surgery* are rejected. Even manuscripts that later resulted in a Nobel Prize have been rejected for publication. For example, *Nature* rejected manuscripts on Cerenkov radiation (used in nuclear reactors) and work on photosynthesis by Deisenhofer, Huber, and Michel (who determined the first crystal structure of a protein that is essential to photosynthesis), and initially rejected, but eventually accepted, Stephen Hawking's manuscript on black-hole radiation. Rejected. Unaccepted. Refused. Declined. Whatever the word, they all have the same meaning. However, authors must remember that it is normal to go through a "grieving process" after receiving a letter of rejection. The purpose of this article is to discuss the process of peer review in scientific manuscripts, to provide pointers on how to tackle rejection and revision, and to offer guidance on how to be a good peer reviewer.

References

陈定安. 1987. 英汉句子结构比较. 香港：中流出版社有限公司.

范仲英. 1994. 实用翻译教程. 北京：外语教学与研究出版社.

胡庚申. 2000. 英语论文写作与发表. 北京：高等教育出版社.

李争鸣，江素侠. 2010. 研究生英语写作教程. 北京：北京师范大学出版社.

陆红. 2011. 研究生英语写作教程. 苏州：苏州大学出版社.

潘文国. 2014. 汉英语对比纲要. 北京：北京语言大学出版社.

庞继贤. 2008. 英文研究论文写作. 杭州：浙江大学出版社.

彭晓林. 2017. 汉语无灵主语句的理解及其英译. 现代语文（5）：153–155.

乔凤和，肖向红. 2010. 专业英语视听说. 北京：中国科学技术出版社.

史文霞. 2012. 学术论文写作与发表. 西安：西安交通大学出版社.

田力平. 2002. 论文写作与网络资源. 北京：北京邮电大学出版社.

杨若东，袁锡兴. 2007. 研究生英语写译教程（提高级/第二版）. 北京：中国人民大学出版社.

郑福裕，徐威. 2008. 英文科技论文写作与编辑指南. 北京：清华大学出版社.

Abed, A. & AI-Jokhadar, A. 2021. Common space as a tool for social sustainability. *Journal of Housing and the Built Environment, 37*: 399–421.

Ahmad, J. 2012. Stylistic features of scientific English: A study of scientific research articles. *English Language and Literature Studies, 2*(1): 47–55.

Allen, A. L. 2016. Law, privacy & technology commentary series: Protecting one's own privacy in a big data economy. *Harvard Law Review Forum, 130*: 71–78.

American Psychological Association. 2020. *Publication Manual of the American Psychological Association* (7th ed.). Washington, DC: American Psychological Association.

Azad, B., Faraj, L. S., Goh, J. M. & Feghali, T. 2009. What shapes global diffusion of e-Government: Comparing the influence of national governance institution. JGIM Final Manuscript ref. Paper 2009-1006-a, *Forthcoming in *Journal of Global Information Management*.

Basturkmen, H., East, M. & Bitchener, J. 2014. Supervisors' on-script feedback comments on drafts of dissertations: Socialising students into the academic discourse community. *Teaching in Higher Education, 19*: 432–445.

Bossetta, M. 2018. The digital architectures of social media: Comparing political campaigning on Facebook, Twitter, Instagram, and Snapchat in the 2016 U.S. election. *Journalism & Mass Communication Quarterly, 95*(2): 471–496.

Cargill, M. & O'Connor, P. 2013. *Writing Scientific Research Articles: Strategy and Steps*. Oxford: John Wiley & Sons.

Chen, Z. M., Wei, X. S., Wang, P. & Guo, Y. W. 2021. Learning graph convolutional networks for multi-label recognition and applications. *IEEE Transactions on Pattern Analysis and Machine Intelligence, PP*: 1–20.

Creswell, W. J. 2014. *Research Design* (4th ed.). London: Sage.

Ding, D. 2002. The passive voice and the social values in science. *Journal of Technical Writing and Communication, 32*: 137–154.

Ding, X. B., Zhang, Y. K., Sheng, F., Li, Y. Q., Zhi, L. L., Cao, X. B., Cui, X., Zhuang, D. M. & Wei, J. Q. 2021. Preparation of $CsPbBr_3$ films for efficient perovskite solar cells from aqueous solutions. *ACS Applied Energy Materials, 4*(6): 5504–5510.

Eliot, R. S., Steven, S., Marlena, R. F. & Selma, S. 2020. Positive emotions, more than anxiety or other negative emotions, predict willingness to interact with robots. *Personality and Social Psychology Bulletin, 1–14*: 234.

Flint, A., Clegg, S. & Macdonald, R. 2006. Exploring staff perceptions of student plagiarism. *Journal of Further and Higher Education, 30*(2): 145–156.

Gasparetto, A. & Scalera, L. 2019. A brief history of industrial robotics in the 20th century. *Advances in Historical Studies, 8*: 24–35.

Gastel, B. & Day, R. A. 2016. *How to Write and Publish a Scientific Paper* (8th ed.). Santa Barbara & Denver: Greenwood.

Giammatte, L., Messerer, M., Oddo, M., Borsotti, F., Levivier, M. & Daniel, R. T. 2018. Cisternostomy for refractory posttraumatic intracranial hypertension. *World Neurosurgery, 109*: 460–463.

Glasman-Deal, H. 2020. *Science Research Writing for Non-Native Speakers of English*. London: Imperial College Press.

Gruzdev, I., Terentev, E. & Dzhafarova, Z. 2020. Superhero or hands-off supervisor? An empirical categorization of Ph.D. supervision styles and student satisfaction in Russian universities. *Higher Education, 79*(5): 773–789.

Guo, J. Q., Yin, Y. J. & Ren, G. X. 2019. Abstraction and operator characterization of fractal ladder viscoelastic hyper-cell for ligaments and tendons. *Applied Mathematics and Mechanics, 40*(10): 1429–1448.

Hartman-Ohnesorge, L. & Ebbe, R. 2021. Europe's green policy: Towards a climate neutral economy by way of investors' choice. *European Company Law, 18*(1): 34–39.

Hesterman, C. M., Szperka, C. L. & Turner, D. P. 2018. Reasons for manuscript rejection after peer review from the journal *Headache*. *Headache, 58*: 1511–1518.

References

Halliday, M. A. K. & Matthiessen, C. 2004. *An Introduction to Functional Grammar*. London: Hodder Arnold.

Huang, L.S. 2013. Academic English is no one's mother tongue: Graduate and undergraduate students' academic English language-learning needs from students' and instructors' perspectives. *Journal of Perspectives in Applied Academic Practice, 1*(2): 17–29.

Hyland, K. 2004. *Disciplinary Discourse: Social Interactions in Academic Writing*. Ann Arbor: The University of Michigan Press.

Kumar, V. & Stracke, E. 2007. An analysis of written feedback on a Ph.D. thesis. *Teaching in Higher Education, 12*: 461–470.

Lara, O. & Ebbe, R. 2021. Europe's green policy: Towards a climate neutral economy by way of investors' choice. *European Company Law, 18*(1): 34–39.

Lea, M. R. & Street, B. V. 1998. Student writing in higher education: An academic literacy approach. *Studies in Higher Education, 23*(2): 157–172.

Li, G. Q., Deng, L., Tian, L., Cui, H. T., Han, W. T., Pei, J. & Shi, L. P. 2018. Training deep neural networks with discrete state transition. *Neurocomputing, 272*: 154–162.

Li, Z., Wilson, C., Xu, T., Liu, Y., Lu, Z. & Wang, Y. 2015. Offline downloading in China. *Proceedings of the 2015 ACM Conference on Internet Measurement Conference*.

Littlewood, W. 1994. *Foreign and Second Language Learning*. Cambridge: Cambridge University Press.

Ma, C., Zhao, Q., Li G., Deng, L. & Wang, G. 2020. A deadlock-free physical mapping method on the many-core neural network chip. *Neurocomputing, 401*: 327–337.

Manoharan, A. P., Ingrams, A., Kang, D. & Zhao, H. 2021. Globalization and worldwide best practices in e-government, *International Journal of Public Administration, 44*(6): 465–476.

Mayberry, D., Bartletta, H., Mossd, J., Davisone, T. & Herreroa, M. 2019. Pathways to carbon-neutrality for the Australian red meat sector. *Agricultural Systems, 175*: 13–21.

Melián-Martel, N., Alonso, J. J. S. & Ruiz-García, A. 2018. Combined silica and sodium alginate fouling of spiral-wound reverse osmosis membranes for seawater desalination. *Desalination, 439*: 25–30.

Morton, J., Storch, N. & Thompson, C. 2014. Feedback on writing in the supervision of postgraduate students: Insights from the work of Vygotsky and Bakhtin. *Journal of Academic Language & Learning, 8*(1): A24–A36.

Neville, C. 2010. *The Complete Guide to Referencing and Avoiding Plagiarism* (2nd ed.). Berkshire: Open University Press.

Newman, I. & Benz, C. R. 1998. *Qualitative-Quantitative Research Methodology: Exploring the Interactive Continuum*. Carbondale: Southern Illinois University.

Ngo, F. & Jaishankar, K. 2017. Commemorating a decade in existence of the *International*

Journal of Cyber Criminology: A research agenda to advance the scholarship on cyber crime. *International Journal of Cyber Criminology*, *11*(1): 1–9.

Okike, K., Kocher, M. S., Nwachukwu, B. U., Mehlman, C. T., Heckman, J. D. & Bhandari, M. 2012. The fate of manuscripts rejected by the *Journal of Bone and Joint Surgery* (American Volume). *Journal of Bone and Joint Surgery* (American Volume), *94*(17): 130–139.

Padilla-Rivera, A., Morgan-Sagastume, J. M. & Guereca-Hernandez, L. P. 2019. Sustainability assessment of wastewater systems: An environmental and economic approach. *Journal of Environmental Protection*, *10*: 241–259.

Pinkham, J. 2000. *The Translator's Guide to Chinglish*. Beijing: Foreign Language Teaching and Research Press.

Popek, S. & Halagarda, M. 2017. Genetically modified foods: Consumer awareness, opinions and attitudes in selected EU countries. *International Journal of Consumer Studies*, *41*: 325–332.

Qiu, H. R., Banerjee, S. S., Jha, S., Kalbarczyk, Z. T. & Iyer, R. K. 2020. FIRM: An intelligent fine-grained resource management framework for SLO-oriented microservices. *Computer Science*, *1–20*: 805–825.

Raissi, M., Yazdan, A. & Kamiadakis, G. E. 2020. Hidden fluid mechanics: Learning velocity and pressure fields from flow visualizations. *Science* (New York, NY), *367*(6481): 1026–1030.

Ramirez, M. D. 2019. Credit, indebtedness and speculation in Marx's political economy. *Economic Thought. World Economics Association, 8*: 46–62.

Schedler, K. & Summermatter, L. 2007. Customer orientation in electronic government: Motives and effects. *Government Information Quarterly*, *24*(2): 291–231.

Shelton-Strong, S. J. 2012. Literature circles in ELT. *ELT Journal*, *66*(2): 214–223.

Shirzad-Ghaleroudkhani, N., Mei, Q. P. & Gül, M. 2020. Frequency identification of bridges using smartphones on vehicles with variable features. *American Society of Civil Engineers, Journal of Bridge Engineering*, *25*(7): 20–41.

Slade, C. 2000. *Form and Style: Research Papers, Reports and Theses* (10th ed.). Beijing: Foreign Language Teaching and Research Press.

Swales, J. 1990. *Genre Analysis: English in Academic and Research Settings*. Cambridge: Cambridge University Press.

Tang, W. Z., Duffield, C. F. & Young, D. M. 2006. Partnering mechanism in construction: An empirical study on the Chinese construction industry. *Construction Engineering and Management, 132*(3): 217–229.

The Writing Center—University of Wisconsin. Madison. 2022. Retrieved July 22, 2022, from The Writing Center—University of Wisconsin-Madison website.

Toma, A., Hamer, M. & Shankar, A. 2015. Associations between neighborhood perceptions

References

and mental well-being among older adults. *Health & Place, 34*: 46–53.

Wallwork, A. 2016. *English for Writing Research Papers.* Cambridge: Springer.

Wallwork, A.& Southern A. 2020. 100 tips to avoid mistakes in academic writing and presenting. Cambridge: Springer.

Weissberg, R. & Buker, S. 1990. *Writing up Research: Experimental Research Report Writing for Students of English.* Englewood: Prentice Hall.

Weixlbaumer, A., Leon, K., Landick, R. & Darst, S. A. 2013. Structural basis of transcriptional pausing in bacteria. *Cell, 152*: 431–441.

Williams, H. C. 2004. How to reply to reviewers' comments when submitting manuscripts for publication. *Journal of the American Academy of Dermatology, 51*(1): 79–83.

Woo, H. & Lee, W. S. 2009. estMax: Tracing maximal frequent item sets instantly over online transactional data streams. *IEEE Transactions on Knowledge and Data Engineering, 21*(10): 1418–1431.

Yang, L., Su, G. & Yuan, H. 2012. Design principles of integrated information platform for emergency responses: The case of 2008 Beijing Olympic Games. *Information Systems Research, 23*(3): 761–786.

Yin, Y. J. 2019. A viewpoint of the tensoral property of coordinate transformation coefficient and analysis on the concept of hybrid tensor. *Mechanics in Engineering, 41*(1): 1–9.

Yin, Y. J., Yeh, H. Y.& Yin, Y. 2006. Stability similarities between shells, cells and nano carbon tubes. *IEE Proceedings: Nanotechnology, 153*(1): 7–10.

Zhang, Y. 2020. An analysis of the class structure of traditional and modern English teaching. In Wu Jiangmei, Peng Gong & Ju Fang'An (Eds.), *Modern Language Teaching and Research.* Beijing: China Renming University Press, 111–115.

Zhang, Y. 2020. An analysis of the information feedback of traditional and modern English teaching. *New Silk Road, 186*(4): 244–245.

Zhou, X., Qu, Y. S., Passini, E., Bueno-Orovio, A., Liu, Y., Vargas, H. M. & Rodriguez, B. 2020. Blinded in silico drug trial reveals the minimum set of ion channels for torsades de pointes risk assessment. *Frontiers in Pharmacology, 10*: 1–17.